The Life and Letters of

VICE-ADMIRAL LORD COLLINGWOOD

Vice-Admiral Lord Collingwood, portrait by Henry Howard.
A posthumous portrait, painted about 1827. The admiral wears
the King's gold medals for the Glorious First of June, St. Vincent,
and Trafalgar. *National Portrait Gallery.*

The Life and Letters of
VICE-ADMIRAL
LORD COLLINGWOOD

Oliver Warner

LONDON
OXFORD UNIVERSITY PRESS
NEW YORK · TORONTO
1968

Oxford University Press, Ely House, London W.1

GLASGOW NEW YORK TORONTO MELBOURNE WELLINGTON
CAPE TOWN SALISBURY IBADAN NAIROBI LUSAKA ADDIS ABABA
BOMBAY CALCUTTA MADRAS KARACHI LAHORE DACCA
KUALA LUMPUR HONG KONG TOKYO

PRINTED IN GREAT BRITAIN
BY EBENEZER BAYLIS AND SON, LTD.
THE TRINITY PRESS, WORCESTER, AND LONDON

*Dedicated to fellow members of
the Navy Records Society
and the Society for Nautical Research*

Contents

Illustrations

facing page

X.   Letter from Collingwood to Captain
     Benjamin Hallowell   205

     Written on 18 April 1809 and referring to the
     work of W. A. Miles (1753–1817) political
     writer. *British Museum.* (Add. MSS. 37425,
     f.96.)

Charts

     The Atlantic and Channel Waters $\Big\}$ folders
     The Mediterranean   at end

Acknowledgements

I owe a great debt to Sir Edward Collingwood, a descendant of the admiral's brother John, for his sustained encouragement and kindness, and for allowing me the range of his collection of family and other documents. His wide knowledge of everything relating to Lord Collingwood has greatly lightened the way of a biographer.

The Council of the Navy Records Society kindly allowed me the use of the late Professor Edward Hughes's edition of the admiral's private correspondence. I am equally indebted to the authorities and staffs of the British Museum, and the National Maritime Museum, Greenwich, for their helpfulness over the use of documents and other material in their charge. The City Librarian, Newcastle upon Tyne, went to much trouble in procuring reference papers and local information not easily obtainable elsewhere, and also put me on the track of a self-portrait of the admiral, the original of which is now at Greenwich, which has not hitherto been reproduced within the covers of a book.

I am also grateful to the Deputy Keeper of Manuscripts at the National Library of Scotland; to Mr. Kenneth Timings of the Public Record Office, London, and to Mr. Piers Mackesy, of Pembroke College, Oxford, for their patience and goodwill when appealed to over matters relating to Lord Collingwood's career. Mr. Edward and Major A. Du Sautoy were good enough to lend me their copies of journals of proceedings of ships in which Collingwood flew his flag, 1799–1800. Commander Anthony Sainsbury supplied valuable information about Admiral Duckworth.

While formal acknowledgements indicate the sources from which my illustrations are derived, they will give no idea of the courtesy met with in arranging for their use. Captain Lindwall, of the Royal Swedish Fortress Administration, was of particular help in respect of Mr. Harry Sjögren's contemporary oil-painting

of the Spanish *Santissima Trinidada* which was engaged by
Collingwood and others in 1797 and finally captured at Trafalgar. She is seen just before she foundered in the storm which
followed the battle. I am grateful to Mr. H. T. Simpson for
information about the last portrait of Collingwood made from
life, which is in his collection.

Finally the Oxford University Press has by its enthusiasm
for the project made matters of production, which can sometimes be thorny, altogether more delightful.

O.W.

ABBREVIATIONS

The following abbreviations are used in references to sources:

Add. MSS.   Additional Manuscripts; British Museum
Col.   Collingwood manuscripts and other material in
the National Maritime Museum, Greenwich
H.   Letters printed in *The Private Correspondence of
Lord Collingwood*: edited by Edward Hughes for
the Navy Records Society (1957)
N.C.   G. L. Newnham Collingwood: *A Selection from the
Public and Private Correspondence of Lord Colling-
wood* (1828)
N. Chron.   *The Naval Chronicle* (1799–1818)
Nic.   Sir Harris Nicolas: *The Dispatches and Letters of
Vice Admiral Lord Viscount Nelson* (1844–1846)
P.R.O.   Documents in the Public Record Office

In quoting Collingwood's letters and other documents, Newnham
Collingwood, his first editor, tried to 'improve' the originals,
and Collingwood's exact wording is not always discoverable.
Professor Hughes, in his edition of the *Correspondence*, indicated by brackets where the Admiral abbreviated or omitted,
and his practice has been followed, as has his general method of
punctuation: Collingwood habitually used a dash where most
later writers would have used a comma. Largely in the interests
of economy of paper, Collingwood did not often paragraph his
letters, and for convenience this has been done where it seemed
appropriate.

Preface

Lord Collingwood's plain tomb stands near Nelson's in the crypt of St. Paul's, which is the proper place for it; but it is only lately, in connexion with memorials to much later sea officers, that it has been reasonably lit. Biographers have not caught up with this illumination. William Davies (1875), Clark Russell (1891), and Geoffrey Murray (1936), who wrote successively about the admiral, had not the advantage of the mass of correspondence and other material now accessible, by and about Collingwood, which has been steadily added, over the decades, to the archives of the British Museum, and the National Maritime Museum, Greenwich.

The two principal collections which have so far been printed are as distant from one another in time as in scholarship. G. L. Newnham Collingwood, the seaman's son-in-law, issued *A Selection from the Public and Private Correspondence of Vice-Admiral Lord Collingwood interspersed with Memoirs of his Life*, in 1828, and with success, for his work became popular. It was even made use of by Alfred de Vigny as material for a chapter in his *Servitude et Grandeur Militaires* (1835). In this striking work, although liberties were taken with the facts of Collingwood's career, a true impression of his character and achievement was conveyed by a French writer of distinction.

Newnham Collingwood's book has disappointed later students, and his inaccuracy was such that he even got his subject's date of birth wrong by two full years. This was stated to be 1750, an error which is also to be found in many respectable works of reference. Had the author consulted the Register of Baptisms kept in the Chapter Office of what is now the Cathedral Church of St. Nicholas, Newcastle upon Tyne, he could have confirmed that the admiral was christened on 24 October 1748. Family records state that he was born on the 26th of the previous month.

This matter, not so trivial as it may seem, since it stresses still further the slow rise of a remarkable man to a rank where he could exercise his gifts, was noted by the late Professor Edward Hughes in the edition of *The Private Correspondence of Lord Collingwood* which he published for the Navy Records Society in 1957. Hughes had what he conceived to be a wrong to redress. This was the view taken by Sir John Laughton in a notice in *The Dictionary of National Biography* (1887), where he wrote Collingwood down as 'an admirable second in command, but without the genius fitting him to rise to the first rank as commander-in-chief'. Laughton did not say, as he could well have done, that Collingwood was unlucky: his strictures were harsher. His opinion differed considerably from that of other historians, and indeed from that of his son, L. G. Carr Laughton, formerly Admiralty Librarian, at least as expressed in private conversation.

In the existent material for a study of Collingwood's life, there are two rather sharp divisions. There is little covering the earlier years, but from 1778, when he and Nelson first served together in the West Indies, there is abundance. For over three decades every major event of Collingwood's life—the Glorious First of June, 1794; the action off Cape St. Vincent in 1797; Trafalgar, and the aftermath—is recorded in his own words. And of all the sea officers of the great era of sail, none excelled Collingwood in three respects: bravery in battle; felicity in written expression; and abiding sense of duty.

The other division is between the public and the private life. For most of his career, Collingwood had no public life, except in so far as the administration of a man-of-war may be said to be such. But during his final years, the range of his responsibilities became so huge that it wore him out. It fell to him to conduct the strategy decided on by his Government throughout the Mediterranean area, and even much of its diplomacy—this without previous training, and with no staff whatever according to the modern idea of the word. The ramifications of the task have been studied, notably by Piers Mackesy in *The War in the Mediterranean, 1803–1810* (1957). Its importance and interest is such that it is likely to attract further commentary.

The present work is biographical; its aim is to present Collingwood, as far as possible, in his own words: his thoughts and actions set against the essential background of his time. His circle was close, private and professional alike, but there were times when he took part in great events, and was brought into touch with men who made a stir in history. The events, and the leading personalities who affected him, are given fresh colour by what he wrote about them.

Duty was long a fashionable word. If it is so no longer, this can scarcely be a matter for satisfaction, and certainly not in a nation which is as dependent as ever on the character of its people. Collingwood was a martyr to duty, and, if he was not an uncomplaining victim, at least he was fortified by the knowledge that his trials benefited those he loved. 'You have no conception of my labour,' he wrote to his sister-in-law towards the end of his life[1] 'and the satisfaction I have is that it is to procure your ease and safety, and I hope it will not fail.' It did not fail.

When, half a century after Collingwood had joined his friend and comrade-in-arms in St. Paul's, Thackeray published *The Four Georges*, he could look back on the ardours and triumphs of their era with adequate perspective. Of Collingwood he was moved to say: '. . . I think since Heaven made gentlemen, there is no record of a better one than that. Of brighter deeds, I grant you, we may read performed by others; but where of a nobler, kinder, more beautiful life of duty, of a gentler, truer heart?' Warming still further to his subject, Thackeray added: 'There are no words to tell what the heart feels in reading the simple phrases of such a hero. Here is victory and courage, but love sublimer and superior.'

If few will be inclined to quarrel with the sentiments expressed, a certain reserve is legitimate about the 'simple phrases' referred to by the commentator. For in fact Collingwood was never a simple character, and, if what he wrote was seldom ambiguous or convoluted in the manner which seemed so inevitable with Howe, it was not, in its essence, unsophisticated. He observed shrewdly, had no illusions, and the years brought him a breadth and complexity of experience unsurpassed by that of any sea officer of his time.

Collingwood inspired no 'school', as did a succession of great sea commanders such as Hawke, Howe, St. Vincent, and

---

[1] H., Letter 152.

Nelson, and he remained a lonely figure, almost as much so in the Navy as in the world at large. He was known to many of his contemporaries, but only Nelson penetrated his reserve. Fate threw them together so often that this was inevitable. A succession of superiors valued Collingwood for his professional ability, in particular Sir Peter Parker, Howe—in spite of one serious lapse in encouragement—St. Vincent, and Cornwallis. His equals and juniors were generally either silent about him, or cautious in their verdicts (except about his bravery) since Collingwood was never expansive. There are, however, three expressions of opinion worth noting, since they came from three brilliant officers of a rising generation.

William Hoste, than whom no frigate captain ever won a finer reputation, the basis of which was founded by Nelson, who gave him his first command, wrote: 'Never shall we find Nelson's equal, and never will the navy of Great Britain furnish a man with half his abilities . . . Collingwood . . . is a very different man . . . but as brave an old boy as ever stood.' This was immediately after Trafalgar, but years later, when there was talk of Collingwood leaving the Mediterranean, and when Hoste had come to know him really well, Hoste told his father: 'I should be sorry to lose so good and able a chief; nor do I know of anyone who is better calculated for the general good of the Service and this important Station than Lord Colling-wood.'[1]

A much colder view was taken by another Nelson pupil, George Elliot, who never knew Collingwood as well as did Hoste, though he was much the same age and had as much battle experience. He wrote:

> That Collingwood was as brave, stubborn, persevering, and determined an officer as was known, everyone acknowledged; but he had few if any friends, and no admirers. In body and mind he was iron, and very cold iron—in heart I believe the same, except one small soft corner, accessible only to his family . . . He was always as kind to me as he could be to anyone, but it did not sink deep; he was naturally so cold.[2]

[1] *Memoirs*, Sir William Hoste (1833), ii. 4.
[2] 'Admiral the Hon. Sir George Elliot' by Rear-Admiral A. H. Taylor: *Mariner's Mirror*, xxxv (1949), 424.

Henry Blackwood's remains perhaps the fairest verdict. It was written to his wife when Collingwood transferred his flag to Blackwood's frigate, the *Euryalus*, after the *Royal Sovereign* had been disabled in battle, and it could scarcely be bettered in its succinct perception: 'a reserved, though a very pleasing good man, and as he fought like an angel, I take the more to him.'[1]

Finally, by a rare and most fortunate chance, a seaman's opinion of Collingwood has survived for posterity in the Memoirs of Robert Hay, who served in the *Culloden* when the Admiral flew his flag in this ship in 1804.

A better seaman—a better friend to seamen—a greater lover and more zealous defender of his country's rights and honour, never trod a quarter-deck. He and his favourite dog Bounce were known to every member of the crew. How attentive he was to the health and comfort and happiness of his crew! A man who could not be happy under him, could have been happy nowhere; a look of displeasure from him was as bad as a dozen at the gangway from another man.[2]

[1] Nic. vii. 226.
[2] *Landsman Hay: the Memoirs of Robert Hay, 1789–1847*, edited by M.D. Hay (1953).

1 *Slow Rises Worth*

A few weeks after Trafalgar, Collingwood was asked by Mr. Joyce Gold, the publisher of the *Naval Chronicle*, for some details of his life. Fame had come upon him suddenly as a result of the battle, and those at home had little knowledge of his service and background. They wanted more. Pressed as he was by business of every kind, Collingwood, with typical consideration, was willing to spare time to provide information for a journal favoured by his own Service, and designed to appeal to outsiders who followed sea affairs with attention. All the same, he did not believe that what he could impart was likely to cause much stir, and he was without the vanity which would have made an account of himself pleasurable to compose.

On 7 January he wrote to Gold from the *Queen*, at sea:

> You have really made a request to me, that notwithstanding I have every desire to comply with your wish, I find a great difficulty in; that is, in writing any thing relating to myself, that can be ever interesting or entertaining to the public:— my life has been a continued service at sea, but unmarked by any of those extraordinary events, or brilliant scenes, which hold men up to particular attention, and distinguish them from those officers who are zealous, and anxious for the public service.[1]

There can be little doubt that when he wrote these words, Collingwood had Nelson in mind, Nelson whose career, though indeed linked with his own at many points, had also included just such 'brilliant scenes' as had attracted notice. There had, for instance, been the spectacular victory of the Nile in 1798,

---

[1] *N. Chron.* xxiii. 380. (The version printed by Newnham Collingwood is inexact.)

which Collingwood had missed. There were also the months, crowded with events (nearly all of them unfortunate) which Nelson had spent at the Courts of Naples and Palermo; and the more bracing campaign and diplomacy in the Baltic in 1801. Collingwood had made good use of what opportunities had come his way, but until now the limelight had never fallen directly upon him. Since he was destined to remain at sea, it would not be long before he was forgotten.

His letter continued:

> I went into the Navy at a very early period of my life, in the year 1761, in the *Shannon*, under the protection and care of a kind friend and relation, the late Admiral Braithwaite, to whose regard for me, and to the interest which he took in whatever related to my improvement in nautical knowledge, I owe great obligations. I served with him for many years, and afterwards with my friend Admiral Roddam.

Collingwood was twelve when he joined Braithwaite's frigate, and thus was afloat during the closing stages of the Seven Years War, when Anson ruled at the Admiralty, and when the Navy was at one of its greatest periods. The 'Year of Victories', 1759, was clearly remembered, distinguished as it had been by Boscawen's chase of de la Clue into the Bay of Lagos, with the loss of five ships to the French; by the amphibious operations of Saunders and Wolfe which had led to the capture of Quebec; by Hawke's annihilation of the fleet of Conflans in the rock-strewn waters of Quiberon, and—on shore—by the army's triumph at Minden. It was a war which might have seemed to settle beyond dispute the pre-eminence of the Georgian Navy, and to have ensured the rapid growth of British power overseas.

The Navy had attractions for a boy with his own way to make in the world, particularly if he was taken under the wing of a captain likely to go far. In fact, Collingwood's earlier career was humdrum, and his patron, Braithwaite, had few chances to win fame. The great events of the current war at sea were over, and Collingwood began to learn his profession under conditions not much different from those of peace. For many years they would so continue, and it was perhaps fortunate that the circumstances of his birth and earlier years were not such as to lead him to believe that life was anything but a struggle.

Cuthbert Collingwood was born at Newcastle upon Tyne in a
street known as the Side. His family had been long established
in Northumberland. A few of its members had landed property:
others were in trade or the professions. His father, who gave his
own Christian name to his eldest son, had served an apprentice-
ship to a local merchant, and then set up on his own in the house
where his children were born. He married Milcah, daughter of
Reginald Dobson of Barwise, near Appleby. She bore him ten
children. The first seven were girls, Mary, Elizabeth, who died as
an infant, a second Elizabeth, Dorothy, Philadelphia, Barbara,
and Eleanor. The last three were boys. Cuthbert was followed
by Wilfred, who also went into the Navy, then by John, who
went into the Customs. Of the girls, only Mary, the second
Elizabeth, and Dorothy survived their youth, and none of them
married. Mary lived to be 77; Elizabeth to be 95; Dorothy to be
89; and John, by far the longest lived of the boys, reached 90.

Cuthbert Collingwood the elder was not a successful man of
business, and when he died, in 1775, his widow and daughters
were not well provided for, the sons stepping into the breach as
well as they could, and continuing so to do. The boys were sent
to the local Grammar School, where the instruction was good,
directed by an excellent master, Hugh Moises. At the time the
future admiral was there, Moises had at least two other pupils
who were later to shine, John and William Scott. John, who was
three years younger than Cuthbert Collingwood, became Lord
Chancellor, taking the title of Eldon. William, who was two
years older, afterwards became Lord Stowell and an authority
on maritime law.

Moises was an exceptional teacher, and, although a strict
disciplinarian, greatly loved. It was said of him that he advised
his boys to read only the works of great authors, and as much
with a view to their style as to their content. He himself had a
passion for the classics, but he made it his business to mark the
special aptitudes of those he taught, and advised them to pursue
only such lines as they were likely to excel in.[1] Certainly Moises
gave Collingwood a love of reading, and from reading, aided by
a natural gift of expression, he wrought his own style. George III
was the first to remark on the grace of Collingwood's Trafalgar

[1] Note supplied by Joseph Cowen to W. Clark Russell for his Life of Collingwood (1891).

dispatch. This he accounted for by having heard from Lord Eldon that the pair had sat together under Moises. It was the sort of information which delighted the King.

Collingwood's attachment to the House of Hanover was never in doubt, and he could have reflected sadly on the consequences of misdirected loyalty, for one member of the family, George Collingwood, who had property at Eslington in Northumberland, had taken part in the ill-supported attempt by the Old Pretender in 1715 to regain the throne for the Stuarts. George Collingwood was hanged at Liverpool for his pains. He had been the friend and companion of Lord Derwentwater, a principal in the rising, whose forfeited estates went to finance Greenwich Hospital. In a contemporary ballad, *Derwentwater's Good Night*, the condemned man is made to say:

> And fare thee well, George Collingwood,
>   Since fate has put us down;
> If thou and I have lost our lives,
>   King James has lost his crown.

In later life Collingwood came to know members of the Forster family, who were also related to those implicated in the rebellion. Thomas Forster was the Stuart's general, and he was taken prisoner, but escaped to France, surviving for many years. At the time of the grant of his peerage, Collingwood wrote to Sir Isaac Heard, Garter King at Arms:

> . . . I have heard from the Forsters, who knew more of the Family than anybody, that when Eslington was forfeited to the crown, my grandfather was much blamed in the county for not endeavouring to get the estate transferred to him, which it was thought, on a proper application to the King, would have been done, as he was loyal. . . .[1]

Such were his circumstances, that, if Collingwood himself was ever to make a fortune, it would be through prize money. This could only accrue in any quantity after promotion to the rank of post-captain, and then only if he were lucky enough to command a successfully engaged ship in time of war. Otherwise the sea profession, though honourable in itself and essential to the

[1] N.C., 5.

welfare of the nation, could provide only a modest living, and a very arduous one at that.

During the years of what were usually described by young men aspiring to commissioned rank as their 'servitude' Collingwood went, as one of Braithwaite's 'followers', from the *Shannon* to the *Gibraltar*, another frigate, the ships being mainly employed in Atlantic and home waters, the *Shannon* sometimes convoying the Baltic trade. In the *Gibraltar*, he came to know something of the Mediterranean as well.

By 1766 he had been rated midshipman, and in the following year, when he transferred to the *Liverpool*, he became a master's mate. In this ship he was once again in the Mediterranean, and in 1771 he made an elaborate survey of the harbour of Port Mahon, duly recorded in his log. In 1772 he was taken into the *Lennox*, Captain Roddam, which was guard-ship at Portsmouth, the captain also taking charge of Wilfred. In 1773 Collingwood made a voyage to Jamaica in the *Portland*, and a well-illustrated log of his survives. At Jamaica he would have seen Admiral Rodney, who then commanded there.

An expectation of operational service came with Collingwood's appointment to the *Preston*, destined for the North American Station. This ship, like the *Portland*, was a 4th rate, a two-decked vessel which, though larger than a frigate, was among the smallest units well enough armed to take her place in the line of battle. The admiral, Samuel Graves, had been one of Hawke's captains at Quiberon, but he gained no further laurels in America.

There could not be much prospect of glory in the war which was clearly about to open with the American colonists, for they had no navy. It was said, moreover, by those who knew little or nothing of the temper and quality of the Americans, the nature of the country, the distances involved, or the capacity of those who would direct the strategy of the Mother Country, that the affair would be over in a few months at most. In fact, the struggle lasted eight weary years, and its protraction offered France, and later Spain, an opportunity of revenge for the humiliations suffered at the hands of Great Britain in previous decades. When the vigour and resolution of the Americans had become plain to the world, and when the embarrassments of the navy and army of George III seemed to increase rather than diminish, it was one which enemies took with eagerness, if with limited success.

Collingwood joined the *Preston* at the time when the first American Congress was preparing to meet at Philadelphia, the result of that assembly being a Declaration of Rights forbidding exports to or imports from Great Britain until grievances were remedied. Within months, actual hostilities followed this assertion of a state of economic war, and Collingwood was soon in action. He described his crossing of the Atlantic, his baptism of fire, and his first significant step in rank in the course of less than fifty words of the letter he addressed to Mr. Gold of the *Naval Chronicle*.

> In 1774 I went to Boston with Admiral Graves, [he wrote] and in 1775 was made a lieutenant by him on the day the battle was fought at Bunker's Hill, where I was with a party of seamen, supplying the army with what was necessary to them.

Although, as an example of concision, this statement has much to commend it, Collingwood took for granted a good deal of background information which, though it would have been tolerably familiar to his own generation and profession, requires some expansion if it is to be understood today.

Admiral Graves had been sent to Boston, which had been the scene of riotous refusal by the colonists of a consignment of tea sent by the Mother Country, on which an import tax was payable, because it was one of the places in North America where a substantial army could be quartered and maintained. The port had been closed to commerce, following the 'tea party', and relations between the troops and the townsmen, which had long been bad, were deteriorating still further. If, for the colonists, the situation had become intolerable, it was not much less so for the British who, though they denied the harbour to any shipping but their own, were in fact besieged.

The culminating act of intransigence of about 1,500 men of Massachusetts, led by Colonel Prescott, was to dig a system of trenches and strong points overlooking part of the harbour, the outcome of a surprise nocturnal foray. When the garrison woke on the morning of 17 June 1775 it was to the sound of guns from H.M. sloop *Lively*, whose captain had decided, on his own

initiative, to demolish the offending 'works' with a round or
two of shot. The action was useless. The Americans had dug
and constructed far too well, and in any case ship's fire was
rarely effective against shore positions.

If Bunker Hill was in rebel possession, it was the firm belief
of William Howe, a general with distinguished service in the
Seven Years War, that a direct assault by nearly 3,000 regular
troops would soon put matters to rights. Colonists, armed with
miscellaneous weapons, and lacking discipline or even uniforms,
could never, so he reasoned, stand up to a bravely-led attack.
Like the captain of the *Lively*, he was wrong. It needed three
separate operations, the first two of which ended in bloody
repulse, before, with the aid of reinforcements including marines
from the Fleet, the Americans were winkled from their entrench-
ments at the point of the bayonet, their ammunition spent.
Collingwood, ensuring that the soldiers had all the powder and
shot they needed, would later describe the action as very fierce,
as indeed it was, the British suffering over a thousand killed
or wounded, including eighty-nine of commissioned rank, as
against less than half that number sustained by the defenders.

It was in every way a costly victory. The loss was due to
Howe's over-confidence in the face of irregulars who had been
told to hold their fire until every bullet hit. 'Men,' so Prescott
is stated to have said, 'you are all marksmen—don't one of you
fire until you see the whites of their eyes.' A more circumspect
commander would have taken his time and turned the position,
but Howe disdained to do this. Although in the end the day
was his, the granite obelisk which rises 220 feet above the little
rise where so many fought and died commemorates a great
achievement. In the following year, the British withdrew from
Boston.

II

When Collingwood said that he was made a lieutenant by
Admiral Graves, the promotion, as a substantive step, was subject to formal confirmation by the Admiralty. Partly in order
to get matters straight, Collingwood was sent to the *Somerset*,
a 74-gun ship-of-the-line, and in her returned to England. It
was from Castle Street, London (within the boundary of the

City), that on 22 March 1776 the seasoned man of twenty-seven addressed the first letter from his hand to have survived, though it was a duller one than most he wrote. His rank had been approved, his seniority dating from the day of the battle. Now he must look for a new ship.

My dear Betsy, [he wrote to his third sister] A few days after I wrote to you last, I left Ports[mouth] in order the sooner to determine by waiting on Lord Sandwich what was to be my destination, and visited Mr. Collingwood first; when I talked on going to N[ew]C[astle] he said it certainly wou'd be the best way if there was no possibility of getting employed, intimating that employment should be the first consideration; and I believe this to be the sentiments of his father, it is a matter I need not much urging to. I know not anything less than the desire to see you my dear sisters that could have made me suspend my application an hour after I was discharged from the *Somerset*. Mr. Palliser's letter show'd the necessity of offering myself, and since I find his opinion corresponds with the sentiments of those who have ever studied my interest, I hesitated not to offer myself to his Lordship as a Volunteer for the American service, and received assurance that I shou'd be presently employed, several new ships are almost ready for launching in the river, all to be immediately commissioned, one of those will fall to my lot. Mr. Coll[ingwood] has promised to endeavour to get me a recommendation to my Lord Howe, if amongst his acquaintance he can find one any ways connected or known to his Lordship. I feel much disappointed that I come not down to you, I once flattered myself I might have been excused from business 2 or 3 months without appearing backward; I see things now in a different point of view, besides I am persuaded employment neglected now will be very difficult to attain 6 months hence.[1]

Those referred to in this opening paragraph were Lord Sandwich, head of the Admiralty in Lord North's administration, who would ordain Collingwood's next move; Mr. Edward Collingwood of Chirton, a cousin, and the most influential member of his own family; Mr. Palliser, who would almost certainly have been a close relative of Rear-Admiral Sir Hugh Palliser, then

[1] H., Letter 1.

serving on the Board of Admiralty; and Lord Howe, elder
brother of the general of Bunker Hill, upon whom sea strategy
in North American waters was shortly to devolve.

From his own affairs, Collingwood turned to those of others,
and in particular to the family of his former captain, Richard
Braithwaite, or Brathwaite as that officer signed it in his own
beautiful script. His description is of interest for what Collingwood noted, and how he set it down.

> I visited Mrs. Brathwaite the other day, the change in that
> family cou'd not escape the most unobserving: she is very
> much altered in her person, is very thin indeed, seems to be
> out of love with the gaiety which once engrossed too much
> of her attention, and become at last quite the housewife:
> Economy has insinuated herself into her family, and seems
> a favourite of the mistresses: she assured me Dick's reforma-
> tion was perfectly accomplished, his Coffee house acquaint-
> ance wholly dropt, and the comfort and happiness of his
> family his only care. You will share with me the pleasure I
> felt while she related this strange change . . .

The closeness which existed between Collingwood and the family
of his old commander was lasting. When Mrs. Braithwaite died,
nearly a quarter of a century later, Collingwood wrote: 'No
woman ever possessed a sweeter temper, or a more benevolent,
affectionate heart. I always loved her as a near relation and
dear friend, and the regard she professed for me I am sure was
unfeigned.' Braithwaite he described as being 'as honest and
honourable man, I believe, as any in England, even in his days
of difficulty and poverty he was always superior to anything
that could tarnish the lustre of a pure reputation'.[1]

Continuing his letter to Betsy on more general topics, Collingwood gave vent to his political views, which had the merit of
being expressed in the clearest terms.

> The Mayor, Aldermen and Common Council, petition the
> King today to cease hostilities against the Americans, and to
> adopt some mode of accommodation. I am out of all patience
> with them, and consider them the supporters of a dangerous
> Rebellion, rather than the assertors of the publick Liberty;

[1] Col., 39–839.

wish from my heart the whole pack were on Mount Pisga,
then their declamations might get them a dinner—they won't
much avail them here.

His missive ended, as would so many in similar terms: 'Pay
my duty to my Mother. Love to all our friends, and believe me
my dearest Sister in all sincerity, Your affectionate, Cuthb't
Collingwood.' When he wrote home, whoever he addressed
himself to, Collingwood thought of his letters as circulating
among family and friends, as in fact they did. From this time
onwards they had an increasing chance of preservation.

Fate, through the channel of Lord Sandwich, indeed sent
Collingwood to a new ship, the *Hornet*, sloop of war, and in her
to the West Indies. Unfortunately, she was put in charge of
Robert Haswell, a hateful character, in the view of his lieutenant, soured no doubt by eighteen years on the lieutenants'
list. Although Haswell had by then been fourteen years a commander, and so, by custom, was addressed as 'captain', he
seemed to have no immediate prospect of 'taking post'—that
is being appointed to a ship large enough to entail post or full
captain's rank, the ambition of every serving officer.

In a letter dated 1777 (*tout court*) to his brother John, Collingwood described what he endured in his new employment.

. . . The *Lively* brings this. Wou'd to God the *Lively* brought
me also for believe me I am heartily tired of my situation,
and cou'd a letter contain half the causes of my disatisfaction
you wou'd not wonder at it.

What a country is this at present to make a fortune in; all
kinds of people are wallowing in their wealth acquired by
prizes and so extraordinary an exception are we that to be as
unfortunate as the *Hornet* is become a proverbial saying, and
the Black girls sing our poverty in their ludicrous songs.[1]

Haswell was the trouble. He had no active spirit, and everyone
detested him. Collingwood's view was that 'there is not a man
or officer in the Ship that wou'd not consider a removal as a
kind of promotion'. Upon the lieutenant devolved all business
but, he complained, 'the fatigue I undergo is inconsiderable to
what I suffer from the insolent manners of a strange compound

[1] H., Letter 2.

of extravagant pride, and abject meanness'. At last, the inevitable row blew up and Haswell, asked for an explanation of
his attitude, had not a word to say. Matters came to a head as
a result of official proceedings, the first of two cases in which
Collingwood was concerned.

A Court martial was held the other day [the letter continued]
for the trial of 3 of our men for desertion and myself with the
other evidences were rather later in our attendance than we
ought to have been; such things will happen in the confusion
of carreening; the president expressed himself displeased and
H. added a speech so replete with virulence, rancour and
animosity that every hearer stood astonished.

Every Capt. there was unknown to either of us, it became
incumbent on us to deface the impression such a declaration
might make on them, and I determined that moment to make
him gainsay all he had said.

The court was no sooner dissolved than we represented to
them our uneasiness that violence should be offered to our
good fame in such an assembly and beg'd them to attend to
the explanation which H. was required to give in order for us
to vindicate us from an aspersion which they would find as
groundless as it was malicious.

The man stood confounded and speechless, and when the
meaning of each part of his declamation was asked, he with
an unparrallel'd effrontery denied having said before the same
assembly every syllable he had advanced: the creature looked
less than man, he was unworthy even of our resentment; it
cooled, and with the mediation of each Capt. ended. He has
drawn his own picture and strongly pencil'd its deformities.

If Haswell had been a zealous officer, something would have
been forgiven him, but this was not so. When possible prizes
were sighted he soon 'left off even the ceremony of chasing
them, and allowed them to pass unmolested sometimes within
½ a gun shot. There's a man to support the honour and interests
of his country; wou'd to heaven I was clear of him,' wrote his
unhappy subordinate.

Before the year was out, Collingwood was himself court
martialled at Port Royal, Jamaica, for what amounted to disobedience and neglect of orders. The case came up in September

1777 and he was acquitted, but the Court, wishing no doubt to uphold at least the principle of authority, remarked on his apparent want of cheerfulness, and recommended him to 'conduct himself for the future with that alacrity which is essentially necessary to His Majesty's service'. This admonition (on the part of those who had never served under Haswell) must have caused Collingwood at least a wry smile or two. He had about a year more to endure in the *Hornet*, but when his fortunes mended, they did so in a full-blooded way.

III

Admiral Sir Peter Parker, who outlived many of those he benefited, deserves to be well remembered as a talent-spotter. He arrived in the West Indies as Commander-in-Chief, Jamaica, in 1778, after service further north against the colonists, and at once matters began to mend for Collingwood. France had by now made her alliance with America, to be followed by Spain, and, although the situation produced more problems and burdens for the British Navy than it could always deal with, it also gave opportunities for officers of promise and activity.

During the year of Collingwood's greatest misery, Nelson arrived on the West Indies Station in the frigate *Lowestoffe*, Captain William Locker. Although he was almost exactly ten years younger, Nelson, who had once had the influence of his uncle, the Controller of the Navy, behind him, was already a lieutenant. He had also seen much of the world, his experience including a spell in the East Indies, and an expedition to the Arctic. The two men, so different in temperament, soon met, and continued what Collingwood later described as 'habits of great friendship'.[1]

Collingwood had everything to complain of—Nelson, nothing. The younger man loved his captain, and the *Lowestoffe* was a crack ship. By good fortune, both Collingwood and Nelson caught the eye of Admiral Parker, who in the summer of 1778 took Nelson into his flagship, the *Bristol*, where he soon rose to be first lieutenant. Collingwood he relieved from his durance

---

[1] They had met as early as 1773, when Nelson was only fifteen, as Collingwood stated in a letter to Walter Spencer-Stanhope of 6 March 1806 (Add. MSS. 52780).

I. Frontispiece of the Log of H.M.S. *Portland*.
Kept by Collingwood while serving in her, 1773. *Collection of Sir Edward Collingwood.*

II. Collingwood as a Post Captain.
A self-portrait, *c.* 1783. *National Maritime Museum.*

under Haswell, putting him into the *Lowestoffe*, where he had
the pleasure of serving a captain whom he and everyone else
could respect.

Nelson's next promotion, made in December 1778, was to the
Badger, brig, which made him a commander at the age of
twenty. Within six months, he had gained the further and most
vital step. He became a post-captain and in charge of the frigate
Hinchinbroke, while still three months short of the age of
twenty-one. Collingwood succeeded him, first in the brig and
later in the larger vessel; and so, from being a badly placed
lieutenant in a sloop-of-war despised on the Station, he was
translated, within a single year, into a full-blown post-captain—
this with a major war proceeding, and while on active service.
It was the biggest stroke of luck that Collingwood and Nelson
could have had. To their dying day, neither of them forgot what
they owed to Parker. They did all they could to repay it, when
their own turn came, by attention to those he recommended.
Parker continued to recommend well, though it is true he promoted Haswell. He could hardly have avoided doing so, for
such was the mortality in the Caribbean that those who survived got on, and the event was put off until Collingwood had
already been three months on the captains' list. This gave him
a comforting seniority over his old tormentor, who in due time
was superannuated.

The advent of Spain into the war exposed her colonies, and
it was considered by the authorities that a successful sortie
could be made into Nicaragua. This might have been so had a
well-equipped force been sent at an appropriate time of the
year. As it was, nothing but misfortune resulted.

The plan was described with Collingwood's usual dryness, in
the account of his services which he afforded to the *Naval
Chronicle*.

The *Hinchinbroke* [he wrote] was in the spring of 1780 employed on an expedition to the Spanish main, where it was
proposed, by the River San Juan, and the Lakes Nicaragua
and Leon, to pass by a navigation of boats into the South
Sea.

The plan was formed without a sufficient knowledge of the
country, which presented difficulties that were not to be
3

surmounted by human skill or perseverance. The river was difficult to proceed on from the rapidity of the current, and the several falls over the rocks, which intercepted the navigation, and the climate was deadly; no constitution could resist its effects.

Collingwood joined Nelson at the port of San Juan, Nelson then being given a larger ship, the *Janus*, owing to the death of her captain. But he himself soon succumbed to fever, and was forced to return to Jamaica; thence he made his way back to England.

My constitution [continued Collingwood] resisted many attacks, and I survived most of my ship's company, having buried in four months 180 of the 200 which composed it. Mine was not a singular case, all the ships that were as long there suffered in the same degree: the transports' men all died, and some of the ships having none left to take care of them, sunk in the harbour; but transport ships were not wanted, for the troops they brought were no more; they had fallen, not by the hand of an enemy, but sunk under the contagion of the climate.

This matter-of-fact account of what was appalling misery, recorded what had occurred in a number of campaigns of a similar kind, from which successive generations of operational planners seemed to learn nothing.

From this scene [wrote Collingwood] I was relieved in August 1780, and in December following was appointed to the command of the *Pelican*, a small frigate of 24 guns. In August the following year, a severe hurricane blew, in which she was wrecked, being cast on the rocks of Morant Keys, in the middle of a most tremendous night; the next day with great difficulty the ship's company got on shore by rafts, made of small and broken yards, and in those small sandy hills, with little food and water, we remained ten days, until a boat went to Jamaica, and the *Diamond* frigate came and took us off.

Morant Keys consisted of a few low islets in the form of a crescent, about 35 miles south-east of Morant Point, Jamaica. Collingwood showed resource in getting his crew to safety, skill in keeping them disciplined, and energy in getting a boat away so soon. He had some good fortune in finding a frigate ready to undertake the rescue work at once, for at Port Royal, Jamaica, over a hundred vessels had been driven ashore, two men-of-war were entirely dismasted, and the general havoc was considerable.

Early in 1782 Collingwood went home, and never ceased his applications to the Admiralty for a new appointment. For some time, these had no result, and he made a letter to his brother John, addressed from London on 22 June, the occasion of another grumble. He had had ill luck, followed by good luck, followed by shipwreck. He felt low.

> It grieves me to the heart [he wrote] that I cannot tell you I am a whit nearer getting a ship than I was the first day I came to town. Interest carries its point in all administrations and God knows no poor wretch ever had less interest than I have. There are at least a hundred Captains scrambling for ships, and I believe I may say *all* the ships for this season are given away except such as fall vacant by chance.[1]

He had also dined with Lord Ravensworth, a leading North-country Whig, where he found two other Collingwoods, one of them a lawyer; Sir Francis Blake, a Durham landowner; and a Captain Dickson, later to get his flag. His host asked if Collingwood had hopes of getting a ship soon, but Collingwood added that he 'did not seem at all disposed to interfere in my favour'. Another contact, which was later to prove invaluable, was with Captain George Bowyer, whom Collingwood heard had married a daughter of Admiral Sir Piercy Brett, in his day one of Anson's most distinguished officers.

> He has given me a very civil invitation to come down to him, [he said] and as it is little more than thirty miles from town I propose going down on Monday next, and if there is good company and I like the place, I shall probably stay a few weeks, unless my good fortune calls me thence to a ship.

The rest of the letter was full of gossip about people he had met both in London and on his earlier visit home. Of one acquaintance he remarked: 'Let a woman alone for a good story. I

[1] H., Letter 3.

begin, John, to think they are more dangerous to encounter than Hurricanes, as they do not give so fair a warning. Wou'd I was abroad again! Better be wrecked a thousand times at sea, than once ashore.'

Collingwood had been needlessly gloomy about his prospects, or perhaps he had better-placed friends than he realized, for, although he had to wait a few months, he was appointed in January 1783 to the *Sampson*, a brand new ship-of-the-line of 64 guns. He was not in her long, being transferred to the *Mediator*, a frigate, also newly built. It was from her that he wrote to his sister, probably Mary, on 9 July, when he was at Portsmouth. He was having difficulty getting enough men, and believed that when he was ready he was likely to go to Antigua.

Matters dragged on, and he was still at Spithead in August, disconcerted at some of the youngsters he had taken charge of, or who had been recommended to him, and—more immediately —with the toothache. He told his sister how he at least settled the later trouble. 'My tooth was so painfull to me,' he wrote,[1] 'that I have just had it taken out, the hollow part fill'd with caddee lead and put in again, and tomorrow I hope it will be as good a tooth as any I have.'

As for the boys: 'Lord knows I have more monkey things now than I well know how to manage; they are a constant plague to me.' Some were good: others would never make officers. All needed attention, and Collingwood, who had himself been well trained by Braithwaite and Roddam, could be relied upon to do his best for those he had taken into his ship. The best of them would become the admirals of the future.

He had heard from Wilfred, back from a spell in the East in the *Asia*. He was also trying to get men for his ship, which was at the Nore, by sending a boat to London. He would have helped the *Mediator* by the same means, had he been given the chance. 'He is never forgetful of me when he has anything nice,' added an appreciative brother.

Collingwood told his sister that 'Wilfred is always call'd old Collingwood and has been taken for fifty,' though he was actually a year younger than Cuthbert, a mere thirty-four. He added that Wilfred was 'already remark'd for his diligence, attention and (the fruits of it) the good order of his ship, and

[1] H., Letter 5.

when people's character begin so early to go abroad there is no
doubt it will soon be establish'd'. When an officer gets talked
about, he is likely to make his mark. It was true in Wilfred's
case, for within the next eighteen months, after a spell on the
Gold Coast, he had been made a commander, his ship being the
Rattler, sloop-of-war, and had been ordered to the West Indies.

Before he himself sailed for Antigua, which was indeed his
destination, Collingwood had time for one more letter to Mary,
dated from Spithead on 15 September, in which he assured her,
with that warmth of affection which was so abiding:

> Whenever it is in my power to contribute to your ease and
> comforts you may trust I will. I have no pleasure in my
> successes, but as they enable me to assist those who need my
> help . . . I have no pleasure equal to the administering the
> means of happiness to you my sisters, and will most willingly
> do whatever is in my power towards it.[1]

There was no prospect of prize-money, for peace had just
been signed at Versailles. American independence had been
formally recognized, Britain was once again in amity with
France and Spain, and Collingwood might have looked forward
to a commission tranquil by comparison with some of those he
had known earlier in his life. In the event, it did not work out
that way at all.

[1] H., Letter 6.

2   *The West Indies Revisited*

The war had brought a change in the affairs of the West Indies which was not appreciated by the inhabitants, least of all by some of those in high places. Formerly, since the communities in British-held islands, and the people of the North American Colonies, had been under the same Crown, commerce between the two areas had flourished. The war had interrupted this, but planters and merchants looked forward to a full resumption of trade, once peace had been concluded. What they did not fully apprehend was the fact that by the Treaty of Versailles the colonists had become not merely independent, but foreigners. Trade could no longer be as before, since under a series of Navigation Laws, going back to the time of Oliver Cromwell, and re-confirmed as lately as the reign of William and Mary, trade could only be consigned in ships registered in Britain, so far as concerned such possessions as her West Indian islands, or in ships registered in the islands themselves, of which there were few with ocean-going capacity.

The Americans had in fact become interlopers, and, since it was the duty of Captains of H.M. ships, serving on the appropriate Station (in this case the Leeward Islands), to prevent their commerce and uphold existing laws affecting the matter, zealous naval officers were likely to run into difficulties if the local authorities insisted that traffic should continue as in the old days.

The way out was to wink the eye. Governors and others were glad to do so, and the admiral, Sir Richard Hughes, would have been happy to agree. What Hughes did not reckon with was the temper of his own captains, conspicuous among whom were Collingwood in the *Mediator*, his friend and senior Nelson, who had been sent to Antigua in the frigate *Boreas*, and, later,

Commander Wilfred Collingwood of the *Rattler*. All three were men of principle, with firm minds, who were determined to do their duty by the home Government, admiral or no admiral. In any case, Hughes was not much of a man. 'He bows and scrapes too much,' wrote Nelson, 'and his wife has an eternal clack . . .'[1] 'Because our diligence reflects on his neglect,' wrote Collingwood, 'he dislikes us.'[2]

The first move against illegal trading was made by Collingwood. On the afternoon of 15 December 1784, while cruising off Antigua, he sighted an American vessel making for the harbour. He at once sent a boat to board her and inquire her business, and was informed that the ship was making for St. Johns. Her master stated that he wished to enter the port to enable repairs to be made to the mainmast, which was unsafe. This was a regular excuse for entry and discharge of cargo.

Collingwood sent his carpenter and bo'sun to examine the mast and report on its condition. They told their captain that the defects were slight, and could be put right, if necessary, by the *Mediator*'s own resources, within a matter of four hours. Collingwood therefore anchored in the roadstead of St. Johns and told the American master to bring his vessel alongside the frigate where the repairs could be carried out, if necessary with naval assistance.

As he had no alternative, the master did as he was told, but he took the opportunity to go ashore to inform the consignees of his cargo what had happened. He also lodged a protest with the Governor, Major-General Thomas Shirley.

Shirley was well aware of the anger and dissatisfaction which would arise among the trading community through Collingwood's action, and, privately at least, he sympathized. But he took the precaution of asking Counsel's opinion on Collingwood's action. The view of the local Solicitor-General, in which the Attorney-General of Grenada, who happened to be on a visit to Antigua, concurred, was that Collingwood had no business to prevent the American putting in to St. Johns, and that what action the Customs and other local authorities took regarding the ship was their own affair, not the Navy's.

. . . I have always apprehended that the coercion for an

[1] Nic., i. 110.   [2] H., Letter 7.

obedience to the Laws of Trade, Navigation or the Revenue is peculiarly committed to the Board of Customs [said Counsel], and to the subordinate officers of the Customs acting under the instructions of this Board. Any military inter-ference without requisition from these officers of the Customs in any port of the British Dominions is certainly very unusual and singular.[1]

Collingwood wrote officially to the Governor about the inci-dent on 16 December, stating the reasons for his action with regard to the American, and making his views in general clear.

For my authority for not suffering her to proceed further, I refer your Excellency to the Statutes (12 Chas: 2 and the 7th and 8th of William and Mary) excluding Aliens from Commerce with the British Colonies, which Statutes I am ordered to put in full force and execution.

I shall take this opportunity of informing Your Excellency I have reason to believe Foreigners (that is Americans) do find means to impose on the Custom House, proofs, which will not stand the test of inquiry, to procure papers authoris-ing them to trade hither.

I shall instance a Brig which sailed this morning having procured such papers, the *Royal Midshipman*, is reported to me by the officer who boarded her to be commanded by an American and navigated by six American seamen, which alone is a violation of the Act of Navigation . . .[2]

Collingwood gave Shirley further instances of illicit traffic, ending his letter: 'Is it amazing that I should, in obedience to my orders, endeavour to restrain to the limits prescribed to it by law?'

Shirley, not unnaturally, referred the whole matter to Hughes, as well as to the home authorities. Seeing that Hughes was Hughes, he issued revised instructions to his captains merely to report the arrival of foreign ships to the local Governor.

If [the order ran] after such Reports have been made and received, the Governor (or his Representative) shall think proper to admit the said Foreigner into the Port or Harbour

---

[1] P.R.O./C.O. 152/64.

[2] P.R.O./C.O. 152/64. *Nelson's Letters from the Leeward Islands, etc.*, ed. G. Rawson (1953), contains a careful examination of the incidents concerned.

where you may then be, You are on no account to hinder, or prevent such Foreign ship or vessel from going in accordingly, or to interfere any further in her subsequent proceedings . . .

This was altogether too much for Nelson, as indeed it was for the home authorities. Lord Sydney, who was then responsible for Colonial affairs, was entirely of the opinion of the naval officers as to the iniquity of the traffic.

My letter to you of 8 January last [he wrote to Shirley later in the year] will inform you that the same suspicions exist among the King's Servants here, as are entertained by Captain Collingwood, that People unqualified to trade have, by eluding the vigilance of the Revenue Officers, or by some other means, obtained a participation of the Trade to our Colonies unauthorised by the Legislature of this country.[1]

Sydney later gave a specific promise to Nelson to defend any suit which might be brought against him which should arise from his activities in the West Indies, though in fact both Collingwood and he were pursued with threats long after their ships had been paid off at the end of their commission.

Unpopular as they made themselves with the local communities, the captains had a firm friend in John Moutray and his wife, Moutray being Commissioner for the Navy Board in Antigua. He was an elderly man, a post-captain who had taken civil employment, and he was not long in office, for his health failed: but while he and his wife remained in the West Indies, Collingwood and Nelson were assured of a welcome in at least one household, and this in spite of the fact that Nelson had once disputed Hughes's authority in permitting Moutray to instruct a junior captain to hoist his pendant as commodore, and had made his point.

Both Collingwood and Nelson greatly admired and valued Mrs. Moutray, who appears to have provided the affection and hospitality they needed amid an increasingly hostile society. They kept up with her for the rest of their lives, and posterity has reason to remember her, for she preserved two little portraits, one of Collingwood by Nelson, the other of Nelson by Collingwood, now at Greenwich, which were done in her house.

[1] P.R.O./C.O. 152/64.

These are astonishing. Collingwood's version of Nelson shows a humorous appreciation of a most unexpected kind. It is close to caricature, which is only partly explained by the fact that at the time Nelson sat, he wore a yellow wig, his head having been shaved as the result of fever, so that Collingwood's remark, made in a letter some five years later: 'My regard for you, my dear Nelson, my respect and veneration for your character, I hope and believe will never be lessened'[1] strikes quite an odd note, since 'veneration' is not a quality apparent in the sketch.

Nelson's silhouette, on the other hand, is serious and accomplished. This is also rather unexpected, since it is said to have been drawn 'in revenge' for Collingwood's effort. It reveals a noble head, bearing out what Nelson wrote to their mutual friend, Captain William Locker: 'What a charming good man Collingwood is . . . a valuable member of society.'[2]

On the showing of these two small works alone, Collingwood and Nelson were an uncommonly clever couple.

Collingwood returned home in the late summer of 1786, leaving Wilfred in the *Rattler* under Nelson's orders as senior officer, for Admiral Hughes also left for England. The little force was increased in November by the frigate *Pegasus*, commanded by Prince William Henry, third son of George III. The Prince was already both a seaman of experience—he had served in battle as a midshipman under Rodney—and a martinet. Nelson got on well with him, though he found him 'volatile' and more than a little taxing, since he drank hard, enjoyed socialities, was extremely conscious of his position, and was hard on his officers, all of whom complained of his unreasonableness.

The Prince was, however, ready enough to fall in with Nelson's policy against the interloping trade, while Wilfred seems to have worn himself out in the same service. He died suddenly, on 21 April 1787, aged only thirty-eight, the event being described in a long letter from Nelson dated 3 May from Nevis.

My dear Collingwood [he wrote sadly and formally, in place of his usual familiar 'Col']: To be the messenger of bad news is my misfortune, but still it is a tribute which friends owe each other. I have lost my friend, you an affectionate brother.

[1] N.C., 17.   [2] Nic. i. 128.

Too great a zeal in serving his Country hastened his end. The greatest consolation the survivor can receive, is a thorough knowledge of a life spent with honour to himself, and of service to his Country. If the tribute of tears be valuable, my friend had them.

The esteem he stood in with His Royal Highness was great. His letter to me on his death is the strongest testimony of it. I send you an extract of it: 'Collingwood, poor fellow, is no more. I have cried for him, and most sincerely do I condole with you on his loss. In him, His Majesty has lost a faithful Servant, and the Service a most excellent Officer.' A testimony of regard so honourable is more to be coveted than anything this world could have afforded, and must be a balm to his surviving friends.

The *Rattler* had been refitting at English Harbour, and when I arrived there in the middle of April, Wilfred was a little complaining, but I did not think, at first, anything dangerous was to be apprehended. But in a few days I perceived he was in a rapid decline. Dr. Young told me to send him to Sea, as the only chance. He sailed on the Tuesday for Grenada, where I was in hopes, could he have reached Mr. Hume's, some fortunate circumstance might turn out; but it pleased God to order it otherwise. On Friday, the 21st of April, at ten at night, he left this life without a groan or struggle.

The Ship put in to St. Vincent's, where he was interred with all Military Honours; the Regiment, President and Council attending him to the grave. I mention the circumstance to show the respect for his character. It is a credit to the people of St. Vincent's, which I did not think they would have deserved. I have directed Wallis not to suffer a thing to be disposed of, but to have everything sealed up the moment he goes on board, and that I will take them on board the *Boreas*, and carry them home.

Adieu, my good friend, and be assured I am, with the truest regard, your affectionate friend   HORATIO NELSON

Mrs. Nelson desires to present her kind compliments and condolence.[1]

The postscript referred to Nelson's newly married wife, formerly

[1] Nic., i. 20.

Frances Nesbit. Collingwood had known before he left the Station of his friend's attraction—and the ill-fated union at Nevis, which took place in March 1787, had been attended by the Prince.

One of the *Mediator*'s midshipmen had been Jeffery Raigersfeld, a son of Baron de Raigersfeld who came to England in 1756 as a member of the Austrian Embassy. Jeffery was a boy of twelve when he joined the ship and he served for the whole of her commission. He conceived the greatest admiration for his captain, and was able to observe the brothers Collingwood at sea together. He wrote:

> During our stay in the West Indies, Captain Cuthbert Collingwood had frequently under his command the *Rattler* sloop-of-war, which was commanded by his brother . . . The brothers resembled each other in nothing but their zeal for the service, which never relaxed, indeed when the two ships were cruising together, I often thought that the sail the *Rattler* carried to keep her station with the *Mediator*, when a strong breeze blew and a lumping sea was going, that that small ship, a sloop-of-war, would be swamped; however the two brothers were always on good terms with each other when they met on board the *Mediator* at dinner, though that was not often. Captain Cuthbert Collingwood was a reserved man, a good seaman and navigator, and well read in the English classics; and most heartily do I thank him for the care and pains he took to make me a seaman.[1]

'Pains' included punishments of various kinds, invariably the result of just consideration, and encouragement was liberally afforded when this was deserved. The punishments included, for the 'young gentlemen', mast-heading, disrating, being turned before the mast, flogging, and being turned out of the Navy for good.

> On board the *Mediator* [Raigersfeld continued], all these punishments were inflicted at various times; and one morning after breakfast, while at anchor in St. John's Road, Antigua, all the midshipmen were sent for into the Captain's

[1] *The Life of a Sea Officer*, by Jeffery Baron de Raigersfeld, edited by L. G. Carr Laughton (1929), pp. 35–6.

cabin, and four of us were tied up one after the other to the
breech of one of the guns, and flogged upon our bare bottoms
with a cat-o'-nine-tails, by the boatswain of the ship; some
received six lashes, some seven, and myself three. No doubt
we all deserved it, and were thankful that we were punished
in the cabin instead of upon deck, which was not uncommon
in other ships of the fleet.

Some time after this another of the midshipmen and myself
were put to mess with the common men, where we lived with
them three months, performing all the offices of the ship boys
such as cooking the victuals, standing the rank at the ship's
copper for the beef, burgoo and pease soup, and cleaning the
mess platters. At first I was indignant at such treatment, but
there was no help for it, therefore I quietly resigned myself to
my fate, and I am very glad I was so placed, as it gave me a
great insight into the character of seamen, and enabled me
to govern them as well as their officers hereafter with advantage to themselves and the country. In so doing Captain
Collingwood did his duty by me, as well as his country, and
I was thankful he so took it into his head, for during those
three months I gained more knowledge of the seamen's
character, than in all the other ships I have since served in
during the trials I have undergone in my profession.

II

After his return home from the West Indies, Collingwood enjoyed the first of the only three extended periods he ever spent
in the North of England between boyhood and death. The time
was described in a single sentence in the arrow-swift account of
his career printed in the *Naval Chronicle*. 'From 1786 to 1790 I
was in Northumberland, making my acquaintance with my own
family, to whom I had hitherto been as it were a stranger.'

As that was indeed so, Collingwood wrote few letters, and his
interests have to be deduced from the series which he addressed
to his sister Mary, which were sent to her from London and
elsewhere between May and October 1790. These arose from the
next excitement in his life. 'In 1790', continued the *Naval
Chronicle* account, 'an armament being prepared against Spain,

I was appointed to the command of the *Mermaid*, and went to the West Indies with Admiral Cornish . . .'

As one of the innumerable war scares in history which came to nothing, the affair of 1790 has not attracted much attention, but it had considerable importance for the Royal Navy. Trouble arose because the officer in charge of two Spanish ships of war seized some British vessels lying at Nootka Sound, off what is now Vancouver Island, which was held to be within waters controlled by Spain. The crews were sent as prisoners of war to a Spanish port, and since, as the result of the investigations of James Cook in his third voyage of circumnavigation (1776–9) British interest in the area had notably increased, and since, moreover, Spanish sea power was held in some contempt, a high tone was taken by the Government of George III, and preparations made accordingly. The then large sum of £3,000,000 was expended in what Collingwood described as the 'armament', and naval officers eager for service had their chance of a ship.

In the upshot, unsupported as she was by France, Spain climbed down, even allowing settlements in certain areas on the American coast of the Pacific, but the stir was notable while it lasted, and the money was not altogether wasted, since, as Edward Brenton remarked, 'it brought forward the naval service, which in a peace of seven years had fallen into much disuse'.[1] Not every captain was as lucky as Collingwood in getting a command. Nelson, for instance, who was at home in Norfolk, was entirely unsuccessful.

By May 1790, Collingwood had made his way to London to ask for an appointment, quartering himself this time at 62 Dean Street, Soho. On the 10th he wrote to Mary to report, and this time he spoke with such confidence that he gave her precise orders about his things.[2]

Here we are in the most delightful confusion. War is inevitable and every preparation making . . . Every body pushing their interest for ships. We who have none must be content to wait until those who have are out of our way, but I think I can hardly miss being employed very soon, therefore have

[1] Edward Brenton, *Naval History of Great Britain, 1783–1822* (1823), i. 71.
[2] H., Letter 8.

enclosed to you the key of my bureau. The keys of my trunks
are in it. Every thing that is in my bureau except the ragged
shirts leave in it, fill it with linnen from the trunk, so as to
prevent its shaking, but with such things as are least heavy.
All the papers that are in it leave just in the state they are,
all the plans and draft books put into the larger chest, with
such books of navigation and signals as are on the book
shelves and, in the drawers under them, three spy glasses.
The shortest night glass not to be packed, it may stay; in a
right hand drawer in the top of the bureau is the great object
glass of the largest telescope, it must be screwed in its place.
My quadrant with the brass at the key hole must be put into
the chest, the glasses might be rolled in the cloaks to preserve
them from injury, a few books might be put in where there is
room, the Spectator and Shakespear. Of plate my plain
spoons, fish things and teaspoons, those I bought last, no
salts, cups nor castors: of linnen, 4 prs of sheets, and my sea
table cloths and breakfast cloths, towels etc. In short, where
I say that my very best things, I wou'd not have come, I
think you will know exactly what I wish shou'd come. My
new shoes are in a box—I do not know where. May I beg of
my brother John to get those things in readiness for me, that
if I am appointed to a ship they may be sent to the port
where she is, by the earliest opportunity that offers.

The letter continued, full of naval gossip and political rumour,
and Collingwood also afforded his sister a glimpse of their kinsman, the important Mr. Collingwood of Chirton, which has its
humour.

I must not forget Mr Coll[ingwood's] commands which have
been so often repeated that I imagine it is of consequence to
his peace they shou'd be exactly conformed to. It is that John
will go down to Chirton and stay with Miss Roddam during
the holy days of Whitsuntide. Every time we have met for
this fortnight past it has been [a] subject [of conversation],
and seems far nearer his heart than any hope of advantage
from beating the Spaniards. I am doing all I can to get
employed, but all that appears matter of perfect indifference
to him.

The allusion Collingwood made in this letter to his reading-matter is informing, for Shakespeare and Addison's *Spectator* were also favourites with Nelson, while everyone of their time and upbringing would have had the cadences of the King James Bible as part of their mental equipment. Collingwood knew the value of good models.[1] Newnham Collingwood printed a letter which the captain wrote to one of his youngsters during his spell at home. 'Read,' said Collingwood, '—let me charge you to read. Study books that treat of your profession, and of history. Study Faulkner's Dictionary, and borrow, if you can, books which describe the West Indies, and compare what you find therein with your own observation. Thus employed, you will always be in good company.'[2] The specific reference (inaccurately transcribed by Newnham Collingwood) was to William Falconer (1732–69), poet, sailor, and publisher of *The Universal Marine Dictionary* in the very year that he was himself lost at sea.

On 29 May Collingwood wrote further to say that 'in the city they seem satisfied there will be no war, yet the naval preparation is making with exertions that seem to imply a different opinion in the Ministers. In short, I believe no man can say at present whether this spark will blaze or not.' Lord Chatham, then presiding at the Admiralty, had already more or less promised Collingwood a frigate, and he had called on Lord Howe, who was expected to serve as Commander-in-Chief:

> . . . this was more complimentary than official [Collingwood confided to his sister], and few have thought it necessary. I took the occasion to offer my service to him, at which he expressed great satisfaction, but if I am employed I do not much care where. If I had a choice it wou'd carry me to Jamaica, but if the Spaniard is bold enough to war with us single handed he can never shew his face on the sea, we must play the ferret and seek them in their hiding places.[3]

Personal and political rumours and comments followed, then came a further injunction to 'keep my things in a state of readiness', and finally an indication of that fondness for animals

---

[1] 'Whoever wishes to attain an English style . . . must give his days and nights to the volumes of Addison.'—Samuel Johnson.

[2] N.C., 15.   [3] H., Letter 9

III. Commander Wilfred Collingwood (1749–87).
Silhouette by W. Willings, 1781, showing him as a lieutenant.
Collection of Sir Edward Collingwood.

IVA. Collingwood by Nelson.

IVB. Nelson by Collingwood.

Portraits done in the house of Commissioner Moutray at Antigua *c.* 1785. Nelson wears a wig. His head had been shaved as the result of fever. *National Maritime Museum.*

for which Collingwood was particularly noted in his later years. 'My dog is a charming creature,' he wrote, 'every body admires him but he is grown as tall as the table I am writing on almost.'

By 14 June, Collingwood's affairs were so nearly settled that he gave precise instructions how his stuff was to be forwarded. Lord Chatham had already offered him a 64-gun ship, which was then ready, or else a frigate. He chose the frigate, for reasons he explained to his sister, who must by this time have understood a good deal about nautical matters.

You will, may-be, wonder that I shou'd prefer a frigate to a line of battle ship where my pay would be two hundred pounds a year more: a 74 I shou'd prefer to anything, but there are many disagreeable things attach'd to the 64 ships. Their most common employment is convoy, which is a constant worry: in the line they are the weakest ships, for which reason when any detachment is made they are the ships, and they are besides the most likely to be sent to India. And as for the difference of emolument; in a frigate the expenses are somewhat less and if I can get her into the W't Indies I will make the Dons pay me the difference once or twice a month I hope. The larger frigates are in general more sought after, but I think I can make mine equal to anything the Spaniards have on one deck, and what is everything I am perfectly content.[1]

Collingwood had been much helped by a fellow-captain, Lord Hugh Seymour, who had praised him to the First Lord, Seymour being an officer with whom he was later to serve in battle, and he gave his sister messages to various people in the North who might help him recruit.

By 15 July he was at Sheerness in charge of the *Mermaid*, and able to issue still more precise directions about his baggage. He was seeing much of his friend Sir Hew Dalrymple, a colonel in the army, and told his sister he had 'as much business as I can lay my hands to, and my spirits rise in proportion to my exercise'.[2] As for his dog: 'My dog is a good dog, delights in the ship and swims after me when I go in the boat.' Later he moved round to Portsmouth, and on 4 October referred to a matter which Mary would have known all about. He had been courting.

And have you been to visit my dear Sarah? [he asked] She

wishes very much to be well acquainted with you but is so shy you must encourage her. I think if you would let her drink tea with you in my Doll's room[1] she wou'd soon loose that reserve that diffident people have at first. Alas! I am going abroad . . . I am quite distressed that I must leave things as they are . . . Pray go and see my Sarah. I have told her you will and she is expecting you . . .[2]

Before the winter had set in, Collingwood was off with his squadron to the West Indies on a cruise which lasted until April 1791.[3] It was a pleasant and, as it proved, uneventful way of spending the cold months on full pay in a climate he enjoyed.

III

'Affairs with Spain . . . being accomodated, and no prospect of having employment at sea again soon,' Collingwood continued in the *Naval Chronicle*, 'I went into the North, and was married, and thought I was settling myself in great comfort, but I was mistaken . . .'

Once the *Mermaid* was back in England, Collingwood lost no time in returning home, and it was well that he did so, for his spell of privacy was so short, considering the responsibilities he took on, and the attachment he felt to all his closer kindred, that every moment became treasured.

Collingwood was married on 18 June 1791, in Newcastle, to his Sarah. She was the daughter of John Erasmus Blackett, Mayor of the city, who was a well-to-do merchant of excellent family. Sarah's maternal grandfather was Admiral Roddam, and her relations included an uncle, Sir Edward Blackett, who became one of Collingwood's favourite correspondents, also Doctor Alexander Carlyle, a well-known writer and divine, nicknamed 'Jupiter' Carlyle from his handsome appearance, the husband of a much-loved aunt of the bride's. Sarah's sister, who became Mrs. Stead, lived further south, and she was also the recipient of many and continued confidences.

The marriage was as happy as it could well be, given the circumstances of Collingwood's later life. Sarah made a devoted

---

[1] 'Doll' was always the most delicate sister, though, as is so often the case, she lived to a great age.

[2] H., Letter 12.   [3] P.R.O./Ad 51/590; captain's log.

wife, and the pair settled in a plain-looking house at Morpeth,
north of Newcastle. There were two children, both girls: Sarah,
born in 1792, and Mary Patience, born the year following, of
whom their father was destined to see little.

The letters which survive from the months at home are
few. Two are to Mary Collingwood. One, from Morpeth, is to
Alexander Carlyle, and one to Nelson. Even the second of those
to Mary, from London, foreshadows the future, since it is much
occupied with the prospect of new employment at sea.

The first letter to Mary, dated on 21 February 1792 from
Musselburgh, at which place the Collingwoods had been staying
with Alexander and Mrs. Carlyle, gave an account of Edinburgh.

> We have been a week . . . visiting and dining with a few
> people but not entering at all into the gayeties which ap-
> proach more to extravagency than I had any idea of. And
> we were every morning at six or five disturbed by the return
> of parties and the rattling of coaches. We left the town a day
> or two sooner on my account, for on one of those cold days
> I was suddenly seized with so violent a rheumatic pain in my
> back that if Mr Blackett had not been with me I do not know
> I shou'd have got home. I am now however quite well again.[1]

Collingwood's observations on the Carlyles, and on the country
he was visiting, were nothing if not frank.

> Mrs Carlyle is in a very weak state of health but she fretts
> herself on every trifling occasion and has so many fears and
> apprehensions about nothing, that I do not think she will
> ever be much better. Her hardy husband seems as if he was
> out of reach of accident. I shall be very glad, and so I believe
> shall we all, to get home again. This has been called the land
> of cakes; it may well be called the land of pensions. There is
> hardly a family of any note, either famous or infamous, who
> have not (some one of them) a pension. Even the Lady
> Augusta Murray who was the other day found in bed with
> the village apothecary has since that by the interest of her
> friend Dundas got a pansion [sic] of 300£ a year. The dowager
> Lady Errol, the young Lady Errol, and Mrs McCoy have each
> pensions of 300£ pr ann; the propriety of the first being aided

[1] H., Letter 14.

by the royal bounty will not sanction the abuse of giving to Mrs McCoy who has a very ample provision what might be so much better bestowed on indigence, or unfortunate industry. I cannot hear the subject mentioned, which however is a very common one, without expression of astonishment and resentment that the munificence of the king shou'd be so abused by the direction of it to objects so very unworthy, a sort of comment that is not much relished.

On 27 September of the same year, Collingwood gave Carlyle his views on the Northumberland weather. 'If you have the kind . . . we have had for this last two months, very cold and very rainy, seldom a day passes without some. We seek comfort at home and a good fire.' Then there was a reference to 'our darling', the infant Sarah, who had been inoculated and had 'taken' satisfactorily. Mr. Blackett, his father-in-law, had been with them for a week, anxious about his 'little Sall'. They had been to the local races, which had caused some entertainment.

We had notwithstanding the deluge, a great deal of company at the races last week to see five gentlemen play the part of jockeys, some of them unskilfull enough. Mr Watson of North Seaton mounted on a good horse, when he found he could not win the race, quitted the ground without riding up to the post, by which he caused considerable betts to be lost to his friends . . .[1]

This was the time of some of the worst excesses of the French Revolution. The newly formed Republic had recently declared war on Austria, and become involved with Prussia. Within six months, Britain would be drawn in as well: and Collingwood left Carlyle in no doubt how he himself felt about foreign affairs. His views were conservative, and were complacent about the virtues of the form of government under which he himself lived.

If the French people are not all mad [he wrote], I pity most sincerely those who have yet retained their senses . . . I hope the miseries of France will be such a lesson to the Patriots of this country as will teach them the danger of reform and shew them the true value of this form of government, which

[1] H., Letter 15.

affords the means of happiness to all who have from nature
dispositions to enjoy it.

These views were emphasized in a letter from Morpeth to
Nelson, written on 14 November, when he said:[1]

> There are great commotions in our neighbourhood at present.
> The seamen of Shields have embarked themselves, to the
> number of 1200 or 1400, with a view to compel the owners of
> the coal-ships to advance their wages; and as is generally the
> case when they consider themselves the strongest party, their
> demand has been exorbitant. Application was made to
> Government for such assistance as the remedy of this evil
> might require. They have sent the *Drake* and *Martin* sloops
> to join the *Race-horse*, which was here before, and some troops
> of dragoons, whose presence, I hope, will dispose the Johnnies
> to peace, without their having occasion to act. But the times
> are turbulent; and the enthusiasm for liberty is raging even
> to madness. The success of the French people in establishing
> their republic has set the same principle, which lurked in
> every state in Europe, afloat; and those who secreted it in
> their bosoms have now the boldness to avow a plan for adopt-
> ing it in the government of this Country, and to recruit
> volunteers for carrying their purpose into execution. In this
> neighbourhood we seem to be pacific. Misery will undoubtedly
> be the consequence of any commotion or attempt to disturb
> our present most excellent Constitution. . . .

All too soon, the war was to engulf Collingwood, for on
17 February 1793 he was in London, writing to Mary about
his prospects of a ship. He had met with an incident which
gave him great annoyance.

> When I called on Mr Brandling one day [he said], not having
> any intention to ask anything of him, he offered his service
> with great civility, and said he would do anything that I
> thought wou'd assist me. Mr Black[ett] had wrote to him
> on the subject before. It was agreed he shou'd write to Lord
> Chatham. He sent me a copy of the letter, which I dare say
> he thought a very proper one—I did not. I felt my pride
> offended that no better claim for his Lordship's attention

[1] N.C., 17–18.

was advanced for me, than that I had a *Vote* for a *Parliament Man*. I am lamenting that he happened to be at home, or that he had not a happier mode of making his requisition, but do not say anything of this, especially to the Squire, for he is not quite in my grace at present.[1]

The 'Squire' was of course Mr. Collingwood of Chirton, who owed him a letter. The Squire had told Blackett: 'he would have answered my letter but did not choose to put me to the expense of postage. If sixpence had been as dear in my eye as it is in his, the reason wou'd have been a very good one: I hope it never will be, and people who are poor do not like to be told of it every day.'

The great news was that Collingwood was to go as flag-captain to his old friend George Bowyer, recently promoted to the Rear-Admiral's list, and he would command the *Prince*. She was the biggest vessel he had ever been given, a three-decked ship-of-the-line of 98 guns, rated in the second class, and almost new. Collingwood came to know her well, but he soon found her 'the most miserable sailer in the fleet, for ever in the rear'. He and Bowyer transferred early in the following year to the *Barfleur*, a much older 2nd rate, completed in 1768 and seasoned in battle under Samuel Hood and Rodney in the American War. Some two years after Collingwood left her, the *Prince* became the first man-of-war of anywhere near her size to be cut in two and lengthened. The alteration did not do her much good, for, although she was to be present at Trafalgar, she was as slow as ever.

First in the *Prince*, then in the *Barfleur*, Collingwood had begun that servitude which, since it had only a single interruption, was gradually to wear him out: but as active service was before him, and bright prospects, he was content. He was nearly forty-five, ripe in sea experience, master of his profession. He could go far.

[1] H., Letter 16: Charles Brandling was M.P. for Newcastle.

3   *The Glorious First of June*

Thanks largely to the 'armament' of 1790–91, the opening of what was to prove, with short breaks, a twenty-two-year-long struggle with France and her various allies found the Navy reasonably well ordered: ships in fair number, and the most active officers recently exercised, though there was the usual shortage of stores, including masts.

There were to be two main fleets, Home and Mediterranean, commanded respectively by Howe and Hood. Both admirals were close upon seventy, and Howe had always reasoned that an officer should not serve operationally at more than sixty years of age, unless specially pressed to do so. Hood had no such reservations, but the history of war shows Howe to have been right.

The King had immense faith in Howe, and personally requested that he should go to sea. There could be no refusal of such a wish. Within the Service, each fleet thought it was being robbed of ships and material in favour of the other, but the general view was that the choice of commanders-in-chief was right: in Howe's case, very right. Alas, the first letter that Collingwood sent home from sea, addressed from Spithead on 22 July 1793 to Sir Edward Blackett,[1] spoke of shortage of men and 'a tardiness every where in the preparation and a sluggishness in the execution that is quite new'. Even the volunteers he had himself procured in the North had been drafted elsewhere, and one of them had written from another ship to complain.

Howe's opening cruise had been marred by an accident to the *Bellerophon*—in which Bowyer had first flown his flag—which was run into by the *Majestic* during a squall and damaged.

[1] H., Letter 17.

This [wrote Collingwood] was not the fault of the ship nor the weather, but must ever be the case when young men are made officers who have neither skill nor attention, and there is scarce a ship in the Navy that has not an instance that political interest is a better argument for promotion than any skill.

Things should be better where his own charge was concerned. 'Admiral Bowyer,' he told his correspondent, 'is very pleased with the order of his ship, but it keeps me, like a bow, for ever bent.'

On 1 August, Collingwood wrote to Mary from Spithead, telling her he thought that letters to his wife (which unfortunately have not survived), 'wou'd give you as good accounts of me as if I had addressed them to you'.[1] He repeated what he had said to Sir Edward Blackett about his ship, 'but I can assure you,' he added, 'it cost me some fat to make her what she is. I am not oppressed with belly now, and was never in my life in better health. Every moment of the day is occupied, and when I go to bed I have always enough to begin upon in the morning.'

He was concerned about 'little Sall', and thought that 'mothers who have their children ever in their sight do not judge so well of change. I hope the salt water will agree with her and make her bear the cutting of her teeth, poor little darling.' Sarah was expecting her second child shortly, and Collingwood was anxious, although he knew she was in good hands. If the baby was a girl it was to be called Mary, after his correspondent, and Patience after Mrs. Stead: if a boy, Cuthbert. Squire Collingwood and Sir Edward Blackett were to be godfathers, and Mary and Mrs. Carlyle godmothers.

By 10 September, when he wrote from Torbay to Mrs. Carlyle, all had turned out well: Mary Patience and her mother were flourishing. 'My heart is full of gratitude to you,' he told this aunt by marriage, who was evidently capable of forgetting her own 'fretts' in an anxious time for Sarah: 'I have no interest in this world superior to the happiness of my beloved wife.' He was well, but his 'unremitted business wears me to a skeleton'. There had been surprise, it seemed, at the sheer size of the French fleet, which had been sighted off Scilly: but confidence

[1] H., Letter 18.

was now more general. 'Lord Howe is high in the estimation of every body who has witnessed his skill,' said Collingwood, 'and no man can judge better what is proper to be done. Who would have thought the British fleet would ever have been surpassed in strength by that of the Republicans?'[1]

On 27 December 1793, Collingwood gave Sir Edward Blackett an account of Howe's winter cruise. He was still in the *Prince*, but in future letters would be headed *Barfleur*, for he and the admiral were on the point of transferring. Howe was being blamed in the press for not bringing on a successful battle. It was the old story: the public wanted news to hearten them, and nothing cheerful had come from sea. Howe had had information that the French were out in strength, but he could not get near them with his main force, so that the cruise as a whole

> ... was a series of vexations, disappointments and bad weather. What is more mortifying than all those is to find on our return that to be unfortunate is to be criminal, and that want of success where it was scarce to be expected, is treated with all the severity of censure of a high offence. I believe no man can serve on a more honourable principle than Lord Howe does: to do good service to his country is the first ambition of his life, but he has no supernatural powers on a winter's day to make the sun stand still, or make an English ship sail fast and a French ship ill.

However things might be at sea, yet when he thought of home, Collingwood's spirits lifted at once:

> ... my little precious girls thriving to a wish. I am sure I have great cause for thankfulness for such a family, a wife that is goodness itself, and two healthy children that with her care and her example can scarce fail to be like her. All my troubles here seem light when I look Northward and consider how well I am rewarded for them.[2]

Collingwood was concerned for the safety of convoys. One, a large body of ships, had been 'cut up' off the coast of America, and he believed that Howe's cruise had saved another. 'The W't India Convoy is sailed, a 64 gun ship and frigate with more than 170 sail of merchant ships. If the French are out, which

[1] H., Letter 19.   [2] H., Letter 20.

is very likely, it is easy to see what will become of them. We must hope all will be well.'

On 2 March 1794 Sir Edward Blackett had the benefit of Collingwood's impressions of the war in general.

This war is certainly unlike any former, both in its object and execution. The object is a great and serious one, to resist the machinations of a mad people who, under the mask of freedom, wou'd stamp their tyranny in every country in Europe, and support and defend the happiest constitution that ever wisdom formed for the preserving order in civil society. The execution is quite mysterious. Great fleets are prepared and lay totally inactive; schemes of conquest are formed and relinquished at the moment when execution is expected.[1]

He had heard of Hood's enterprise in occupying Toulon, but this had been followed by withdrawal, ghastly massacre of friendly people, and failure to destroy French ships-of-war in the harbour before leaving. Nelson was with Hood, but his high praise of the admiral's qualities in his letters home found no echo in Collingwood's. Of Toulon Collingwood said: 'Lord Hood was in good luck to get possession of it, but was not General enough to discover how critical his situation was there.' He spoke of 'gross mismanagement,' and attributed the lack of success in destroying the enemy ships largely to Sir Sydney Smith, an officer against whom there was already much prejudice.

No preparation was made either for the destruction of ships or arsenal, and at last perhaps it was put into as bad hands as cou'd be found. Sr Sid. Smith, who arrived there a few days before, and had no public situation, either in fleet or army, but was wandering to gratify his curiosity. You know how it was executed. The ships shou'd have been prepared for sinking as soon as he got possession of them, loading them deep with ballast and stones and making a port hole in them near the edge of the water, and then place the ships in those parts of the harbour which wou'd most effectually injure it. If the necessity of sinking them did not arise, the

---

[1] H., Letter 21.

ships would be uninjured; if it did, they might all have been put under water in half an hour. The squadron in the Mediterranean are very much in the dumps. Lord H's ambition far exceeding his abilities gives rise to many unpleasant circumstances.

Collingwood found small comfort anywhere except at home, and there everything seemed perfect in his eyes.

In all our operations there is nothing pleasurable to be found. I must look for that at home, where I hope and believe I shall never be disappointed. My good wife and her two darling little girls who, they say, are as fine healthy children as ever were, are well. Your goddaughter has been inoculated, had the small pox very plentifully and is recovering as well as can be wished. Mr Blackett is very well and so fond of them and so kind to them, that I think they are as happy a family as can be found. I wished very much to have gone down to them for a fortnight, but cou'd not obtain leave.

Within three months, even the professional's clouds had lifted, for Collingwood had taken part in his first major sea battle, that of the Glorious First of June, 1794. The engagement, which took place far out into the Atlantic, was given a name which, in the circumstances, was somewhat grandiloquent, since the main action was the culmination of a whole series of operations, some successful, some not. But it was the King himself who sanctioned the use of the adjective Glorious, and the action gave the utmost pleasure to both Navy and nation.

There are no better accounts of the day itself than Collingwood's.

II

The cruise which led to Howe's victory began on 2 May 1794 and had three aims. The first was to cover outward convoys from England; the second was to intercept a convoy of 117 ships bound from America to France with badly needed foodstuffs; and the third was to meet and if possible cripple the main French fleet, which would certainly be employed to cover their merchantmen. The first and third of these objects were accomplished. The second was not, and Villaret-Joyeuse, the French commander-in-chief, considered the loss, on 1 June, of seven ships of the line, six captured and one sunk, a price well worth paying to get grain safely to France. So did his Government.

The size of Howe's fleet, 32 ships of the line, with frigates and smaller craft, and with an attendant hospital ship, the *Charon* (ill named), was reminiscent of the days of the seventeenth-century wars with the Dutch. So was the galaxy of flag-officers: Howe himself, Thomas Graves, Sir Alexander Hood, younger brother of Lord Hood, George Bowyer, Benjamin Caldwell, Alan Gardner, Thomas Pasley, and George Montagu. The junior admiral, Montagu, was reserved for detached duty with the convoys. In the outcome, he protected his own charges satisfactorily, but had no success in intercepting the French.

Howe sailed from Spithead, with 26 ships of the line as his battle force, Montagu, with six others, being detached soon after the fleet was off the Lizard. On 5 May, while off Ushant, Howe learnt that the main French fleet had not yet sailed. The frigates *Latona* and *Phaeton* made a close reconnaissance and reported two ships of the line, two frigates, and two brigs at anchor under shore batteries. Twenty-two larger ships were seen within the Goulet.

Howe did not want to prevent the French from putting to sea, since he was as eager to defeat them as to capture the convoy. He therefore made no attempt to watch the port, but advanced south-westerly, putting himself between the grain ships and their covering force, and thus in a position to deal with them first and to fight Villaret-Joyeuse later.

A week passed, and Howe met nothing. Retracing his course, he went back to Ushant, off which he arrived on 19 May. His frigates reported that Brest was empty, and they brought the added news, gleaned from coastal shipping, that the French, 25 of the line, had sailed three days earlier. Villaret-Joyeuse had been joined at sea by one more ship, and had actually passed close to Howe, unseen in the prevailing foggy weather.

Having missed the French, Howe's first idea was to steer after Admiral Montagu, but late at night on 21 May the flag-ship *Queen Charlotte* nearly ran down a brig, the *Argo*, which was boarded. She proved to be one of a convoy to Newfoundland which had just been snapped up by the main French fleet. The only escort had been Captain Thomas Troubridge of the frigate *Castor*, who had had to surrender to overwhelming numbers. Many of the vessels were recaptured, and Troubridge himself was among those later released. His former ship fell to the *Carysfort* even before she reached France, so she was not long lost to the Navy.

Meeting with the *Argo* decided Howe that he must be near the French, so he held a westerly course. Early in the morning of 25 May, two corvettes out of Brest were sighted. They were steering after the French fleet, and mistook the British for their own. Both ships were taken and burnt, Howe having no men to spare for prize crews, particularly in view of an imminent battle. Early on 28 May, with a rough sea running, frigates sighted the enemy. They were to windward, and about ten miles away. The relative position was important, since, with the advantage of the weather gage, Villaret-Joyeuse could refuse action if he so wished, or attack in his own time. It was now apparent that he was between Howe and the grain convoy.

At first, the French held on, but when they discovered the size of Howe's fleet they hauled their wind. Howe had formed his fastest sailing ships into a flying squadron under Admiral Pasley in the *Bellerophon*. At 8.25 on the 28th, Howe signalled Pasley to 'reconnoitre or make discovery of the enemy or strange ships in view, and signify the same to the Admiral'. Being a diligent officer, Pasley was soon not merely reconnoitring, but in action.

As the French were distant, it was not until nearly two o'clock that Howe made the signal: 'Take suitable stations for mutual support and engage the enemy as arriving up in succession.' Five ships managed to get into action with the French rear, one of the enemy ships, the three-decked *Revolutionnaire*, being so badly mauled that, had it not been for nightfall and some misunderstanding, she would have been taken. One British ship, the *Audacious*, was also badly damaged, but, like the *Revolutionnaire*, she made port safely.

Next day, 29 May, Howe was still to leeward of the enemy, and his object was to gain the weather gage. He determined if possible to break through the French line from his leeward position. The van failed in this object, thanks largely to wretched handling of the leading ship, the *Caesar*, by Captain Molloy, but Howe in the *Queen Charlotte*, Pasley in the *Bellerophon*, and Lord Hugh Seymour in the *Leviathan* went through towards the enemy rear and cut off three Frenchmen. Other ships, including the *Queen*, whose captain lost a leg, the *Barfleur*, and the *Glory* did well in this action.

In order to save his damaged ships, Villaret-Joyeuse bore down to their defence with the rest. He saved them indeed, though they were unfit for further immediate fighting: but the second round was decidedly with Howe, since he had reduced the opposition and, even more important, had gained the weather gage. Howe could now attack, with his whole force, whenever he wished, provided the enemy stood his ground. If he did not, he could be chased across the broad ocean, and there would be stragglers in plenty for pursuers to take prize.

30 May was foggy, and Howe was content to keep contact, while Villaret-Joyeuse gradually edged away to leeward, skilfully enough to give his crippled ships a chance to get away, and for the convoy he was protecting to gain distance. He was also lucky enough to be reinforced by five ships from the west, so that his strength was brought up to at least what it was when he was first sighted.

Soon after midday on 31 May the fog lifted, but Howe, with the moral strength which marks a great commander, decided to postpone his attack until next day, to make sure of the result. The action of 29 May had shown that some at least of his captains needed the force of example, and this he meant to give. Before nightfall, he had got his ships into precise battle order, and thus they stayed all through the hours of darkness, ready to pursue if the enemy decided to run for it. By the late afternoon, when it had become apparent that Villaret-Joyeuse was a brave and determined man, Howe was seen to smile, and the news spread like wildfire round the flagship. 'Black Dick', as the men called him from his complexion, never smiled without reason.

On 1 June, hands were piped early to breakfast.

At ½ past 7 [to quote the log of the *Barfleur*],[1] haul'd to the

---

[1] P.R.O. Ad/51/90.

wind and formed a line close and compact—at 8 the Admiral
made the signal that he means to pass through their line and
engage them to leeward. At 9 the Admiral made the signal
for each ship to steer for and engage the ship opposite to her
in the enemy's line, at 10 the action began.

Howe's prophecy was that he would take a prize for every
ship of his fleet which obeyed his signal to break through the
French line, and he was exactly right. He noted the meritorious
six in his private journal—the *Queen Charlotte, Defence, Marlborough, Royal George, Queen*, and *Brunswick*, three of them
flag-ships and three-deckers. Six Frenchmen were taken, and
another, the *Vengeur*, was sunk after a fierce gun-duel with the
Brunswick. Well before midday the main fighting was over, and
the French in flight.

Collingwood had the industry to write a number of accounts
of the action in the days which immediately followed it. Several
have survived, and all are of value. They are remarkable as
giving an admirable idea of events as a whole, even from the
necessarily restricted point of view of a single ship. The first,
written at sea on 5 June, when battle-damage had scarcely been
made good, was to his father-in-law, John Erasmus Blackett,
who could be trusted to circulate the information where it
would be best appreciated.[1]

My dear Sir

When the Admiral's despatches came away, I
was unable, from fatigue and hurry, to write more than a
few lines to my wife, to tell her that I was well; but as no
doubt you will be desirous to know the particulars of our
success, I will first give you the outlines of our cruise previously to the 1st of June, and then all the satisfaction I can
as to the proceedings of that day.

It is a narration full of incident, and I feel myself very
unequal to describe a battle unlike any thing that perhaps
ever happened before, for we had three days' hard fighting
before we were crowned with victory, by the total defeat and
flight of a fleet superior to our own, and sent out for the
express purpose of destroying us.

[1] N.C., 19–23.

Well, then, after seeing the convoys down the Channel as far as the Lizard, and detaching Rear-admiral Montague, with six sail of the line, for their further protection, we stretched across the Channel to Brest, and sent in two frigates, covered by two ships of the line, to see what force was there; when they found the French fleet at anchor, and counted twenty-four sail of large ships. Unsettled weather, and the wind hanging to the north-eastward, set us to the southward, so that it was fourteen days before we got off Brest again, and then found that the enemy's fleet was gone.

How the Admiral got his intelligence I do not know, but he did get a very exact account of their route; for we immediately made all the sail we could for 150 leagues to the westward, retaking about fifteen English merchant vessels, some Dutch, and a few French cruisers, in our way; all of which were immediately burnt, as it was impossible, under the circumstances in which we were, to spare a man, or to be encumbered with prizes.

In that situation we cruised for a few days, like disappointed people looking for what they could not find, until the morning of little Sarah's birthday, between eight and nine o'clock, when the French fleet of twenty-five sail of the line, was discovered to windward. We chased them, and they bore down within about five miles of us.

Admiral Pasley commanded the advanced squadron of four sail, viz. *Bellerophon, Russell, Marlborough* and *Thunderer*. They were much nearer; and about three o'clock they began to exchange fire with the enemy's rear, which increased as they advanced, and continued very hot until nine at night, when the detached ships joined the fleet. On the 29th, the French fleet was to windward about three miles, and as it showed no disposition to come down, we tacked about six in the morning, in the hopes our van would bring their rear to close action; but they only fetched within a long shot, which the French kept up pretty smartly.

About eight, they wore, which again brought them in a line parallel to us, and their van continued a sharp cannonade on ours for two hours or more; when the Admiral, finding there was no chance of bringing them to close action but by a dash, made a signal for the van to tack, and the rest in

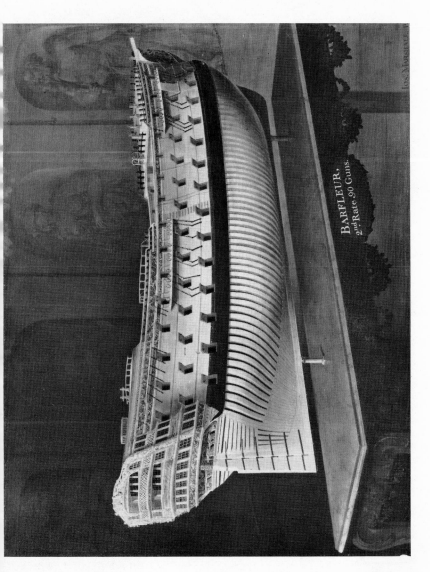

V. H.M.S. *Barfleur*, 90 guns. Perspective painting (showing the ship as a model) executed in 1774–5 for King George III. Collingwood commanded the *Barfleur* at the Glorious First of June, 1794, and later flew his flag in her. *Science Museum*.

ADMIRAL *the Earl of S* VINCENT

VI. Admiral the Earl of St. Vincent, drawing by Bouch.
A drawing made in Lisbon in 1797, the year of his victory over
the Spaniards. *National Portrait Gallery.*

succession to follow them; and we then led in amongst them in very fine style.

Admiral Gardner led the fleet, and suffered a good deal; but we cut up their rear effectually. They skilfully enough covered their disabled ships, and made an assault on ours (the *Queen* and *Invincible*); but Admiral Graves, in the *Royal Sovereign*, and ourselves stood between them, and had very smart work, for an hour and a half, with one of their first-rates and two 74 gun ships, when they all bore away.

On the 30th, we first saw them far to leeward, but it was foggy and bad weather, so thick that we could scarce see the length of the ship until the 31st, in the afternoon, when it cleared, and we observed the enemy to leeward forming their line. We bore down to them, and formed ours, which took us all the evening. The night was spent in watching and preparation for the succeeding day; and many a blessing did I send forth to my Sarah, lest I should never bless her more.

At dawn, we made our approach on the enemy, then drew up, dressed our ranks, and it was about eight when the Admiral made the signal for each ship to engage her opponent, and bring her to close action, and then down we went under a crowd of sail, and in a manner that would have animated the coldest heart, and struck terror into the most intrepid enemy.

The ship we were to engage was two ahead of the French admiral, so that we had to go through his fire, and that of two ships next him, and received all their broadsides two or three times before we fired a gun. It was then near ten o'clock. I observed to the Admiral, that about that time our wives were going to church, but that I thought the peal we should ring about the Frenchman's ears would outdo their parish bells. Lord Howe began his fire some time before we did; and he is not in the habit of firing soon.

We got very near indeed, and then began such a fire as would have done you good to have heard. During the whole action the most exact order was preserved, and no accident happened but what was inevitable, and the consequence of the enemy's shot. In ten minutes the Admiral was wounded; I caught him in my arms before he fell: the First Lieutenant was slightly wounded by the same shot, and I thought I was

5

in a fair way of being left on deck by myself; but the Lieutenant got his head dressed, and came up again. Soon after,
they called from the forecastle that the Frenchman was
sinking; at which the men started up and gave three cheers.
I saw the French ship dismasted, and on her broadside, but
in an instant she was clouded with smoke, and I do not know
whether she was sunk or not.[1] All the ships in our neighbourhood were dismasted, and are taken, except the French
Admiral, who was driven out of the line by Lord Howe, and
saved himself by flight.

At about twenty minutes past twelve, the fire slackened,
the French fled, and left us seven of their fine ships—*Sans
Pareil*, 84; *Juste*, 84; *L'Achille*, 74; *Northumberland*, 74;
[*L'Impetueux*, 74;] *L'Amerique*, 80 and *Le Vengeur*, 74, which
sank the same evening; so that you see we have had as complete a victory as could be won. Our condition did not admit
of a further pursuit; indeed, to take possession of what we
had got required exertion. Two of our ships were totally dismasted, and many of us very much crippled. We left off in
admirable good plight, having sustained less loss than could be
expected, considering the fire we had so long on us. We had
nine men killed, and twenty-two with severe wounds, a few
others slightly hurt; our masts &c all in their places, though
much wounded.

We have not obtained this victory without losses that must
long be lamented. Admiral Bowyer and Admiral Pasley have
each lost a leg; Admiral Graves is severely wounded in the
arm, and as he is seventy years of age, or nearly, it is hard
to say what will be the consequence. Captain Montague was
killed; and Captain Hutt, of the *Queen*, lost his leg.[2] Several
Lieutenants are killed and wounded: and this, altogether,
has been the severest action that has been fought in our time,
or perhaps ever. It did not last very severely much more than
two hours, when ten of the enemy's ships were dismasted,
and two of ours. They were superior to us in ships, men, and
guns, sent out for the express purpose of destroying us. Four
of their ships were provided with furnaces for red-hot shot,
one of which stuck in the *Royal Sovereign*, but I have not
heard that they did any mischief in any part of the fleet by

[1] She did not sink.   [2] Captain Hutt later died of his wound.

them. We understand their orders were to give no quarter;
and, indeed, they fought as if they expected none.

June 13. We are just arrived at Spithead. A thousand
blessings on you all.

> I am ever, my dear Sir
> Your truly affectionate Son.

It was Collingwood's references to his Sarah in this letter which
so appealed to Thackeray, and indeed, with its blend of the
general and the personal it is hard to see how this, the earliest
description Collingwood produced of the battle, could be improved except in unimportant particulars. In later letters, he
was able to add a few details, and Newnham Collingwood included a note in his book[1] to the effect that from a document
in his possession it appeared that in making their approach to
the enemy line, those in the *Barfleur* noted that the vessel
immediately opposed to them was much crippled in her masts
and rigging.

> The *Invincible* having been severely engaged [Collingwood
> stated] we made the signal to change places with her, that
> she might take the crippled ship, and we might have a fresh
> one. The *Invincible* stuck as close to us in going down, and
> during the whole action, as if she had been lashed to us, some-
> times having her jib-boom over our taffrail.

Dr. Carlyle was early in Collingwood's mind as a recipient
for news, and a letter to him was begun on 10 June, well before
the *Barfleur* anchored.[2] Much of the information was the same
as Collingwood had given his father-in-law, but the concluding
paragraph extended the writer's observations to the war as a
whole.

> I hope this battle will be attended with happy consequences,
> and tend to promote a peace; it certainly must give a security
> to our trade which has lately suffered exceedingly. But is it
> not astonishing that the French, who we have despised,
> ruined in their finances, supplied with great difficulty with
> stores, and almost all Europe at war with them, shou'd meet
> us at sea with a fleet superior to ours? It is leaving too much
> to fortune and chance. Great as the skill of Lord Howe is,

---

[1] N.C., 24.   [2] H., Letter 22.

and we have had nothing like him, it is not right to oppose us to a force that chance might give a victory to. I hope however their naval force is done for this summer; those that remain must be in a ruined and shattered state.

I am extremely distressed at the misfortune that has befallen Admiral Bowyer. The country will lose the service of a very gallant and intelligent officer. He bears it with a great deal of calmness, and is in a fair way of recovery. The accident will make a revolution in my affairs, for as this will always be an Admiral's ship, whoever comes will nominate his Captain. I do not know any person with whom I wou'd be in the same capacity, yet I think they cannot supercede me here, without appointing me to a ship to my wish.

Bowyer in fact lived another six years, enjoying his fine house at Radley, where a flag is still flown in his honour on 1 June. As for his own future, Collingwood had always wished to have charge of a 74-gun ship, and, if such should be his next appointment, he would be well content.

Meanwhile, there were other correspondents who must be given news, Edward Collingwood of Chirton among them. He was duly favoured with a very complete account,[1] and, by the time Collingwood addressed him, letters were beginning to arrive on board the *Barfleur* congratulating her captain on his part in the success and on his safe return. He had already begun to learn something about the immense drive which had enabled the Revolutionary Government of France to put a fleet of the strength of Villaret-Joyeuse's to sea. Much had been due to Jean-Bon Saint-André, officially a Navy Commissioner, who had sailed in the flagship *Le Montagne* and had had a say in all decisions. He was in fact a political commissar of a type known in far more recent revolutionary forces.

Not all that Collingwood heard was strictly accurate. For instance, in his undated letter to Chirton (the first missive from his naval cousin that 'the Squire' preserved), Collingwood remarked that 'six thousand have been guillotined at Brest for showing a backwardness, or endeavouring to get clear of the Service'. This was almost certainly an exaggeration, but at least it indicated the zeal with which Saint-André and his fellow

---

[1] Add. MSS. 52780.

doctrinaires had set to work, and it was already common talk
that if Villaret-Joyeuse had allowed the convoy from America
to be taken or destroyed, he would have lost his head.

To Sir Edward Blackett, Collingwood gave further expression
to his concern for Admiral Bowyer, and of his admiration for
Lord Howe, in a letter written on 15 June:[1]

. . . at the time we have so much to rejoice at, I have much
to lament in the sufferings of my friends, particularly Admiral
Bowyer, whose misfortune has quite checked joy in me. He
is a brave and gallant man, and was so raised by the success
of the day that he made his own misfortune of little consideration; and I believe he would have done himself material
injury by his spirits if I had not at last shut him up and
prohibited every body but the surgeon and necessary attendants going near him. We carried him on shore yesterday,
and I hope he is in a favourable way. It was early in the
action when he was wounded by a great shot, and I caught
him in my arms before he fell to the deck. It is a great misfortune to me: for the more we were engaged in business, the
more we were attached, and I believe he had full and implicit
confidence in me.

We who were seamen were well acquainted with the great
professional abilities of Lord Howe; but he has outdone all
opinion that could be formed. The proceedings of the 1st of
June were like magic, and could only be effected by skill like
his.

III

There were certain disappointments connected with Howe's
battle, generously as Collingwood and others viewed the skill
of the Commander-in-Chief. As regards the progress of the war,
the failure to intercept the French convoy can be put down
chiefly to the dispositions and to some extent the ill fortune of
Admiral Montagu and his detached ships, though if Howe himself had been able or willing to pursue Villaret-Joyeuse relent-
lessly back towards Brest, as the more eager thought he should
have done, the convoy or part of it might have fallen to him

[1] H., Letter 23.

as well as Villaret's unluckier ships of war. Howe's reasons for
not exploiting his success to the utmost were that those of his
ships which were least damaged, and so best able to pursue,
were the unlikeliest, from the way they had been handled in
battle, to be the most successful in a chase; moreover, Howe
liked to conduct all fleet operations by close control, which he
could not have exercised had he allowed an extended pursuit.
The final disappointment was in the nature of the public recog-
nition of those who had fought, a matter about which Collingwood felt as keenly as any man in England.

Howe's original announcement of the victory was in the form
of a Letter to the Admiralty, composed on 2 June while the
Fleet was still well out to sea, which was taken to England by
Sir Roger Curtis in a frigate and rushed to Whitehall by the
fastest available means. The Admiralty published the letter the
moment it was received, and the King made up his mind to
visit the Fleet in person, to congratulate the victors on the first
resounding success of the war up to that date. In the official
Letter, high praise was given to the fleet as a whole, but only
two individual services were referred to, those of Sir Roger
Curtis, who was Howe's First Captain or Chief of Staff, and
those of Sir Andrew Douglas, the second or flag-captain, who
was in charge of the *Queen Charlotte*. Howe was soon pressed
on all sides to add further names, at least those of the most
meritorious admirals and captains. This he did with some hesitation, not from any wish to withhold public approbation but
because, with long experience in such matters, he well knew
that any such supplementary letter would cause offence to those
not mentioned therein, and might well do more harm than
good.

The composition of the second letter was believed to have
been largely the work of Sir Roger Curtis, who was not a popular
character in the Fleet, and who undoubtedly had his prejudices.
The offending paragraph (which was intended so entirely otherwise), ran as follows:

> The commander of a fleet, their Lordships know, is unavoid-
> ably so confined in his view of the occurrences in time of
> battle, as to be little capable of rendering personal testimony
> to the meritorious services of officers who have profited, in a

greater extent, by the opportunities to distinguish themselves on such occasions.

To discharge this part of my public duty, reports were called for from the flag officers of the fleet, for supplying the defects of my observance, under the limited circumstances above mentioned. These officers, therefore, who have such particular claim to my attention, are the Admirals Graves and Sir Alexander Hood; the Rear Admirals Bowyer, Gardner and Pasley; the Captains Lord Hugh Seymour, Pakenham, Berkeley, Gambier, John Harvey, Payne, Parker, Henry Harvey, Pringle, Duckworth and Elphinstone. Special notice is also due of the Captains Nichols of the *Sovereign* and Hope of the *Bellerophon*, who became charged with, and well conducted, those ships, when the wounded flag-officers, under whom they respectively served therein, were no longer able to remain at their posts; and the Lieutenants Monckton of the *Marlborough* and Donnelly of the *Montagu*, in similar situations.

Some of the edge of this particularization would, it was hoped, be softened by the next sentence, which ran:

These selections, however, should not be construed to the disadvantage of other Commanders, who may have been equally deserving of the approbation of the Lords Commissioners of the Admiralty, although I am not enabled to make a particular statement of their merits.

Two features of the statement of services at once leapt to the eye of those most concerned. One admiral, Caldwell, was omitted, and one captain who had taken charge after his flag-officer had been wounded, Collingwood. Both men felt it as a personal affront, but, as it was recognized that Caldwell's large ship, the *Impregnable*, had not been more closely engaged than others whose captains were omitted, there was perhaps some logic in leaving him out. There appeared to be none in the case of Collingwood, and he was wounded to the heart.

Sir Edward Blackett was one of the earliest to be told exactly how Collingwood felt, for he wrote to him on 30 June[1] in reply to a letter which had asked him to take charge of a youngster in whom Blackett was interested.

[1] H., Letter 24.

I will take Mr Wise into my ship with a great deal of pleasure
[he wrote], rate him Midshipman, and do everything in my
power to bring him forward in the Service, and doubt not,
notwithstanding Lord Howe's supplemental letter, he may
learn his duty as an officer in my ship as well as any other.

That extraordinary production of Sr Roger's pen threw
the fleet into the utmost consternation and astonishment.
There was not a cool heart amongst us except Molloy's, whose
conduct is past defence,[1] and though the situation of the
ships in so large a fleet must necessarily be very different on
such a day, there was not, I believe, a suspicion in the mind
of any man that all had not done their duty well.

The appearance of that letter had nearly broke my heart,
but I still trusted the facts wou'd stand their ground against
any insinuations to their disadvantage: I went immediately
to Sr Roger Curtis and demanded to see Lord Howe who,
however, I have not yet seen with opportunity to talk on the
subject. I told Sr Roger that I considered the conduct of the
Barfleur had merited commendation when commendation
was given to zeal and activity and that an insinuation that
either had been wanting was injurious and unjust, nor do I
believe any ship was more warmly or effectively engaged than
the *Barfleur* from the beginning of the action to the end of it.
That the Frenchmen did not knock our masts away was not
my fault. He assured me no disapprobation was meant to be
implied, but that in the selection the Admiral was pleased
to make, he must stop somewhere, and the good conduct of
the fleet was summed up in a latter sentence. All that cou'd
be said to that was, that it was a most unfortunate style.
Those who were mentioned in this letter were almost as much
offended as those who were omitted.

Collingwood's observation was true, for Newnham Collingwood records[2] that Captain Pakenham of the *Invincible*, one of
those specially mentioned, used to say: 'If Collingwood has not
deserved a medal, neither have I; for we were together the
whole day.' The allusion to 'medals', as well as public mention

---

[1] Molloy, of the *Caesar*, came under general criticism, and as a result of a
later court martial he was dismissed his ship.
[2] N.C., 24.

of services, concerned the King's announcement, made when he visited the Fleet, that gold medals would be conferred upon all admirals and captains named in Howe's letter. As Howe's was the first major fleet action for which such medals were granted, and as, from this event, a system of honours and awards for services in action grew up which has since continued, the matter is of more than passing importance, particularly as, in Collingwood's case, though in his alone, there was a happier sequel, nearly three years into the future, which will in due course be described.[1]

Even the King's visit had its disappointments. Collingwood told Sir Edward Blackett that Lord Hugh Seymour had protested to Howe that the feelings of the captains had been wounded by their exclusion from the flagship when the Admiral was given a commemorative sword. All, later, were introduced to the sovereign and his Queen, and kissed hands. Later still, said Collingwood, 'we all dined with his Majesty and surpassing my expectation had a very pleasant day. He was cheerful and good humoured to all, and there was as little ceremony as at the table of a private gentleman.'

Collingwood could not resist a final dig at Curtis in his letter. Lord Howe is less blamed for his letter than his Captain [he wrote], who has ever been an artful, sneaking creature, whose fawning insinuating manners creeps into the confidence of whoever he attacks, and whose rapacity wou'd grasp all honours and profits that come within his view. The letter was an attempt upon the credulity of the world to make them believe the *Queen Charlotte*, with very little help, defeated the French fleet.

When Collingwood wrote to Dr. Carlyle on 9 July he was still feeling low, 'unfit to write pleasantly,' as he put it, 'which I wou'd always wish to do to you.'[2] He repeated much of what he had said to Sir Edward Blackett, adding: 'it was an ill told story, a story which has given me more pain than even my poor Admiral suffered from his misfortune. Not many are better

---

[1] For a detailed account of the rewards, see *Mariner's Mirror*, Vol. 37, No. 4 (Oct. 1951), 'The Flag Officer's and Captain's Gold Medal, 1794–1815' by Commander W. B. Rowbotham.

[2] H., Letter 25.

pleased than myself and while all England was rejoicing in a great victory, the hearts of those who won it were sinking with disappointment.'

The royal visit had 'cleared out sky a little', he continued, and he had had a message from Lord Chatham, by way of Lord Hugh Seymour, that he should have 'a ship of the rate I was entitled to'.

> In the uncertain state I am at present [he wrote], I hardly wish to see my Sarah here. God knows where I may have to move to, and the vexation I have lately had has made my brows wrinkle, and made me fret. And yet I think nothing wou'd fret me when my darling blesses my eyes: indeed she is a blessing to me and when peace comes—if ever peace comes—I will be happy in spite of the slights of any man.

That Bowyer had been in no doubt as to the virtues of his flag-captain is shown by a letter he wrote to Admiral Roddam in October 1794. 'I do not know a more brave, capable or a better officer, in all respects, than Captain Collingwood,' he said. 'I think him a very fine character; and I told Lord Chatham when he was at Portsmouth, that if ever he had to look for a first Captain to a Commander-in-Chief, I hoped he would remember that I pledged myself that he would not find a better man than our friend Collingwood.'[1]

The mystery of Collingwood's omission may never quite be solved, but some little light on it is shed in a note in the great collection of original documents concerning Howe's and later battles which were presented by the Admiralty to the British Museum.[2] Among the reports included is one from the unfortunate Admiral Caldwell, who in his Letter of Proceedings concerning 1 June wrote: 'At 1 Lord Howe made the signal to open secret instructions.' Howe himself underlined this, and wrote in the margin opposite, in that curious script which is quite unmistakable:

> No such signal made in the *Queen Charlotte*. But appeared to have been made by the captain of the *Barfleur* when Rear Admiral Bowyer was wounded, through inattention to the times and words of the instruction referred to.

[1] N.C., 24–25.   [2] Add. MSS. 23207.

Howe's irritation at such an error (if indeed it was Colling-wood's) would have been natural. Signalling was his special care, and for captains to have been distracted during or shortly after battle by opening secret instructions—which usually re-ferred to the rendezvous to be kept if and when ships became separated—would have gone counter to all his principles. But there is no entry in the log of the *Barfleur* to confirm the Commander-in-Chief's note, and without further evidence Col-lingwood must be acquitted even of misunderstanding, unless a remark of Howe's in an interview which shortly took place may be interpreted as an oblique criticism.

4 *Mediterranean Man*

Collingwood's future service was to take him to the Mediterranean, where he would once more be in touch with Nelson. He had not visited that sea since the old days of the *Gibraltar*, and a good deal was to happen before he left home waters. His new appointment was to the *Hector*, 74 guns. She was ten years old, and had been present at Ushant under Keppel in his action with the French in 1778, during the War of American Independence. The manner of his being given the ship was flattering, for when he visited the Admiralty he was told by Lord Chatham that he should 'have as good a 74 as was at that time disposable'. Asked where he would like to go, he told the First Lord:

> my object was to go to sea as soon as possible and with Lord Howe in preference to any other situation, when I did not doubt I shou'd soon raze from his mind any unfavourable ideas he may have conceived of me, and, if it please God, so I will. For what is ill founded cannot have stability.[1]

Collingwood was still persuaded of the virtues of Lord Howe, though he complained to Carlyle: 'There is such a parade and ceremony in everything done here that the French squadrons, which are now very numerous, threaten to destroy our trade while we are making our arrangements.' He wrote thus from Portsmouth, on 3 August 1794. During the previous month he had made the long journey to Northumberland, just to catch a glimpse of his darlings. His wife met him on the road, and for forty-eight hours he forgot all his cares and vexations. Then a message from the Admiralty recalled him, and he went back to Portsmouth at once.

[1] H., Letter 26.

I am delighted with my little daughters [he told Carlyle], who quite met my expectations. Sarah seems to possess all the sweet gentleness of her mother, mildness and sensibility are marked in all her childish actions. That child will be a comfort if we live old. Mary Pat: possesses more fire, a quicker temper; she will be a spirited dame, but with proper training and the example she will have ever before her, I doubt not we shall have an inexhaustible source of joy. How thankful I am for such blessings.

On 7 August Collingwood wrote to Sir Edward Blackett[1] to tell him that he had at last spoken directly to the Commander-in-Chief about the matter which still rankled.

I went yesterday to visit Lord Howe, [he said] who received me very graciously, lamented that the Admiralty had put nice[2] officers into the fleet who were unacquainted with his signals and general discipline, and hoped my ship would soon be in a condition to join him. I told him how much I had been disappointed and hurt, after all the exertion I was capable of, not having obtained that testimony of his approbation which he had given to others, and which I hoped for; but doubted not on some future day it wou'd not be denied. He talked of the disadvantages the fleet laboured under by the windward situation of the enemy, and what we shou'd have done if we had had the good fortune to have had the wind of them at first meeting, steering clear of any explanation which related particularly to me. I believe he heartily wishes his letter had never been wrote.

Collingwood was finding great difficulty in manning the *Hector*, and, for all his professional admiration for Howe, he was worried and critical about the dilatory methods which seemed to obtain in the Fleet. 'It would be reckoned nonsense,' he wrote, 'in anyone but his Lordship.'

As the manning problem continued intractable, Lord Chatham offered to transfer Collingwood to the *Excellent*, another 74, to which he was able to move at the end of the year. This was one of Chatham's last acts before leaving the Admiralty,

---

[1] H., Letter 27.
[2] Cf. *Northanger Abbey*, ch. XIV, on the contemporary use of the word 'nice'.

where he was replaced by Earl Spencer. 'I have to say,' wrote Collingwood to Carlyle from his new ship on 3 January 1795,[1] 'I have received great civility and kindness from him [Chatham] and am thankful to him that he has left me nothing to ask the new Lord.' Perhaps some of the favour was less to be wondered at when it is recalled that Chatham and Howe were not on the best of terms, and that a captain wronged by the one would have a special claim on the attention of the other: even so, Chatham had long been partial to Collingwood, almost certainly for himself. He never failed to regard his wishes, and even remembered that, although Collingwood had once liked to serve in the West Indies, on his last visit to that area he had found the climate less agreeable.

The change of ships enabled Collingwood to make another visit home, this time of '8 or 9 days amongst my darlings in great comfort,' as he wrote to Carlyle. Then he had been faced with an immense journey to Plymouth, from which his letter was addressed.

On 20 March he wrote to Carlyle from Spithead,[2] telling him that:

> Lord Howe is very ill and has been so ever since that severe day we had at Torbay, the 13th of February, when I assure you I had dreadfull apprehentions for the fate of the fleet. It blew a violent gale of wind, many ships parted their cables, others broke their anchors, and at one period we were driving about in a most lamentable way. The Admiral was on deck almost the whole day and the severity of the weather brought on gout and all mischiefs attending it.

Howe had indeed done his last extended service at sea. He was given leave to recuperate at Bath, and the Fleet was put in charge of Alexander Hood, who had by now become Lord Bridport, Howe retaining nominal authority as Commander-in-Chief for the time being.

Collingwood wrote again to Carlyle on 2 July,[3] complaining of the high cost of provisions, and wondering how the poor lived: 'We give 45 & 50 shillings for sheep which before the war were sold for 30; hay £7. 10 shillings a ton; a bad fowl for half a crown.' He praised Spencer's invigoration of the Navy, and

---

[1] H., Letter 31.   [2] H., Letter 33.   [3] H., Letter 34.

gave Carlyle his own views on his elder daughter, whom his correspondent had lately seen:

> Your account of little Sall quite delights me [he wrote], I felt every word you said of her quite at my heart. I pray she may ever be a blessing to her darling Mother, the gentlest and kindest of all human creatures. I would rather she was good looking than handsome, and possessed of plain good understanding, than wit. Kindness of heart and gentleness of manners she will catch from the example of her instructress. I believe children, like all other animals, ought to be taught very young; the impression is easier made, it is not the effect of study. In her case there is no danger of bad impression.

When Collingwood next wrote it was from Leghorn, to which he had been ordered in charge of a convoy. This he conducted 'without damage of any kind or loss of one'. He seldom slept more than two hours at a time during the entire passage, and when the voyage was over all the Masters came on board the *Excellent* to thank him for his care. He reached Leghorn at the end of August.[1]

II

The safe-guard of his convoy was Collingwood's chief immediate satisfaction, for matters were not going well in the Mediterranean, either ashore or with the Fleet. Ashore, the French seemed everywhere victorious. At sea, no success of any note had been won, and although the British were predominant and could use Corsican as well as Italian bases, there was no spirit of optimism. To make things worse Spain, once an ally, was on the point of changing sides.

Collingwood had scarcely arrived in Tuscan waters when he heard from Nelson, who was operating off the coast with what amounted to a small but independent inshore command.

> My dear Coll [ran the letter],[2] I cannot allow a Ship to leave me without a line for my old friend, who I shall rejoice to see; but I am afraid the Admiral will not give me that pleasure at present. You are so old a Mediterranean man, that

---

[1] H., Letter 35.   [2] Nic. ii. 77–78.

I can tell you nothing new about the Country. My command here is so far pleasant as it relieves me from the inactivity of our fleet, which is great indeed, as you will soon see.

From the event of Spain making peace, much may be looked for—perhaps a war with that Country: if so, their fleet (if no better than when our Allies) will soon be done for.

Nelson was blockading: 'however cruel it may appear to be to deprive poor innocent people of provisions,' he wrote, 'if the inhabitants have plenty, so will the Enemy.' He thought little of Hotham, now commanding in Lord Hood's place. 'Our admiral, *entre nous* has no political courage whatever,' he told his friend, 'and is alarmed at the mention of any strong measure; but, in other respects he is as good a man as can possibly be.' The letter ended as warmly as it had begun.

I hope, my dear friend, you left Mrs. Collingwood well. How many children have you? Did you see Mrs. Moutray lately? Her dear, amiable son was lost by serving under me. I have a stone on board, which is to be erected in the church of St. Fiorenzo in his memory. I hardly ever knew so amiable a young man. Believe me, ever, my dear Collingwood,

Your most affectionate friend
HORATIO NELSON.

Tell me a great deal.

This was exactly the sort of welcome Collingwood needed. The reference to young Moutray recalled days in Antigua a decade earlier. It was just a year since Moutray, a lieutenant in the *Victory*, had served ashore in Corsica with Nelson, and caught fever, from which he died. Shortly before that sad event, Nelson had himself lost the sight of his right eye in action in the same campaign.

Collingwood thought nothing of Corsica and the Corsicans. The island had been gained at much cost, and was now being administered under the British crown. He knew the people of old.

Their manners are savage, their ignorance is gross [he wrote to Sir Edward Blackett at the end of August],[1] but the part of their character of most consequences to us is the

---

[1] H., Letter 35.

inveterate hatred they on all occasions express to the English. Every man of them travels in the country with a rifle, gun and a dagger, with which he kills with admirable dexterity such game or Englishmen as he may chance to meet in his way—the ships of war have lost several men stabbed by these fellows—and do it with the same composure that an old butcher kills a pig. The *Gibraltar* had four seamen stabbed the last time they were there, three of them died.

Final disadvantage in Collingwood's view—the cost of administration in the island exceeded that of Gibraltar, and its use would end with the war.

As for the Fleet, it was little more than a month since Hotham had had an inconclusive action with the French—his second that year. A quick chance of decision had been missed, and Nelson and other eager spirits were still feeling disheartened that they had had no victory to compare with the Glorious First of June.

We should be careful and slow in censure, [Collingwood warned his correspondent, when describing Hotham's encounter], because men of weakest judgment are most prompt to question what perhaps their want of intelligence makes them not comprehend, and in this instance, because the Commander has been esteemed a skillful, good, officer. Yet the opportunity seemed a good one to ruin the French naval force in this country.

Collingwood ended his letter on a somewhat comic note.

I met an old friend today [he wrote], Sigr Spannochi who commands one of the Neapolitan ships, he hugged me in the most public street until I was quite ashamed. It is twenty four years since I saw him; he is about to quit the sea service, being appointed Governor of Leghorn.

Spannochi had learnt seamanship, like Collingwood, from Roddam, and (however effusive his manner) it could scarcely fail to be useful to have another contact who could be relied upon for news.

Alas, Spannochi's spell of official favour did not last. Within a year, Nelson wrote to Collingwood to report that his old friend

6

was in prison.[1] The French had by then established themselves
as paramount in Tuscany, and Spannocchi had fallen foul of
Bonaparte. The Duke of Tuscany (perhaps for Spannochi's own
safety) had sent him to Florence and locked him up.

The winter of 1795 was spent watching in the Lion Gulf, an
employment with which Collingwood, Nelson, and their fellows
were becoming once more grimly familiar as the war unfolded.
In March 1796 Collingwood wrote from Ajaccio to his father-in-
law to tell him of a typical misadventure, typically overcome.

On the night of the 27 February [he wrote],[2] in a squall, when
it was very dark and rainy, the *Princess Royal* ran on board
of us. I was on deck, and luckily saw her coming right on us
in time to sheer off a little, or she would probably have cut
us down to the water's edge: as it was, she carried away the
bowsprit and foremast, and left us a complete wreck.

It was fortunate that we got clear so soon, for there was
sea enough to thump our sides in. We had scarce cleared ourselves of the wreck of our masts, before a hard gale of wind
came on at S.E. getting us into the Gulf of Lyons on a lee
shore. The fleet kept company with us as long as it was safe
for them to do so, and they left a frigate to attend us.

Jury masts were put up, and course set for Ajaccio, but another
gale came on, and it was not before 3 March that the *Excellent*
was safe.

I have been forty-eight hours on deck [continued Colling-
wood], and scarce sat in that time to eat. I am not much the
fatter for it, nor a bit the worse, thanks to a good hard constitution. I have now replaced my lost masts, and hope to be
ready for sea in about a week.

Ajaccio seemed to Collingwood 'still more barbarous than San
Fiorenzo: the least offence offered to one of the inhabitants is
resented by a stab, or a shot from behind a wall'. Some of the
carpenters in the naval yard had been dismissed as 'not wanted':
next day, Sunday, they took a shot at the Navy Office Commissioner as he walked in his garden, but missed.

Before March was out, Collingwood was able to report that he
had rejoined the Fleet which was 'in exceedingly good order, and

[1] H., Letters 38 and 39.   [2] N.C., 26–27.

my *Excellent* one of the best sailers in it'. In May, he was again cruising off Toulon: 'not a service on which we shall get fat,' he told his father-in-law, 'and often do I wish we had some of those bad potatoes which old Scott and William [Ireland] used to throw over the wall of the garden, for we feel the want of vegetables more than anything'.[1] He feared that the success of the French would soon bar the fleet from every port in Italy.

> Whatever happens [he continued], we shall make the best of it; for we now have activity in the fleet, and seem to act upon a settled plan. Formerly, all the good or ill that happened was by chance, and there seemed no forethought to secure the one, or prevent the other.

The transformation had been effected by the zeal of the new Commander-in-Chief, Sir John Jervis, a blessing to the efficient and a scourge to the rest.

Collingwood, with his thoughts so often of his home, was most fortunate in his father-in-law, whose devotion to Sarah and her little girls was as constant as ever, and whose attention in sending news to the Mediterranean was unremitting.

> I am very thankful to you, my dear Sir, [wrote an appreciative man], for all your kindness to me, to Sarah, and to my darling girls. They do not know the want of a father's care while your protection is over them: and I hope they will live to tell you of their gratitude when they can reason on your goodness themselves.

At the end of August, Collingwood sent a glowing account of Jervis to Sir Edward Blackett.[2]

> The enemy seem to have given up all naval operations in this sea . . . So impatient does the Adml appear to be to get at them, that were they to venture from their anchorage the protection of such forts as they have along the shore would not much avail them. They have an equal number of ships to ours . . . but I fancy find it easier to discipline men to their army than qualify them for the various duties of the navy. Our fleet is in excellent order, well provided with everything, in which the Admiral, Sir J. Jervis, takes wonderful pains,

[1] N.C., 29–31.   [2] H., Letter 39.

and the consequence is we are remarkably healthy after being twenty eight weeks at sea.

A month later, Collingwood told his father-in-law that the Fleet, with their 'brown shirts and scanty dinners', wanted something to comfort them, for Leghorn and Genoa were at last closed to supplies, and affairs in Corsica were such that the tricolour cockade had appeared among the people. 'All our naval stores are embarked in ships,' he added, 'because the people are so hostile to us that they can no longer be left with safety on shore.'[1]

Preparations were in fact being made to leave the island, and Collingwood for one was not sorry. The French had been conscripting Austrian deserters and prisoners who had been on service at Genoa, and sending them to France: 'but', wrote Collingwood, 'we stop the ships that carry them, take them out as subjects of our ally, the Emperor, and make sailors of them; so that, in my ship's company, I have some of all the States in Germany—Austrians, Poles, Croats and Hungarians—a motley tribe!'[2]

With every month that passed there was in fact less and less possibility of keeping a fleet profitably in service in the Mediterranean, in whatever condition ships and men appeared to be.

We are remarkably healthy [Collingwood wrote], and the ships were never more fit for service, as the French and Spaniards will experience, if they venture out.

Sir John Jervis is indefatigable in keeping this station, and while we keep it, the Mediterranean is a sea only for our friends; yet I fear our friends will have nothing to do here soon, and if the war goes on, I have no doubt that the French will assault the coasts of England, and we shall be wanted nearer home.

Before the year 1796 was out, Collingwood was writing from Gibraltar. The decision had been taken in London that the Mediterranean was tenable no longer. It was defeat without a battle. The French were irresistible ashore and, for the time at least, there was little a fleet could achieve, and no remaining base from which to supply it.

[1] N.C., 32.　　　　[2] N.C., 33.

5 *Valentine's Day 1797*

The year 1797 was gloomy for Great Britain, with few breaks in the clouds. The threat of invasion to which Collingwood had referred to continued real. A descent on Ireland, made by the French late in 1796, had been foiled by appalling weather, not by the vigilance of Bridport's fleet, and there was soon to be another on Wales, equally unsuccessful, but indicative of what could be done. Financially, there was a run on the Bank of England; there were two mutinies in the Fleet, one of which was very serious; and continental allies were everywhere defeated.

One of the breaks was Jervis's victory over the Spaniards off Cape St. Vincent. This was rather against expectation, for the winter had begun badly with him, from what were normal marine hazards. The *Courageous*, *Zealous*, and *Gibraltar* all became victims of storm damage, the *Courageous* being lost with most of her people. As if this were not enough, the *Bombay Castle* ran aground and was wrecked in the Tagus—Jervis was using Lisbon, which was friendly, as his principal base—and the *St. George* damaged her bottom on a shoal. Only the *Zealous* and *St. George* could be patched up locally, given time: meanwhile, the admiral's effective strength in ships of the line had been reduced by five, and it was not until 6 February that thrice welcome reinforcements reached him from home, bringing his battle force up to fifteen.

The re-formed squadron was somewhat top-heavy with flag-officers, for in addition to Jervis himself there were two vice-admirals, Charles Thompson and William Waldegrave, a rear-admiral, William Parker, and a commodore, Nelson. On the other hand there were no less than six three-decked ships, an exceptionally high proportion, and only one ship of as few as

64 guns. The officers from home were an unknown quantity, but the core of Mediterranean captains, familiar with Jervis's ways, comprised some of the best officers in the navy.

With Lisbon to the north and Gibraltar to the south of Cadiz, Jervis was well placed to watch the Spanish port and to intercept any force which might be ordered to reinforce the already large French concentration at Brest. There, 30 ships of the line and 14 frigates were ready, when the wind served and troops were embarked, for another attempt on Britain.

Juan de Cordova, the Spanish admiral destined for invasion service, replaced a less enthusiastic flag-officer. He sailed from Cartagena on 1 February with a big fleet—28 of the line, including the four-decked *Santissima Trinidada* of 132 guns, the largest ship afloat, 6 three-deckers, two ships of 84 guns, and eighteen of 74 guns. There were appropriate frigates, of which the Spaniards were never short.

De Cordova had two objects. The first was to take his fleet from Cartagena to Cadiz, as a first step towards combination with the French. The second was to ensure the safe passage of a convoy from Malaga past Gibraltar. The merchantmen were also destined for Cadiz; and it was their presence which precipitated the battle.[1] Captain Richard Bowen, Senior Naval Officer at Gibraltar, sent a message to Jervis, who was patrolling at sea, to let him know that fleet and convoy had passed the Rock on 5 February. The report reached Jervis by the *Viper*, cutter, four days later, and found him in readiness to meet anything. Disparity of numbers was of no account, for he believed (in this like Nelson and Collingwood, with their previous experience of fighting Spain) that while the 'Dons', as they called them, could build splendid ships, they had lost the capacity for training good officers and men to handle and fight them.

A levanter or strong east wind blew the Spanish fleet and convoy well to leeward of their port, and Cordova could not take up his proper course till the wind changed to the westward on the morning of 14 February, St. Valentine's Day.

The convoy, which had its own escort, and which was also the special care of Admiral Moreno, who flew his flag in the

---

[1] The significance of the convoy is a later discovery; treated in the *Mariner's Mirror*, Vol. 40, No. 3 (Aug. 1954), 228–30: 'The Battle of Cape St. Vincent' by Rear-Admiral A. H. Taylor.

112-gun *Principe de Asturias*, consisted of *urcas*, which were defensively armed merchant ships, laden with an immensely valuable cargo of mercury. This came from Almaden, about 150 miles north of Malaga, which was then and is still the site of one of the world's largest quicksilver mines. The metal, which was used in amalgamating precious metals found in Spain's New World possessions, was probably destined to cross the Atlantic in due course, an essential contribution from the mother country to that wealth which Spain drew from the South American continent, upon which her economy so much depended.

Jervis knew nothing of the value of this convoy: even had he done so, his first business was to defeat the enemy fleet, and that—considering the difference in numbers—was likely to take all his skill, and all the brief hours of winter daylight.

He was sheltering under the lee of Cape St. Vincent when continuous and reliable news of Cordova's movements began to come in to him, and it soon became clear that he would have a splendid opportunity of engaging an enemy who, whatever the size of his armament, had no great skill in preliminary dispositions and manœuvre.

The main events of the battle itself were described, with his usual clarity, by Collingwood, in the first of many letters to his wife which appeared in Newnham Collingwood's memoir.[1] He wrote three days after firing ceased.

> *Excellent*, off Lagos, February 17, 1797.
>
> My dearest Sarah,
>
> I am sure you will be glad to hear from me after such a day as we have had on the 14th (Valentine's Day). It was indeed a glorious one, and it seldom falls to the lot of any man to share in such a triumph.
>
> First, my love, I am as well as I ever was in my life, and have pretty well got the better of my fatigue. Now for history.
>
> We were cruising off Cape St. Vincent, with fifteen sail of the line, when the Admiral first received information that the Spanish fleet, twenty eight sail of line, were come down the Mediterranean; and a day or two afterwards that twenty seven sail were in our neighbourhood, one being left at

[1] N.C., 35–37.

Gibraltar [Algeçiras] with ten or twelve frigates, making in all thirty seven or forty sail.[1] We were fifteen and four frigates. He determined to attack them.

On the night of the 13th, the weather being fine but thick and hazy, we heard their signal guns, which announced their vicinity, and soon after day-light we saw them very much scattered, while we were a compact little body. We flew to them as a hawk to his prey, passed through them in the disordered state in which they were, separated them into two distinct parts, and then tacked upon their largest division.

The *Culloden* and *Captain*, Commodore Nelson's ship, were the first that brought them to close action. I by chance became the Admiral's leader (for the circumstances were such as would admit of no regular order), and had the good fortune to get very early into action.

The first ship we engaged was the *San Salvadore del Mundo*, of 112 guns, a first rate; we were not farther from her when we began than the length of our garden. Her colours soon came down, and her fire ceased. I hailed, and asked if they surrendered; and when, by signs made by a man who stood by the colours, I understood that they had, I left her to be taken possession of by somebody behind, and made sail for the next, but was very much surprised on looking back to find her colours up again, and her battle re-commenced.

We very soon came up with the next, the *San* [Y] *Sidro*, 74, so close alongside, that a man might jump from one ship to the other. Our fire carried all before it; and in ten minutes she hauled down her colours; but I had been deceived once, and obliged this fellow to hoist English colours before I left him, and made a signal for somebody behind to board him, when the Admiral ordered the *Lively* frigate to take charge of him.

Then making all sail, passing between our line and the enemy, we came up with the *San Nicolas* of 80 guns, which happened at the time to be abreast of the *San Josef*, of 112 guns; we did not touch sides, but you could not put a bodkin between us, so that our shot passed through both ships, and, in attempting to extricate themselves, they got on board each other.

[1] Collingwood included in his total the convoy and its close escort.

My good friend, the Commodore, had been long engaged with those ships, and I came happily to his relief, for he was dreadfully mauled. Having engaged them until their fire ceased on me, though their colours were not down, I went on to the *Santissima Trinidada*, the Spanish Admiral Cordova's ship, of 132 guns, on four complete decks—such a ship as I never saw before.

By this time, our masts, sails and rigging, were so much shot, that we could not get so near her as I would have been; but near enough to receive much injury from her, both in my men and ship. We were engaged an hour with this ship, and trimmed her well; she was a complete wreck. Several others of our ships came up, and engaged her at the same time; but evening approaching, and the fresh Spaniards coming down upon us, the Admiral made the signal to withdraw, carrying off the four ships that had surrendered to our fleet.[1]

The ships longest and most engaged were *Culloden*, Captain Tro[u]bridge; *Captain*, Commodore Nelson; the *Blenheim*, Captain Frederick; and *Prince George*, Rear Admiral W. Parker and Captain Irwin. I had eleven men killed, and many wounded—every body did well.

I am persuaded there will be no complaints of this little fleet; and when the disparity of force is considered, the taking two first rates, with two flag officers, is a new thing. I have got a Spanish double-headed shot, fired from the *Santissima Trinidada*, which I intend as a present to your father, to put amongst his curiosities: it weighs 50 lbs. These are no jokes, when they fly about one's head.

God bless you! my dearest love; may you ever be happy . . .

The Spanish shot had to wait to begin its journey to Northumberland, but three further accounts of the battle, all dated 22 February, followed hard upon Sarah's. In his letter to his father-in-law[2] Collingwood wrote that he felt he had given her an imperfect account: few would agree.

It is a very difficult thing [he continued] for those engaged in such a scene to give the detail of the whole, because all

---

[1] *Salvador del Mundo*, 112 guns; *San Josef*, 112 guns; *San Nicolas*, 80 guns; *San Ysidro*, 74 guns.

[2] N.C., 38–39.

the powers they have are occupied in their own part of it.

As to myself, I did my duty to the utmost of my ability, as I have ever done: that is acknowledged now, and there is the only real difference between this and the former action. Take it altogether, it is perhaps the most brilliant action upon record; and I cannot help feeling an almost spiteful satisfaction that Lord Howe is outdone. His 1st of June (grand as it was) bears no proportion, in any respect, to this. There, the number of ships was nearly equal; here, the enemy was nearly double. . . .

The battle brought Jervis the Earldom of St. Vincent and much deserved renown, but surely no admiral was ever paid a greater compliment than the words of Collingwood in this letter: 'should we not be grateful to him, who had such confidence in his fleet, that he thought no force too great for them?'

In his letter to Edward Collingwood, a passage, hitherto unpublished, described the disappointment over the Spanish flagship.

I had an envious longing for the *Santissima Trinidada* [he wrote][1] which is the largest ship in the world, a four decker, and at one time had no doubt of her . . . three ships that *Excellent* engaged were not more distant than the breadth of your dining room, so that we literally burnt their whiskers . . . the protection of Providence was great, considering what a scene we were engaged in. I have got the picture of *San Ysidro* the Patron of my ship, the least I could do for his holiness after he had given up his charge to me was to give him a good berth in my Cabbin . . . you shall see him at Morpeth some day I hope.

In each of his letters home, Collingwood confirmed Nelson's extraordinary services on Valentine's day. In his letter to Dr. Carlyle[2] Collingwood wrote:

When I left *San Nicolas* they fell on board the *Captain* (the Comm'r's ship) which was very much disabled in the severe service she had had, when the Commodore, whose judgment supported by a most Angelic spirit is equal to all circumstances that arise, boarded the *San Nicolas*, and having reduced her to

[1] Add. MSS. 52780.   [2] H., Letter 41.

obedience sword in hand marched on to the *San Josef*, which was fast on the other side of her; the resistance they made was not great, a sort of scuffle in which a few lives were lost, and there on the quarter-deck of a Spanish first rate, he received the submission and swords of the officers of the two ships, one of his seamen standing by him, and making a bundle of them with as much composure as he would tie a bundle of faggots.

Nelson and Collingwood's written accounts bear one another out in every particular, and breathe the same spirit.

At this time [Nelson wrote of one fierce stage of the battle][1] the *Salvador del Mundo* and *San Ysidro* dropped astern, and were fired into in a masterly style by the *Excellent*, Captain Collingwood, who compelled the *San Ysidro* to hoist English colours, and I thought the large Ship *Salvador del Mundo* had also struck; but Captain Collingwood, disdaining the parade of taking possession of beaten enemies, most gallantly pushed up, with every sail set, to save his old friend and mess-mate, who was to appearance in a critical state. The *Blenheim* being ahead, and the *Culloden* crippled and astern, the *Excellent* ranged up within ten feet of the *San Nicolas*, giving a most tremendous fire. The *San Nicolas* luffing up, the *San Josef* fell on board her, and the *Excellent* passing on for the *Santissima Trinidada*, the *Captain* resumed his position abreast of them, and close alongside.

Almost immediately after the battle, there was a warm exchange of notes between old friends:

My dearest friend [wrote Nelson from the *Irresistible* (into which he had exchanged)].[2] 'A friend in need is a friend indeed' was never more truly verified than by your most noble and gallant conduct yesterday in sparing the *Captain* from further loss; and I beg, both as a public officer and a friend, you will accept my most sincere thanks. I have not failed, by letter to the Admiral, to represent the eminent services of the *Excellent*. Tell me how you are: what are your disasters. I cannot tell you much of the *Captain's*, except by

---

[1] *N. Chron.* ii. 500.   [2] N.C., 41–42.

note of Captain Miller, at two this morning, about sixty killed and wounded.

We shall meet at Lagos; but I could not come near you without assuring you how sensible I am of your assistance in nearly a critical situation.

Believe me as ever,

Your most affectionate

HORATIO NELSON.

Collingwood answered the same day, probably by the same boat:

Excellent, Feb. 15, 1797

My dear Good Friend,

First let me congratulate you on the success of yesterday— on the brilliancy it attached to the British Navy, and the humility it must cause to its enemies—and then let me congratulate my dear Commodore on the distinguished part which he ever takes when the honour and interests of his Country are at stake. It added very much to the satisfaction I felt in thumping the Spaniards, that I released you a little.

The highest rewards are due to you and *Culloden*: you formed the plan of attack, we were only accessories to the Dons ruin; for, had they got on the other tack, they would have been sooner joined, and the business would have been less complete.

We have come off pretty well considering; eleven killed, and fourteen wounded. You saw the 4-decker going off this morning to Cadiz—she should have come to Lagos to make the thing better, but we could not brace our yards up to get nearer. I beg my compliments to Captain Martin [of the *Irresistible*]: I think he was at Jamaica when we were.

I am ever, my dear friend,

Affectionately yours

C. COLLINGWOOD.

Two other notes relating to the battle were treasured by Collingwood, and like Nelson's they were received on 15 February. One was from Captain Dacres of the *Barfleur* and the other from the Admiral who flew his flag in her, the Hon. William Waldegrave. Both men remembered that the *Barfleur* (like the *Orion* and *Culloden*) had been in Howe's victory as well as Jervis's, and they also remembered the wound caused by the fact that while Bowyer got a baronetcy, a thousand-a-year wound pension, and a gold chain and medal for the First of June, Collingwood had been slighted.

My dear Sir [wrote the generous Dacres from Collingwood's old ship],[1] I have just time to request you will accept of my congratulations upon the immortal honour gained by the *Excellent* yesterday. The Admiral joins very sincerely in my ideas. God bless you, and may we all imitate you.

> Yours ever sincerely,
> J. W. DACRES.

Admiral Waldegrave could not let the boat go without a line to support his flag-captain.

My dear Collingwood [he wrote], Although Dacres has in a great degree expressed all I feel on the subject, yet I cannot resist the satisfaction of telling you myself, that nothing, in my opinion, could exceed the spirit and true officership which you so happily displayed yesterday. Both the Admiral [Jervis] and Nelson join with me in this opinion; and nothing but ignorance can think otherwise. God bless you, my good friend; and may England long possess such men as yourself—it is saying everything for her glory.

> Truly yours,
> WILLIAM WALDEGRAVE.

Jervis was much too well aware of the pain which had been caused in 1794, by Howe's discrimination, to make the same mistake, and his public dispatch named only two officers, Captain Foote of the frigate *Niger*, for his vigilance in keeping watch on the Spaniards, and Calder, his Captain of the Fleet who, like Curtis three years earlier, was sent home with the good news, and was duly knighted. Illogically, since the troubles arising from Howe's 'Supplemental Letter' had been common talk in the Service ever since it appeared, there was complaint that Jervis had not been more specific.

Actually, he was indeed so, but confined his observations to

---

[1] N.C., 43.

a private letter to the First Lord. It is a striking proof of Collingwood's judgement that it coincided so nearly with that of his Commander-in-Chief. In his letter to his wife, Collingwood specifically mentioned the services of Troubridge, Nelson, Frederick, Rear-Admiral Parker, and his flag-captain, Irwin. Jervis, writing on 16 February, stated 'the correct conduct of every Officer and man in the Squadron . . . made it improper to distinguish one more than another in my public Letter' and went on to mention Troubridge, a captain for whom he had the greatest admiration, as had his very old friend Nelson, the *Blenheim* (Frederick), *Prince George* (Rear-Admiral Parker and Captain Irwin), *Irresistible* (Martin), and *Colossus* (Murray). Nelson and Collingwood came in for special praise, and so did Hallowell, who was serving on board the *Victory*, the Fleet flagship, as a volunteer.

'The Ship's returns of killed and wounded,' wrote Jervis, 'although not always the criterion of their being more or less in Action is, in this instance, correctly so.'[1] The *Captain* had the largest casualty list, with 24 killed and 56 wounded. Then came the *Blenheim* with 12 killed and 40 wounded; then the *Excellent*, followed by the *Culloden* with 10 killed and 47 wounded. The same four ships also expended the most powder and shot.

'What is particularly happy in this great event', wrote Collingwood in his letter to Carlyle, 'is that there is no drawback, no slander: though all were not equally engaged, all did what was in their power to reduce them . . . I understand the Admiral has wisely avoided all partial praise of particular acts, which might insinuate to the disadvantage of those whose ill luck prevented their getting into conspicuous situations.'

Collingwood was a little previous: there was, for instance, a good deal of feeling about the way in which Nelson wrote up his own remarkable exploits, especially on the part of Admiral Parker, a relative by marriage of Collingwood's: but as regards the medal, there was no distinction made this time. All flag-officers and captains received it, and, in the view of Nelson and others, this gold medal was worth a king's ransom, since it could only be won by intrepid conduct on the part of a commander in a major action. Even Nelson's own Star of the Bath,

[1] Nic. ii. 336.

which the occasion brought him, could be given to peer or
politician: no one but a sea officer could wear the coveted medal.
'Chains and medals are what no fortune or connections in
England can obtain,' Nelson told his brother.

When Collingwood was told by Jervis that he was to receive
his gold medal with the rest, he replied, with great firmness,
that he could not consent to receive it while that for the 'First
of June' was withheld. 'I feel,' he said, 'that I was then im-
properly passed over; and to receive such a distinction now
would be to acknowledge the propriety of that injustice.' Jervis
replied: 'That is precisely the answer which I expected from
you, Captain Collingwood.'[1] In fact, it had been anticipated in
the Admiralty that Collingwood would make some such stand,
and that Lord Spencer at least was on his side admits no doubt,
for he was later sent two gold medals, respectively inscribed on
the reverse:

CUTHBERT COLLINGWOOD ESQUIRE, CAPTAIN OF H.M.S. THE
BARFLEUR ON THE IST OF JUNE MDCCXCIV. THE FRENCH
FLEET DEFEATED

and:

CUTHBERT COLLINGWOOD, ESQUIRE, CAPTAIN OF H.M.S. THE
EXCELLENT ON THE 14TH OF FEBRUARY MDCCXCVII. THE
SPANISH FLEET DEFEATED

The medals, in a large size for flag-officers and a smaller size
for captains, were executed at the Mint by Lewis Pingo from
an earlier design by his father, Thomas Pingo. The obverse
showed a figure of Victory, standing on the prow of an antique
galley, placing a wreath of laurel on Britannia.[2]

The original medals for the First of June were not ready to
be sent off to the captains concerned until November 1796, and
the suspicion is allowable that even by that time the Admiralty
were prepared to extend the award to Collingwood, for Lord
Spencer, in sending him his two medals together, wrote:

I congratulate you most sincerely on having had the good
fortune to bear so conspicuous a part on two such glorious
occasions, and have troubled you with this letter, only to say,
that the former medal would have been transmitted to you

[1] N.C., 46.
[2] *British and Foreign Medals Relating to Naval and Maritime Affairs*
(Greenwich, 1950), p. 199.

some months ago, if a proper conveyance had been found for it.[1]

At last, honour was satisfied. On 3 June Collingwood wrote to Dr. Carlyle from off Cadiz:

His Majesty has been graciously pleased to make me all the amends he can, by ordering that distinction to be done away which was made between those named in his [Howe's] plagued letter and those not, by sending me the Medal for the Victory of June with that for Febr. last.[2]

In the same letter he begged that his letters home about the action and its aftermath should not be generally shown: 'it has too much the appearance of trumpeting, which I detest.' For once, the views of Collingwood and Nelson did not coincide. Nelson was always his own best public relations officer.

[1] *Mariner's Mirror*, Vol. 37, No. 4 (Oct. 1951), 263. N.C. 46.
[2] H., Letter 42.

6 *The Long Watch*

Discussing some aspects of the battle of St. Vincent in the same letter to Carlyle which had given his correspondent news of the receipt of the medals, Collingwood showed himself a student of such technical literature as came his way. One of the more remarkable works of its time was an illustrated *Essay on Naval Tactics* by a Scots layman and amateur artist, John Clerk of Eldin (1728–1812), who set himself to answer the question why naval battles had so often been indecisive, concluding that it was from keeping to a too rigid system of lines of battle. Break the line—ensure a *mêlée*: a result was then at least more likely. Clerk's treatise, privately printed in 1782, was published in 1790 and enlarged in the year of the victory, though not as a result of it. Clerk, naturally enough, always hoped that the leading admirals would acknowledge that they owed something to his ideas: certainly his work was read in the Fleet: both Collingwood and Nelson knew it.[1] Collingwood told Carlyle:

> I admire Clerk's tactick very much. There is much ingenuity in his system which is supported by mathematical demonstration and by experience, but the fact is we did not proceed on any system of tacticks. In the beginning we were formed very close and pushed at them without knowing, through the thickness of the haze, with what part of their line we should fall in.
>
> When they were divided, and the lesser part driven to leeward, the Admiral wisely abandoned them, made the signal to tack, and afterwards stuck to the larger division of their fleet, which was to windward, and could not be joined by their lee division in a short time.

[1] *Barham Papers*, ed. J. K. Laughton (Navy Records Society), iii. 398.

After this we had neither order nor signals, for the Admiral was so satisfied with the impetuosity of the attack made by the ships ahead of him that he let us alone, and the only signal he made was to the *Irresistible* and another to cease firing lest they should cripple me, when I was alongside the *Salvador*.

Greatly as he praised their respective skills as leaders and tacticians, an attitude in which he never wavered, Collingwood's admiration somewhat cooled, later, both for Howe and Jervis. Howe he had found altogether too meticulous in his 'arrangements' for the conduct of a large fleet, a fact which arose both from a passion for order and from a distrust of the capacity of his subordinates. Jervis's discipline Collingwood came to find harsh and eccentric, and he was not alone in this view. Jervis, for his part, had the greatest respect for Collingwood, a regard which never lessened. Collingwood's feeling for the newly created Earl of St. Vincent began to change as a result of the tedious and protracted service on which he was engaged for a very long time after the battle, though with his unshakable fair-mindedness he never lost sight of the Earl's wonderful qualities. 'They also serve who only stand and wait.' As a well-read man, Collingwood had every opportunity, over the next few years, to savour the bitterness as well as the truth of Milton's line. And yet he would not have been engaged otherwise than he was. 'How often do I bless my Sarah,' he wrote to Carlyle,[1] 'that she is not importunate about my being here or there, she does not love me less than any Lady in the land her husband, but has too much sense to make my absence from her more painful than it is by a teazing complaint of what ought to be and [it] is her pride—that when my country needs my service I am devoted to it.'

On 13 April Collingwood wrote more fully to Nelson, in a letter which was full of interest.[2]

My dear Friend [he wrote], I hope you are not angry that I have not been on board the *Captain*[3]—but consider how little you are with us; only just long enough to communicate with the Admiral, and away again; and generally our movements

---

[1] H., Letter 42.   [2] Add. MSS. 34906, f. 22.

[3] Nelson had rejoined his former ship at the end of March and had been promoted Rear-Admiral of the Blue by seniority.

are so sudden and uncertain that I have got a habit of staying on board, perhaps more than is required of me. But I am satisfied that you know my heart, that there are none in the fleet, few in the world that I meet with more pleasure than yourself.

If the Spaniards were in a state to come out, I should be sorry you were going from us, but your going is the strongest indication that the Admiral is certain they cannot come soon, or he would not part with such a precious limb from his body. Whatever you are going about, God bless you with success— I have no doubt of it.

When I heard the Spanish American convoy was arrived at Teneriffe I thought it a probable thing that the Admiral would make a detachment to that quarter, to try how far they were vulnerable there, and if he did, who could he send but one whose name is poison to a Spaniard? Perhaps that is your service; there or wherever you go, may your good fortune never forsake you.[1]

I must always think that Lord Howe's letter was the fruit of a weak understanding. It was highly injurious to me and not to me alone. It was an excruciating anguish to my soul, under which I was supported by a consciousness of the rectitude of my conduct; for who could contend with him, mounted on his pinnacle of greatness? There were those in his fleet who would have monopolised all the credit of his action to be divided amongst themselves; he was their dupe, silly man . . .

Mrs. Moutray is in Ireland on a visit to O'Burne, who is a bishop—he was the Duke of Portland's private secretary. My darlings (heaven bless them) are all well, and very glad to hear I have got my head on. Sarah says you are a most excellent creature and wishes she were acquainted with you. I wish she was.

I think whenever the Spaniards come out, 14 more will be hanged, which is about as many as we shall leave for them to execute.[2] What a fine promotion it will make in the Spanish

[1] Nelson was in fact sent to cover the transports taking off the British garrison then at Elba. He was sent to Tenerife in July to try to capture a Spanish treasure ship but his luck forsook him and he lost his right arm.

[2] An allusion to the report that Spanish officers were hanged as a result of their defeat on 14 February.

Navy! I have a great desire that our Admiral should be a marquis this summer, both because his bright honours will reflect on all of us, and I should delight to see him Lord Howe's superior and become so from naval achievement.[1] Remember me most kindly to Mrs. Nelson and thank her for remembering me.

I am ever, my dear Admiral.

Yours faithful and truly affectionate

CUTHB. COLLINGWOOD.

One of the results of Valentine's day was that Cadiz came under close and continual watch. On 18 April 1797 Collingwood wrote to his father-in-law:[2]

We are not contented with having beat the Spaniards at sea, but have now blocked up their port and are parading under the walls of Cadiz, as we did last year before Toulon . . . The Spaniards have thirty-two sail of great ships ready, or nearly so—enough to devour us, if they knew but how to carve. We have heard that their seamen were offered double pay if they would exert themselves against us, which they decline, as a hopeless undertaking, and have refused to come to sea: but I think they must come, or Spain is lost as a maritime power.

In May, Collingwood heard of the refusal of the seamen at Spithead to take their ships to sea, during the first and lesser of the two mutinies which occurred that summer. The disaffection is considered by historians to have been almost entirely the result of the pressure of bad conditions afloat, not of sedition, and of what has been called the longest pay pause in history. Seamen's wages in the Navy had been unchanged since the time of the Commonwealth. Collingwood, long out of touch with home affairs, had his own ideas on the subject, once a modest increase in pay had been given.

I think I can discover [he wrote to his father-in-law],[3] that the advance of pay, and other advantages which have been

---

[1] Howe was in fact offered a marquisite after the Glorious First of June, but declined it. He would have preferred the Garter, but Pitt had half promised the only vacant Stall to the Duke of Portland for political services. Howe had his Garter in 1797. *The Later Correspondence of George III*, ed. A. Aspinall (1963), Letter 1093, and p. 224 *note*.

[2] N.C., 43–44. [3] N.C., 44–45.

conceded to the Navy, are not received as acts of favour, but as rights extorted from Government; and instead of reposing in thankfulness for these benefits, they seem to be occupied, having felt their power, in considering what next may be demanded. The times are convulsed and full of danger: peace alone can restore us to harmony. Heaven grant it!

Peace seemed as far away as ever: but the war with the Spaniards had an altogether different atmosphere about it than the far more deadly affair with France.

We have almost daily correspondence with the Spaniards by letter [Collingwood told Blackett], and ours is a curious situation: the Spanish officers, who come with the flag of truce, dine with the Commander of the advanced [inshore] squadron; and they invited the Spanish ladies to a ball, but they did not come.

Collingwood told Carlyle: 'their fishing boats, which have always been unmolested, come on board daily to supply us with fish, and sometimes vegetables: perhaps, paying better, we have the preference to their own people.'

By the end of June, Collingwood had heard of the spread of trouble to the ships at the Nore.

The seamen [he wrote to his father-in-law],[1] I am persuaded, would never have revolted from good order: but consider, with such a fleet as we now have, how large a proportion of the crews of the ships are miscreants of every description, and capable of every crime; and when these predominate, what evils may we not dread from the demoniac councils and influence of such a mass of mischief! The best chance that we have here of escaping the anarchy that prevails in England is, that we have been longer established in order. No symptom of irregularity has yet made its appearance, and I hope that blessed peace will stand between us and civil discord.

The Earl of St. Vincent had a short way with mutineers, and so had Collingwood. Their thoughts were alike on the subject. 'Send them to Collingwood,' the Commander-in-Chief would sometimes say of an uncertain reinforcement in men from home.

[1] N.C., 47.

'He will bring them to order.' It was St. Vincent's view that Collingwood had the art of keeping men both attentive and happy. 'They have always preserved the order of a regulated family,' he wrote later of one of Collingwood's ships' companies, 'rather than of men kept in subjection by discipline: their duty seemed to be what most interested them; they have done it faithfully and well . . .'[1]

That this was not invariably so with his 'youngsters' appears from the same letter to Blackett in which Collingwood gave his views about the Nore. A midshipman who was a protégé of his father-in-law, perhaps suffering from that sense of frustration which afflicted all ranks at times, became so impertinent to Collingwood that he was ordered from the deck. Next day the offender wrote a note not excusing but justifying his conduct, and asked to be discharged into any other ship.

> But when [wrote Collingwood], after taking a day to cool a little, I gave him to understand, that having calmly considered the nature of his offence, and the necessity, under the present circumstances of the fleet, of giving a prompt check to the first instance of disobedience that tended to mutiny, I felt that the justice I owed to the public service outweighed the regard I ever had for his interests and his family, and that I only hesitated about bringing him to trial by Court Martial from the apprehension of the fatal consequences that might follow—he began to think very differently of the affair, was exceedingly dejected, hoped something might be done short of a Court Martial, as he knew what would be the probable event of that, and, if I would allow him, would quit the Service for ever. I told him I would consider further; and very much distressed and mortified I am at his conduct. He was not, I believe, sober at the time; but that will not do to plead in excuse for such violence.
>
> I know how sorry you will be on this occasion—not more than I am; but he shall never do duty in my ship again.

On 7 August, still from 'off Cadiz', Collingwood wrote to his sister Mary, giving her the news that Nelson was 'on an expedition, I believe, to Teneriffe', a fact which was true enough, though sad in the outcome. He gave Mary a description of St.

[1] Quoted in Hughes, 82n.

Vincent's way with mutineers which may have reassured her, but also in all probability, caused a shudder:

> ... we saw strong symptoms of convulsions but by the timely application of the only good remedy we were immediately restored to reason and firmness [wrote Collingwood].

> A plan was discovered on board the *St. George* to new model the fleet, *à la Nore*, only a few hours before the proposed time of putting it into execution. The ringleaders were seized promptly, four brought to trial, and being condemned to die late on Saturday night, hoped for Sunday's respite, but the case was urgent and admitted of no delay, they were hung in the face of the Spanish fleet before 9 on Sunday morning, and we have had the most perfect order ever since.[1]

The last surviving letter of 1797 was addressed to Dr. Carlyle from Lisbon on 16 December. Collingwood had been in Portugal since the end of the previous month, after eight months at sea, and he was in hopes, which were not realized, of an early return to England. There were still apprehensions about a junction of the Spaniards and French:

> but [he wrote],[2] when they get together they make but a heterogeneous sort of a compound and can never act with that forcible effect that a neat little active fleet does, the celerity of whose movements is likely to get part of them into a situation where the rest cannot relieve them.

This was a striking prophecy of the tactics which were to be employed by Nelson at Trafalgar.

In January 1798 Collingwood gave his father-in-law his opinion about the gravity of the war. Britain, so he considered, was fighting for survival.

> There never was a time, [he wrote][3] that required so much the unanimity of a nation. The question is not merely, who shall be conqueror, with the acquisition of some island or colony ceded by a treaty, and then the business concludes; but whether we shall any longer be a people, whether Britain is still to be enrolled among the list of European nations, whether the name of Englishman is to continue an appelation

---

[1] H., Letter 43.   [2] H., Letter 44.   [3] N.C., 63–64.

of honour, conveying an idea of every quality which makes human nature respectable, or a term of reproach and infamy, the designation of beggars and of slaves. Men of property must come forward both with purse and sword; for the contest must decide whether they shall have anything, even a country, which they can call their own.

Collingwood himself had had a compliment from St. Vincent. In the absence of certain flag-officers in England, he had been ordered to hoist a broad pendant as Commodore, which brought him an addition of ten shillings a day during the few weeks he held the appointment.

> My wits are ever at work [he wrote], to keep my people employed, both for health's sake, and to save them from mischief. We have lately been making musical instruments, and have now a very good band. Every moonlight night the sailors dance; and there seems as much mirth and festivity as if we were in Wapping itself. One night the rats destroyed the bagpipes we had made, by eating up the bellows; but they suffer for it, for in revenge we have made traps of all constructions, and have declared a war of extermination against them.

On May Day 1798 Nelson arrived off Cadiz, recovered from his wound at Tenerife. He was at once sent on the detached service which was to lead to his victory at the battle of the Nile, but not before he had delivered letters for Collingwood from Sarah and her father, or before the pair had had a talk. 'I never saw my friend Nelson look so well,' he reported: 'he is really grown fat, and not the worse for losing an arm.' Fat was a relative term, and what flesh Nelson put on during his convalescence in England was soon lost in the ardours of his next campaign.

The news from England included details of a voluntary subscription in aid of the finances of the war, a fact which drew a characteristic comment from Collingwood in his next letter to Blackett.

> The Flag-officers and Captains [he wrote][1] have made a subscription amounting to 5000 pounds, which was very well, considering how few of us are men of fortune.

[1] N.C., 65–66.

I confess the subscriptions of ship's companies at home give me no satisfaction: there is much danger in accustoming great bodies of men, whose service should be merely personal, to deliberate on any subject, but particularly to canvass the propriety of any political measure. It has always been a maxim with me to engage and occupy my men, and to take such care of them that they should have nothing to think of for themselves beyond the current business of the day.

In other words, politics were for the politicians and men of property, not for the common herd. These words may strike strangely on the ear today, but Collingwood lived before the time of wide enfranchisement, and the only examples he had had before him of democracy in action were in North America and in France. On each occasion, he had served the opposing side. However wise he came to be, from the experience of increasingly high command, he did not change his view that he lived under the best constitution known to him, imperfect though it might be.

Repeating the same sentiments about the situation of his country as he had expressed to Blackett, Collingwood wrote by the same ship to his cousin at Chirton that he had heard: 'every luxury goes on at full speed in the Capital; and while men shou'd be sharpening their swords, they are disputing points of little moment, hunting down a miserable fox, or listening to the squalling of an Italian Castrata . . .'[1] This seemed a poor recommendation of at least a fair proportion of those who were supposed to govern or at least to think.

By June, Collingwood had gathered the purpose of Nelson's detachment up the Mediterranean, which was, in his words to Blackett, to counter 'the execution of a plan which has long been in contemplation in France, for the opening a trade with India by the Red Sea, and supplying Europe with the produce of the East without the long, circuitous journey around the Cape of Good Hope.' Bonaparte himself had sailed with a great French armada for Egypt. 'I hope,' said Collingwood, 'Sir H. Nelson will dispose of their army and fleet in a way to be no longer troublesome in Europe.'

Collingwood might himself have been sent as part of his

----

[1] Add. MSS. 52780.

friend's picked force, but there were at least three good reasons why he was left behind. The first was that he was invaluable to his chief. The second was that the *Excellent* was overdue to go home, St. Vincent having already written to the Admiralty to say that this should be done before the winter. The third was that Collingwood was senior to Troubridge of the *Culloden*, and St. Vincent wished that Troubridge should go with Nelson, preferably as his second in command. This could not in fact be arranged, since Sir James Saumarez in the *Orion* had that honour: but to send two captains senior to Troubridge, as would have been the case had Collingwood gone, was more than the Commander-in-Chief would allow. It was, in fact, only after Nelson's sensational success against the French fleet that Collingwood began to feel aggrieved, and by that time, there was such dissatisfaction in the once harmonious force watching Spain that Collingwood was merely one of a number of malcontents.

His connexion Admiral Parker was among them, so was Sir John Orde, who was peremptorily sent home. Perhaps trouble was inevitable in a squadron employed month after month guarding against a supine enemy, but the immediate cause of friction was unquestionably the fact that Sir Roger Curtis had joined the Fleet and had become second in command in place of Orde, and that Nelson, still a very junior flag-officer, had been given charge of some of the best two-deckers of the Fleet, and sent off on a mission that any admiral would have wished to conduct, since it was in effect independent. That Nelson was the best possible choice, both in the opinion of St. Vincent and of Lord Spencer at the Admiralty, weighed not a straw in their consideration. Nelson had shown brilliance in battle, but his only experience as a flag-officer on detached duty, his attempt at cutting out the treasure convoy at Tenerife, had been a disastrous failure, in which both he and Troubridge had shared.

The fleet [wrote Collingwood to Blackett on 22 July] is . . . in a most unpleasant state; and now, all that intercourse of friendship, which was the only thing like comfort left to us, is forbidden; for the Admirals and Captains are desired not to entertain, even at dinner, any who do not belong to their ships.

They all complain that they are appointed to many unworthy services, and I have my share with the rest: but I
place myself beyond the reach of such matters; for I do them
with all the exactness in my power, as if they were things of
the utmost importance, though I do not conceal what I think
of them. In short, I do as anybody does—wish myself at home
very much.[1]

The battle of the Nile had been fought on 1 August 1798, but
it was some weeks before the news reached St. Vincent, and not
until October that Collingwood was able to write congratulating Nelson and also his boyhood friend Alexander Ball of the
Alexander, who had done well in the action. 'Many a victory
has been won, and I hope many are yet to come,' he said, 'but
there never has been, nor will be perhaps again, one in which
the fruits have been so completely gathered, the blow so nobly
followed up, and the consequences so fairly brought to account.'[2]

It was indeed a charming thing [he wrote later to Carlyle].[3]
It was the promptitude, as much as the vigour of the attack,
which gave him [Nelson] the superiority so very soon, the
Frenchman found himself assailed before he had determined
how best to repel the assault, and when victory had decided
on our side the fruits of it were carefully gathered in.

When Collingwood wrote on 3 December, it was to Sir Edward
Blackett, and from Spithead. The *Excellent* had at last been
ordered home, and Collingwood reported himself as 'restless and
unfit for anything' until he had seen his Sarah.[4] He still had
much to say about St. Vincent's arrogant ways with his flag-
officers and others, amplified in a letter to his Chirton cousin,
written on 14 December.[5]

The station I left was latterly rather disagreeable, [he wrote].
The strange innovations which the Chief made in all the
ordinary modes of discipline, and the high hand with which
he carried himself towards some officers, made it very
unpleasant for all. For my part, I had the good fortune to
keep clear of all disputes, nor do I know he ever said an unkind thing to me or of me, and that is a very singular case,

[1] N.C., 70.   [2] N.C., 72.   [3] H., Letter 46.
[4] H., Letter 45.   [5] Add. MSS. 52780.

for very few escaped the asperity of his temper. And his not
sending me with the reinforcement to Lord Nelson when of
right I ought to have gone . . . gave me so much dissatisfaction that from that day I looked to my return to England
with my great impatience . . . He treated Sr Jn. Orde very
ill. I never cou'd discern what was the cause, but when two
proud Dons meet, it is not difficult to find a cause of difference. I believe Sr Jn. Orde is as zealous in the publick
service as himself, but in his manners and style of living
there was a magnificence that the Chief was perhaps jealous
of, and so in a very unprecedented way he sent him home.

Although Orde's cause of dissatisfaction was largely the same
as Parker's and Collingwood's, where he had differed from them
was that he had carried complaint beyond what St. Vincent
believed to be the bounds of what was tolerable to a Commander-in-Chief.

On 8 January Collingwood was still at Spithead, slowly dis-
charging men, since the *Excellent* was to pay off, and somewhat
sad that he had not arranged for Sarah to join him. Foreseeing
that he would soon be home, he had wished to spare her the
long journey in mid-winter, with the prospect of a second soon
afterwards to rejoin the children. 'I am now quite sick at heart
with disappointment and vexation,' he told Blackett, 'and
though I hope every day for relief, yet I find it impossible to
say when I shall be clear.'[1]

He had been at a Twelfth Night party at Lady Parker's
house, 'where all the gentlemen's children of the town were at
dance and revelry; but I thought of my own, and was so completely out of spirits, that I left them in the middle of it.'

Lord Spencer had offered him command of the *Atlas* of 90
guns. 'She is ready for sea and may sail in a few days,' he wrote
to Carlyle on 11 January.[2] 'I had no hesitation in declining it.
I would not for the world have done what I believe would have
given so much pain to my darling Sall, as unexpectedly going
to sea without seeing her, and after my long absence from
England it cannot reasonably give offence.'

The season, he reported, had been severe everywhere: 'such
has rarely been known in England. Good fires and a warm house

---

[1] N.C., 75–76.   [2] H., Letter 47.

must make a climate for you. I was dismantling my ship during
the severe frost and truly neither me nor my men seemed to be
so sensible of the cold as other people were.'

He had made the *Excellent* a ship to be remembered. He had
achieved his aim, by arduous training, of delivering three broadsides within a period of a minute and a half, a phenomenal rate
of fire to have been reached in battle. His Spanish opponents
thought they were doing well if they took no more than five
minutes over a single broadside. It is no wonder that the name
of Collingwood's ship is commemorated in the Navy's school of
Gunnery.

At last, towards the end of the month of January, after an
absence of nearly four years, Collingwood was free to go north,
to be 'let loose to the greatest enjoyment a human creature is
capable of, the sweet caresses of a beloved wife and children (for
I expect they will make much of me) & the affectionate regards
of a family and friends that are very dear to me.'[1] If ever a man
had deserved his leave, it was he.

II

Before Collingwood wrote his next letter to Dr. Carlyle, he had
been promoted Rear-Admiral of the White. He was fifty years
of age, and at the height of his professional powers. The appointment dated from 14 February 1799, exactly two years
after the battle off St. Vincent. It was part of a large extension
of the flag-list, and Collingwood passed clean through the grade
of Rear-Admiral of the Blue, the list at that time being divided
into squadrons, red, white, and blue being the order of seniority.
Only a month before his name appeared he had written in a
disgruntled way: 'The Army is the line of *promotion*, the Navy
the field for *service* . . . I suppose it is very right, but I do not
pretend to understand it.'[2]

When he wrote from Morpeth, on 25 February 1799, to answer
Carlyle's congratulations,[3] he was able to tell him:

Since I arrived at Newcastle I have been so visited and visiting that I have scarce sat half an hour at a time, except at a
feast. I am very much flattered by the kind reception I have

[1] H., Letter 47.   [2] H., Letter 47.   [3] H., Letter 48.

met from everybody at Newcastle, and at this place. We came here on Saturday and shall stay but this week. I shall then set off to London.

Even after his years of ardour, relaxation would not do, or so he felt, any longer than was necessary to restore him to a balanced frame of mind. The times were altogether too menacing.

I have spent a month in great happiness [he continued]. Every body and every object contributes to it. My Sarah is all that is excellent in woman, my two girls as sweet children as ever were. They are pretty creatures and appear to me to have the greatest affection for each other, and for their mother, and to possess tempers that promise them a fair share of happiness, so that if this great promotion which the King has made in the Navy should exclude me from serving at sea, and check my pursuit of professional credit, I have as many comforts, and sources of normal happiness, to resort to as any person. But I shall never lose sight of the duty I owe to my country.

Collingwood had already written to Lord Spencer to offer his services, and, if his application was taken up, he did not propose to return to Morpeth, but to ask Sarah to come south, if his ship should be in home waters.

It is impossible to have a peace which would not be more dangerous to a country than a continuance of the war [he added]. I have health and strength in me at present for any thing. Our operations at sea are those of most consequence to the defence of the country. I should feel it a great diminution of my own importance not to be in employment.[1]

He expressed himself as 'sick with abhorrence' at the French. 'Every year they grow in strength, and how or where their tyranny is to end human foresight is too limited to form conjecture.' He prophesied a long continuance of the war, and expected, since the Navy had proved invincible in battle, that the enemy would soon 'make war on our finances'. This was foreshadowing the measures taken to cut off British trade with other countries, which was to be a feature of the next decade.

Lord Spencer and Collingwood got on well together, and the

[1] H., Letter 48.

First Lord appreciated the admiral's offer of immediate service, though he indicated that it might be some time before he was able to hoist his flag. While in London, Collingwood took the opportunity to attend a Drawing Room, of which he gave a characteristic glimpse to his father-in-law in a letter dated 14 March 1799:[1]

There were a great many people . . . yesterday, and a good number of naval officers who kissed Her Majesty's hand on the same occasion as I did. It was an entertaining sight, to so new a courtier, to observe the pleasure that sprang into the countenances of all, when Her Majesty was graciously pleased to repeat to them a few words which were not intended to have any meaning; for the great art of the courtly manner seems to be to smile on all, to speak of all, and yet leave no trace of meaning in what is said.

After the circumscribed excitement of contact with royalty, Collingwood was able to return, for a time at least, to Morpeth, where he spent the month of April and a little of May. He had insisted to the First Lord that he wanted a sea appointment only. 'I have no desire to command in a port,' he wrote to Carlyle,[2] 'except at Morpeth, where I am only second.'

The Collingwoods were expecting a visit from the Carlyles when his letter was sent off, on 26 April. 'Sarah wou'd add a few lines to her aunt,' he concluded, 'but she says her fingers ache with her work. She is making a new cover for her sofa against her friends come—always industrious.' He had visited Sir Edward and Lady Blackett at Thorpe Lee, near Egham, when he had been in the south, and in a letter from Morpeth dated 4 May he referred to a horse which Sir Edward had given him, and to the fact that his little girls, now seven and six respectively, had been taken from their school at Newcastle to be taught at home.

Collingwood was beginning to be restive, despite his happiness. 'I cannot in the present state of things suppress an impatience to be in the exercise of my profession,' he confessed to Sir Edward Blackett,[3] 'and this will increase when the newness of my present situation wears off. There is a nothingness in a

[1] N.C. (Additional letter; 1837 edition.)
[2] H., Letter 49.   [3] H., Letter 50.

sailor ashore at such a time that will, if it lasts long, weary me;
but I rather think it will not last long.' He was right. Within a
day or two he was summoned to serve with the Channel Fleet
under Lord Bridport, hoisting his flag for the first time in the
Triumph on 27 May. He was then detached with a reinforcement of ships under Sir Charles Cotton, which was to be sent
to the Mediterranean to join Lord Keith. A large French fleet
was at sea, and Keith was in hopes, never in fact realized, of
meeting them.

Collingwood's *Triumph* was a 35-year-old 74-gun ship which
had been present at Duncan's victory over the Dutch at
Camperdown in 1797. She was not properly fitted out for a
flagship, but she had to serve him until the following year, when
a larger vessel became available. Like the *Prince* of earlier days,
she was a bad sailer. 'I do not like my ship at all,' Collingwood
wrote to his sister, 'she sails so very ill, so much worse than the
Excellent on her worst day, that if the fleet were not to stop for
me a little I should be left.'[1]

III

The French, under Bruix, were at large from the end of April
to the late summer of 1799. The cruise of his fleet, and the
likelihood that he would be joined by ships from Spanish ports,
caused the gravest concern to Bridport's and St. Vincent's
officers. They had no fears about meeting Bruix in battle, but
of the harm the enemy could do if not encountered, or if met
with in hopelessly inferior numbers. Undefeated, Bruix might
support another attempt at invasion. He could certainly interfere with convoys, attack possessions overseas, and overwhelm
isolated detachments. In Collingwood's view (which was somewhat jaundiced), the situation was badly handled, and he made
no bones about saying so in letters home.

He found the ways of the Channel Fleet slack; he deplored the
fact that—owing to ill-health—St. Vincent conducted Mediterranean strategy from ashore at Gibraltar: as for Lord Keith, he
knew little about him, and decided that what he did know he
did not much approve of, and that, moreover, if Keith were
successful in beating Bruix, St. Vincent would be jealous of his

[1] H., Letter 51.

success. It was Collingwood's view that St. Vincent regarded what was, in the upshot, Keith's failure to meet with the enemy not merely with complacency but with satisfaction.

The strangely depressed, bitter, and even cynical tone of his letters during the cruise of 1799 may partly be accounted for by the fact that Collingwood was in one of the least satisfactory situations offered by the Navy—that of a Rear-Admiral, subordinate to seniors in the Fleet, accommodated in a slow, two-decked ship, with a captain whose ways he did not consider were up to the mark, but whose routine he could not, by custom of the Service, entirely upset. Collingwood was himself so much master of his trade that his position would have been felt all the more acutely. He had too much time to think; too little chance to act. An independent command of any kind would have made all the difference, but for that he had a long and weary wait before him.

Collingwood's account of how the French got out of Brest was contained in a letter written from near Gibraltar on 12 June.[1] This includes one of the more memorable items of purely naval information with which he enlightened his sister, and incidentally gave her an idea of what he preferred in the way of victuals.

I was bustled off in a great hurry [he wrote], but I prefer that to lounging about a length of time in a state of uncertainty. I am not well provided with necessaries, but I shall always be able to get a sheep, a pig and some fruit, and rather than have been absent from this campaign I wou'd have been content with a piece of old salt beef, and it is not a thing I like.

Off Brest (between ourselves) they made a horrible bungling work. The look out frigate saw the French fleet come out— the weather was thick and hazy—the signals he made could not be distinguished for some hours after. By the thickness of the weather, and their increased distance as they went on their voyage, Capt Percy lost sight of them and unaccountably taking it into his head (which I shou'd imagine is something like the weather) that they were all gone into port again, as if the French fleet wou'd come out merely to shew

[1] H., Letter 51.

8

how well they cou'd go in again, he anulled all the signals he had made, as if the whole had been an miscomprehension of his, and their circumstance, which he had indicated by his signals, had not occurred.

The Comm'r in Chief [did] indeed make his sign'l to come to him to explain the matter, but at the same time set so much sail in his ship that the frigate cou'd not get up to him until towards midnight, and then they determined to look into the port and see if they really were gone, and found it clean swept, and by that time sufficiently advanced to be out of danger of being overtaken.

A letter written to Sir Edward Blackett after his return to England, addressed from Torbay on 17 August,[1] expressed disgust at the ill-success of the voyage, which had included a vain search for the enemy at Minorca.

I am afraid we shall be very unwelcome to England, [he wrote] returning from so fair a field for great deeds, having effected nothing. The fleets of France and Spain seemed to be in our power, at least to combat them, and we had a force that promised everything, but the truth is our efforts were not great. I do not pretend to give reasons why they were not—the way of them was obvious to everybody, but we did not go that way . . . To those in the fleet who only looked how best their country's interest might be supported, whose only object was the destruction of the enemy's fleet, it has been a continued series of vexations and disappointments.

Next day, Collingwood wrote to his father-in-law:

We have made a most unfortunate voyage of it. In all reasonable expectation, the French fleet ought not to have escaped us; and I had always hopes of our coming up with them until we sailed into Port Mahon, which is a very narrow harbour, from which you cannot get out without great difficulty. There we remained, until the enemy had got so far from the start, that it was not possible to come up with them. We arrived at Brest the day after them, and finding them snug, came here: at all of which there has been great lamentation in the fleet.[2]

Keith had indeed been over-anxious over Minorca, the capture

[1] H., Letter 52.   [2] N.C., 77.

of which had not been Bruix's object, and Nelson, who at that
time was defending the possessions of the King of Naples, declined to detach ships to the island, though in so doing he was
rightly censured for disobeying Keith's orders.

Settling down for service in Home Waters, based on Torbay,
the anchorage where Hawke had so often sheltered his Fleet
during the blockades of the Seven Years War, a place which
Howe had also favoured, Collingwood could find little cause for
satisfaction, either in the state of Europe in general, in the
Navy, or even in the *Triumph*.

> Our security in great and imminent dangers is skill and sea-
> manship [he wrote to his sister Elizabeth (Bess) on 21
> September].[1] By the increase of the Navy, such numbers of
> unqualified, ignorant people are introduced into it that my
> astonishment is that more accidents do not happen. I was
> never so sensible of this truth as since I came into this ship.
> She is one of the noblest in the navy, but has been in bad
> hands, neglected in all points, the effect of not knowing much
> about the matter.

There had been rumours of Spanish detachments moving to join
the French, and Collingwood, with a fellow admiral, Berkeley,
had been off Brest, but they had had 'very bad blowing weather
. . . not such as wou'd suit the Dons at sea, so the Adml very
wisely brought the fleet in here'.

In November he wrote to his father-in-law about a youngster
recommended to his care, a type with whom he always took
pains.

> Has he been taught navigation? [he asked Blackett][2] If his
> father intended him for the sea, he should have been put to
> a mathematical school when twelve years old. Boys make
> very little progress in a ship without being well practised in
> navigation; and fifteen is too old to begin, for very few take
> well to the sea at that age. If, however, Mr. —— is deter-
> mined, he should lose no further time, but have his son taught
> trigonometry perfectly before he begins navigation. If the
> boy has any taste for drawing, it will be a great advantage to
> him, and should be encouraged.

[1] H., Letter 53.   [2] N.C., 78.

A more cheerful note was struck in a letter to his 'Sister', presumably his usual correspondent Mary, to whom Collingwood wrote towards the end of October.[1] A frigate had taken a Spanish vessel with 1,411,500 dollars on board. As a flag-officer, Collingwood stood to share in the prize, though with six others of his rank. 'What the Captain and officers of the ship will do with their money I don't know,' he added: 'I wish they may have strength of mind to keep their senses.' Digby, the captain concerned, certainly kept his, so Collingwood reported later, as well as 'four score thousand pounds by his prizes this war:'[2] but as he was 'a fine young man, one of those active spirits that maintains the credit of the navy', Collingwood was far from grudging him his luck. The other officers' share would have been so much smaller that no problems could have arisen from it. He reckoned he himself might get about £2,000: 'no bad Michaelmas goose', as he described it. He was now reaping some at least of the blessings of his rank.

On 6 November, Collingwood told Carlyle he thought that the French still had a 'great design' on Ireland in mind.

> Their fleet will carry an army of 30,000 men, without taking a transport ship, and if they can reach Beerhaven 24 hours before us they may establish themselves so strong on shore as to give perfect security to their fleet in that port. But I think we shall overtake them at sea.[3]

The ships, which were criticized for being at Torbay too much, were short of stores and men, but were in readiness for short cruises.

Carlyle had heard of the possibilities of prize money, and had congratulated his correspondent.

> It is a comfortable thing to be at ease in pecuniary matters [Collingwood replied][4] but I do not consider it as a thing that has any relation to our happiness, and I believe Sarah feels very much as I do on that subject. Your sentiments of her brought a pleasure to my heart that the prizes never did. It is that calm and wise temperament of mind that can adapt itself to our circumstances, whatever they may be, that makes

---

[1] H., Letter 54. [2] H., Letter 58.
[3] H., Letter 55. [4] H., Letter 56.

my wealth. I am persuaded were they more confined she
would possess a peaceful composure under them, and if ever
our good fortune advances them, no body will use them more
creditably to themselves or more beneficially to their society
than she will. But I do like to hear my wife praised & reckoned
a Philosopher of the right cast.

Collingwood had heard rumours that St. Vincent might shortly
supersede Bridport as Commander-in-Chief, and he was not
averse from the prospect, in spite of his earlier strictures.
The Channel Fleet, so he told Carlyle:

> is at present in a very very relaxed state, so different from
> what I have been used to, that it often gives me pain to see
> with what indifference the service is done, such as you might
> expect from Spaniards, in the dog days. I have a Captain
> here, a very novice in the conduct of fleets or ships. When I
> joined her I found she had been twice ashore, and once on
> fire, in the three months he had commanded her, and they
> were then *expecting* that the ships company would mutiny
> every day. I never saw men more orderly, or who seem better
> disposed, but I suppose they took liberties when they found
> they might, and I am afraid there are a great many ships
> where the reins of discipline are held very loosely, the effect
> of a long war, and an overgrown navy.[1]

Collingwood was concerned, so he told his correspondent, that
his little girls should not be too provincial in their speech; he
was 'not insensible of the great disadvantage of an uncouth
provincial dialect and corrupt pronunciation', but to find the
right corrective was not always simple. 'Their hearts, their
minds, are of much more consequence than their tongues'—such
was his view.

In his Christmas letter to Sir Edward Blackett, he dwelt
longingly on the prospects of peace.[2]

> Then I will plant my cabbages again [he wrote], and prune
> my gooseberry trees, cultivate roses, and twist the woodbine

[1] Punishments recorded in Collingwood's Journal of his period in the
Triumph (27 May 1799 – 20 January 1800) are limited to a single sentence:
12 lashes to Richard Clay at Port Mahon during Keith's cruise for 'contemp-
tuous behaviour'.

[2] H., Letter 57.

through the hawthorne hedge with as much satisfaction in my improvement as ever Dioclesian had, and with the same desire and hope that the occasion never will recurr to call me back to more important but less pleasurable occupations.

The next important letter to have survived was dated 8 April 1800: Collingwood was in a new century and on board a different ship. His flag flew from the *Barfleur*, from which he had been absent nearly six years. Now he could occupy the spacious admiral's quarters he had known so well when he had served as flag-captain to Bowyer. It was a welcome change from the *Triumph*, in which he had spent over seven months, during which he had seen no action. He was soon to test the *Barfleur's* sea-keeping qualities when, during a gale which was among the worst he had experienced for twenty years, he was able to tell his father-in-law 'this ship bore it as well as any, but I believe we are all much strained'.[1]

Collingwood continued to be concerned with a possible threat to Ireland, and he also had views on the Act of Union between Great Britain and Ireland which was then before Parliament and in its later stages. On 17 April he gave Carlyle his ideas on the character of the Irish people which certainly did not flatter them.[2]

I can judge ill of nice political questions, but I believe no union of government, however nicely devised and closely knit, can ever effect a union of sentiment, and opinions, and general manners in the people, who appear to be as distinct a race from the Britons as a Mexican from a Parisian, who have nothing alike but the feathers they wear in their caps— hot, hasty and inconsiderate: they are governed by no principle of right and wrong, lazy as savages, but more ferocious and cruel in their resentments. Even education does not eradicate this disposition, it only checks its impulse and slightly veils a mischief which is innate. Twenty Irishmen in a ship give more trouble than five hundred English. They seldom ever become seamen and I believe only are good in battle, because it is so much like that mischief which is innate. If they are here twenty years their manners change no more than the colour of an Ethiopian would by looking on the snow.

[1] N.C., 79.   [2] H., Letter 60.

In September Collingwood told Carlyle of a landing made by a military force at Ferrol, where there had been but slight resistance. In his own view, far more could have been made of the advantage gained by the initial surprise, which was scarcely exploited at all. He thought little of military methods and indeed, so far as the main campaigns were concerned, the glories of the Army were still all in the future: the soldiers had done very little in the earlier years of the war.

What seems odd to us [he wrote],[1] who are not conversant in land affairs and the etiquette to be observed by armies, is, that they were in possession of the arsenal, amongst the naval store houses, and where ships were building, and did not burn them. Perhaps they had not carcases, links and port fires, and it wou'd not have been military to have struck a light in a tinder box. They sailed from thence to Vigo, which they also looked at, but did not land. Some of the ships' boats cut out a French privateer that was lying there. . . . They sailed from thence towards the Mediterranean and every body here seems very thankful they are so far off. Yet I wish they were in England, or a few here to compleat the complements of our ships.

125879

At one period during the summer of 1800 Collingwood had a brief change of ship, for he wrote a letter in August from the *Neptune*, off Brest. She was another fine vessel of 98 guns, like the *Barfleur*, and was only three years old, but she did not bring him comfort.

Nothing good can happen to us short of peace [he told his father-in-law].[2] Every officer and man in the fleet is impatient for release from a situation which daily becomes more irksome to all. I see disgust growing round me very fast. Instead of softening the rigours of a service which must from its nature, be attended by many anxieties, painful watchings, and deprivation of every thing like comfort, a contrary system is pursued. . . . What I feel is a great misfortune is, that there is no exercise of the military part of the duty, no practice of those movements, by a facility in which one fleet is made superior to another. Whoever comes here ignorant in

[1] H., Letter 61.   [2] N.C., 79–80.

these points, must remain so; for he will find other employment, about blankets, and pig-sties, and tumbling provisions
out of one ship into another. How the times are changed!
Once, when officers met, the first question was—What news
of the French? Is there any prospect of their coming to sea?
Now there is no solicitation on that subject, and the hope of
peace alone engages the attention of every body.

Collingwood was aware of the acidulation of his own temper
caused by his employment: constant vigilance, unseasoned by
action, and irritation with those less competent than himself.
His letters were becoming more than a channel of communication with those he loved: they were his principal release from
care.

Great allowance should be made for us when we come on
shore [he wrote home on 4 October,[1] once more from the
Barfleur], for being long in the habits of absolute command,
we grow impatient of contradiction, and are unfitted for the
gentle intercourse of quiet life. I am really in great hopes that
it will not be long before the experiment will be made upon
me, for I think we shall soon have peace; and I assure you
that I will endeavour to conduct myself with as much modera-
tion as possible. I have come to another resolution, which is,
when this war is happily terminated, to think no more of
ships, but pass the rest of my days in the bosom of my family,
where I think my prospects of happiness are equal to any
man's.

Collingwood was mistaken, for even the one uncertain treaty
which was to make a pause in the long struggle was still many
months off, and so indeed was that reunion in Northumberland
to which he so much looked forward. Instead, there were
rumours of changes in the Fleet: Sir Hyde Parker was said to
be coming to the Channel Command, and in November Collingwood was able to tell his sister what he believed to be the nature
of the man.

I cannot but wonder [he wrote],[2] the Admiralty shou'd be so
anxious to have him employed, for in the little I have seen
of him I could only discover a good tempered man, full of

[1] N.C., 80-81.   [2] H., Letter 62.

vanity, a great deal of pomp, and a pretty smattering of ignorance—nothing of that natural ability that raises men without the advantages of a learned education.

This thumb-nail sketch was not jaundiced but exact. Parker had but one stern test of his character as an admiral, when he was sent to the Baltic to speed the disintegration of a dangerous Northern Coalition which was threatening the interests of his country. Had it not been that the Admiralty thought fit to send Nelson as his second in command, his mission would have failed dismally. Even as it was, he was sent home, and never employed again. He committed the unforgivable sin of ordering action to be broken off, just as it was beginning to succeed: the occasion of Nelson turning a blind eye to his signal.

Collingwood found himself increasingly often at Cawsand Bay, at the western entrance to the sheltered waters of Plymouth, and it was from there that he wrote to Carlyle, on 7 December[1] prescribing for an ailing fellow admiral ashore. 'If I was his Physician,' he said, 'I should prescribe a cheerful friend or two, who could be merry without being loud, light and nourishing food, and a bottle (at least) of good claret after dinner.'

As for his own physical condition, a week later he told his sister: 'I used to be complaining often, bilious and nervous, and subject to violent disorders in my stomach and bowels, of which I have very little now, and which I attribute chiefly to wearing a flannel waistcoat. Since I used it I seldom get cold.'[2] Yet there were worse ailments than colds. On 4 January 1801 he told the same correspondent about his 'weak nerves'.

God knows how much I suffer from them [he complained], what hours of sadness and depression of spirit I pass heavily away.[3] I endeavour to correct it by exercise and cheerful company, but this requires an effort, for languor and indisposition to any thing gay is a part of [the] disease. In us I believe it is in great measure constitutional. I have been very poorly lately, weak in the greatest degree, and never sleep at nights. The only time I am free of this weight, this oppressive something, as if I bore a mountain on my shoulders, is the few hours that I am dispatching my business, and at that time I know no ill, all is brisk with me then.

[1] H., Letter 63.   [2] Col. 39–839.   [3] H., Letter 65.

The wretched sailors, cooped up eternally and involuntarily in their ships, with no amenities such as could be provided for admirals and captains, were in much worse case, and there was trouble in the *Téméraire*, where the men believed that they were to go on distant service. Examples had to be made, and Collingwood assured Carlyle that these were *absolutely* necessary, underlining the word. He believed that half the trouble arose from free postage. 'The intention was kind and considerate, but the allowing seamen's letters to pass free of postage has done infinite harm. Of a hundred letters not more than five are from wives or relations, but either scrawls from the nannies, or plans of resistance from other ships.'[1]

Personal news at this time was both good and bad: good because Sarah had been arranging to buy their house at Morpeth, which until then had been rented, and the notion was agreeable; bad because the Newcastle lads in the *Barfleur* were disappointing. One of them, a protégé of Mary Collingwood's, 'young Emerson' would, in the admiral's view, 'never make a sailor. He never comes on deck but when he is sent for by some officer, and does nothing below. And yet he messes with some as fine boys as are in the Navy. The Newcastle boys do not prosper, at least in my hands.'[2]

The brightest news of all came in mid-January, when Collingwood heard that his Sarah had been intrepid enough to start on the 500-mile mid-winter journey which was to take her from Morpeth to Plymouth. She brought her eight-year-old daughter with her, leaving Mary Patience under the care of the ever attentive Blackett and the Collingwood aunts. The negotiations over the property were in a state satisfactory enough to leave in the lawyer's hands, and Collingwood could scarcely trust himself to express what he felt at the prospect of a little family life. 'There is a dreadful languor that I cannot quite shake off,' he wrote to Blackett,[3] 'but when Sarah comes, when I see her, I shall then be well.'

Sarah was indeed on her way; so too was Nelson.

---

[1] H., Letter 66.   [2] H., Letter 65.   [3] N.C., 82.

IV

It was Nelson's fate to bring stir of some sort into Collingwood's life, and his arrival at Plymouth certainly did so, 'Lord Nelson is here,' Collingwood wrote to Blackett on 25 January, 'and I think he will probably come and live with me when the weather will allow him; but he does not get in and out of ships easily with one arm. He gave me an account of his reception at Court, which was not very flattering, after having been the admiration of that of Naples. His Majesty merely asked him if he had recovered his health, and then, without waiting for an answer, turned to General —————, and talked to him near half an hour in great good humour. It could not have been about *his* successes.'[1]

The meeting of such old and tried friends could not but have been happy in itself. Collingwood did not find Nelson changed, but in fact the younger man was wretched. He was a Vice-Admiral and a Peer of the Realm, his breast sparkled with orders, but he had just parted from his wife for ever, Emma Hamilton was bearing his child, and many of his friends shook their heads over him. His sightless eye was inflamed and painful, and he was about to sail as second in command to Sir Hyde Parker, an officer about whom Collingwood had lately expressed himself in no uncertain terms. The mission would be to destroy or intimidate the fleets of the Northern Powers, which had banded together in an Armed Neutrality whose object was to resist the belligerent right of search, and whose attitude was favourable to France.

As for Collingwood, he had not known the heady wine of fame, such as Nelson had enjoyed ever since the Nile, and the weary time he had spent in Channel and Atlantic waters had indeed worn him down, as he often said. The one great hope he had, that he would soon see his beloved, was realized at the very moment when he and Nelson were dining together.[2]

'Collingwood's wife and child arrived last evening,' Nelson wrote to St. Vincent on 28 January, the Earl then exercising command of the Channel forces from ashore at Tor Abbey.[3] A

---

[1] N.C., 83.   [2] N.C., 85.   [3] Nic. vii. ccxxix* (*Addendum*).

week later, from Torbay, to which he had suddenly been sent,
Collingwood wrote to Blackett:[1]

> Sarah will have told you how and when we met; it was a joy
> to me that I cannot describe, and repaid me, short as our
> interview was, for a world of woe I was suffering on her
> account. I had been reckoning on the possibility of her arrival
> that Tuesday, when about two o'clock I received an express
> to go to sea immediately with all the ships that were ready;
> and had we not then been engaged at a court martial, I might
> have got out that day: but this business delayed me till near
> night, and I determined to wait on shore until eight o'clock
> for the chance of their arrival.
>
> I went to dine with Lord Nelson; and while we were at
> dinner their arrival was announced to me. I flew to the inn
> where I had desired my wife to come, and I found her and
> little Sarah as well after their journey as if it had lasted only
> for the day. No greater happiness is human nature capable
> of than was mine that evening; but at dawn we parted, and I
> went to sea. Lord St. Vincent has, however, been so good as
> to promise that I shall go to Plymouth whenever I can be
> spared from the fleet.

The flurry had been caused by the escape of a small squadron
from Brest. Sir Robert Calder had been sent after them, and
Collingwood had been ordered to take Calder's station at
Torbay. On 8 February, Nelson wrote a kindly note to Sarah
Collingwood to tell her: 'I own I should have sent my friend
after the French Squadron, because I think him much fitter than
the one sent, and I do not believe there are two opinions on the
subject. Hoping you may soon see my dear friend . . .'[2]

Nelson had at last caught a glimpse of the felicity known to
the Collingwoods. Writing later to Mrs. Moutray, with whom
Collingwood and Nelson always kept up, Collingwood said:
'How surprised you would have been to have popped in to the
Fountain Inn and seen Lord Nelson, my wife, and myself sitting
by the fireside cosing, and little Sarah teaching Phillis, her dog,
to dance.'[3] It would have seemed to all three of them an age
since the sunlit days at English Harbour, Antigua, in the 1780's.

---

[1] N.C., 84–85.   [2] Nic. iv. 283–4.

[3] Quoted in W. Clark Russell, *The Life of Lord Collingwood* (1895 ed.), 97.

Then, the two men had been young and ambitious captains: now they were seasoned and principal officers in one of the largest naval armaments their country had ever assembled.

While her husband was at sea, Sarah settled in lodgings at Plymouth, where she found everyone attentive, though she was surprised at the cold, which she found more trying than that of the north.

The weather here is very severe,[1] [she wrote on 15 February to her uncle, Sir Edward Blackett] I never suffered so much from cold, and have been confined to the house some days with rheumatism, but hope soon to get out again.

I wish I could give you any account of Admiral Collingwood . . . in the meantime, I have the satisfaction of knowing how much my husband is respected here by the very great kindness and attention that everybody shows me. I might, if I pleased, be engaged out every day; but as I have my little girl with me, that would not answer at all, as it would be leaving her too much, so I shall now stay more at home . . .

I have received great kindness and attention from Sir Thos. Pasley, the Port-Admiral here; he has two public days in the week, and I was to have dined there yesterday, but was obliged to send an excuse, being so poorly, and this morning he has sent me some books to amuse me.

It was Pasley who, with his flag in the *Bellerophon*, had done so well with the advanced squadron in the preliminary fighting before the Glorious First of June.

Collingwood was off Ushant all through February and for part of March, and it was from there, on 6 March, that he wrote to Sarah's father:

I have little chance of seeing her again, unless a storm should drive us into port, for the French fleet is in a state of preparation, which makes it necessary for us to watch them narrowly. This cruise is the most tiresome of all I ever experienced; for, independently of the reasons which I now have for desiring to be in port, no regard is paid to letters coming or going, which was always an object of the first consideration with Lord Bridport, Lord St. Vincent and Sir Allan Gardner. I do

---

[1] Ibid. 102.

not know that one of the many letters I have written since
my sailing is gone, and I have not heard from any one these
three weeks. Of public matters we know nothing, for we do
not even get a newspaper. We are immured within the sides
of our ships, and have no knowledge of the world or its ways.[1]

Collingwood's allusion to changes in the Fleet were apropos, for
Cornwallis had succeeded St. Vincent as Commander-in-Chief,
and St. Vincent had gone to the Admiralty as First Lord. But
by 15 March the *Barfleur* was at anchor again, and Collingwood
was able to report to Carlyle that his Sarah had:

managed her affairs and made out very well. All the families
have been very kind and attentive to her and she is already
much better acquainted with their histories than I am. I
cannot tell you what my delight has been for the four days
I have been here, with my wife and little Sall. My former
disappointment heightened the pleasure I have felt now, and
I hope to remain with them some days to come, as Lord St.
Vincent was so good as to say I should stay here as long as
the state of things, fleets &c wou'd allow, which however
cannot be very long, as at Brest they seem to be quite ready
for sea.[2]

St. Vincent had gone to Whitehall at the invitation of Addington, who had succeeded Pitt as Prime Minister. Collingwood
was pleased at the appointment.

The navy, I doubt not, will be ably directed by Lord St.
Vincent [he wrote]. His ambition, which has ever been his
ruling passion, has kept him all his life in the continual
exercise of his powers, and established him in habits of business which will enable him to keep the Admiralty as active
as his predecessor, with more knowledge of the character and
ability of all the officers. I do not know how the changes can
affect me. Under the present circumstances I am satisfied with
my station in the fleet, but I believe Lord St. Vincent is very
kindly disposed towards me, and if he thought some other
situation might be more advantageous to me I do not think
he wou'd ask me anything about it.

[1] N.C., 85–86.   [2] H., Letter 67.

When Collingwood wrote to his Chirton cousin at the end of
March he confirmed this opinion.

Our late Chief, [he wrote][1] has now arrived at the summit of
his ambition. No man in England is more capable of conducting the Naval department than he is, besides his having the
advantage of much professional information which cannot be
so well understood by landmen. He has more hours for business than most men, having little taste for pleasure, and
seldom sleeps more than 4 or 5 hours in a night.

Collingwood also told his relative about the only recorded
time when the Sarahs, great and less, were at sea. 'They came
on board the *Barfleur* in Cawsand,' so he reported, 'and unluckily a hard gale of wind came on which made them very ill
and not a little glad to get on shore again as soon as the storm
abated.' Collingwood was sorry for the effect on his wife. 'I do
not think I shall prevail on her to trust herself on board again,'
he wrote. 'It was unlucky.' But at least the incident had given
Sarah some idea of how her husband lived during his long
absences from her.

Soon afterwards, mother and daughter went to stay at
Paignton, which Collingwood described as 'a very pleasant
village near Torquay'. His hope was that 'some good gale might
have driven us in there', but this did not happen.

In April Collingwood was once more off Brest, and on the
20th of the month he wrote to his father-in-law to tell him that
he had just heard the news of Nelson's exploit in destroying
the Danish fleet at Copenhagen, which had occurred nearly
three weeks earlier. This, he said, had 'almost turned my head
with joy'. A thankful impulse made him ask Blackett to 'send
Scott a guinea for me, for these hard times must pinch the poor
old man, and he will miss my wife, who was very kind to him'.[2]
Scott had helped in the Morpeth garden.

Thinking further about Nelson's success in the Baltic, and of
his friend's qualities in general, Collingwood wrote later in the
year to Carlyle:

Lord Nelson is an incomparable man, a blessing to any
country that is engaged in such a war. His successes in most

[1] Add. MSS. 52780.   [2] N.C., 86.

of his undertakings are the best proofs of his genius and his talents. Without much previous preparation or plan he has the faculty of discovering advantages as they arise, and the good judgement to turn them to his use. An enemy that commits a false step in his view is ruined, and it comes on him with an impetuosity that allows him no time to recover.[1]

This tribute, one of many made during Collingwood's service life, is additionally pointed as having been written not as the result of Nelson's later glory, but as an immediate assessment by an officer not much below Nelson in rank, and with a galaxy of other admirals, still in mid-career, with whom to compare him.

In July, Collingwood wrote to his sister to thank her for sending news of Mary Patience. He was:

happy to find you are all well, and that my precious Mary is so spritely and so gay after the little jauntings she has had, which I dare say will strengthen her and do her health good.

Poor little Sarah is very much troubled with her eyes, which inflame upon every little cold she takes and even exposure to the wind makes them very sore, and particularly the sea air. I am convinced from what I saw at Plymouth that bathing in the sea is not proper for her. None of the applications to her eye has done it good. Doctor Trotter disapproved of them all and recommended small quantities of sulphur and honey to be taken merely as an alternative, which one may reasonably hope wou'd correct that sharp humour which causes the inflammation, which I hope it will in time.[2]

The Doctor referred to was Thomas Trotter, Surgeon to the Fleet. He was a great admirer of Howe. He had been present at the battle of 1794 in the hospital ship *Charon*. He also had much regard for Collingwood. In his *Medicina Nautica*, which first appeared some years later, he wrote of a ventilating device which Collingwood had had designed and installed in the *Barfleur*: 'and the Admiral, with great justice, attributes a large share of the improved health of his ship's company to this flue for conducting from the lower parts of the deck, the air vitiated

---

[1] H., Letter 69.   [2] H., Letter 68.

by respiration'.[1] Shortly after he had attended little Sall, Trotter took up private practice at Newcastle upon Tyne, no doubt encouraged by Collingwood, and made a great success of it.

It appeared as if Collingwood had been right about St. Vincent looking after his interests. 'I never was so well supplied or taken care of in any of my former cruizes,' he told his sister.

In August Sarah was still at Paignton, as Collingwood still expected to anchor in Torbay, but she had a disappointing wait there and at the end of it returned to Plymouth, for Collingwood, who was still off Brest on the 24th of the month, sent a message ashore to say it would be best for her to return to the quarters she had left. He wrote to Carlyle on that day: 'Thank God I am now very well, but have been more out of health this cruize than I ever was, which I attribute very much to the long confinement. This is the third summer that I have hardly seen the leaf of the trees, except through a glass at a distance of some leagues.'[2]

He and Sarah had a spell together during September, and in October, though Collingwood was once more with the Fleet, he wrote to his father-in-law to tell him with what happy expectations they had parted, before she made her long journey back to Northumberland.[3]

I cannot tell you how much joy the news of the peace gave me [he wrote on the 16th of the month]. The hope of returning to my family, and living in quiet and comfort among those I love, fills my heart with gladness. The tidings came to us at the happiest time. I was to take leave of my wife after breakfast, when William [Ireland, his servant] came running in with one of his important faces on, and attempted to give his information in a speech; but after two or three efforts, which were a confused huddle of inarticulate sounds, he managed to bring out, Peace! Peace! which had just as good an effect as the finest oration he could have made on the subject . . .

The moment the French in Brest heard the preliminaries were signed, they sent out a flag of truce with the informa-

[1] *Medicina Nautica* (1804) reprinted in *The Health of Seamen*, ed. C. Lloyd (N.R.S.), 1965, p. 288.
[2] H., Letter 69.   [3] N.C., 87–88.

9

tion to Admiral Cornwallis, and their congratulations on the
approaching amity of the two countries. The English officer
who was sent in with a return of the compliment was treated
with the greatest hospitality and kindness, both by the
French and Spanish. They feasted him all the time he staid
there, and carried him to the plays and places of entertainment, I hope now we have seen the end of the last war that
will be in our days, and that I shall be able to turn my mind
to peaceful occupations.

Glad as he was, Collingwood's own release was still some six
months off, and he had another whole winter at sea before him,
including a spell at Bantry Bay, which he described as 'the
most miserable part of the King's dominions. Nothing can
exceed the nakedness of the country and the wretchedness of
the inhabitants, but it is a fine port, where the ships lie safely,
and I conclude we shall stay here until all the conditions of the
peace are settled by the definitive treaty.'[1]

The last months of active service were a particularly testing
time for the tempers of officers and men, and the punishment
records of the *Barfleur* tell how discipline was upheld, the flog-
gings ordered by the captain being duly noted in Collingwood's
journal.[2] One of them was merely for 'mutinous expressions'.
Between the beginning of October 1801 and May 1802, when
Collingwood struck his flag at Spithead, 23 seamen and marines
suffered the lash, the maximum sentences being 24 strokes for
'neglect of duty and contempt for their superior officer'.

As a captain, Collingwood, though undoubtedly humane, never
unduly spared the lash if and when it was warranted, a fact
which may be discovered even in the pages of Newnham Collingwood, who would have had his readers believe that his father-
in-law differed in this respect from most of his contemporaries.[3]
Collingwood was in fact a man of his age in that he believed
that the sailor or marine must remain a sternly subordinated
being, to be governed with an unrelaxed vigilance. He had seen
the results of mutiny, and approved of how St. Vincent, in that
respect a pattern to him, stamped it out in every fleet he commanded, without sentiment, without mercy, without regard to

[1] H., Letter 71.   [2] Col., 13a/0310.
[3] N.C., 52, where punishment records are printed relating to the *Prince*.

any consideration but the fighting efficiency of his ships. To him, war was never a business for half measures.

It is a melancholy thing [Collingwood wrote to his sister-in-law, Mrs. Stead, from Plymouth, early in January 1802],[1] but there is no possibility of governing ships, so as to make them useful to the state, but by making examples of those who resist the execution of their orders, and I hope this will have such an effect upon the whole fleet that we shall have no more commotions amongst them.

Later in the same month, Collingwood wrote a revealing sentence in a letter to his cousin at Chirton, referring to the grim series of punishments and sentences with which he had become involved. 'I am not yet hard enough to witness the infirmities and misfortunes of men, without suffering much pain from such human frailty and deficiency.'[2]

It will be seen from this confession that it was not the horrific spectacles afforded by the infliction of the lash, and hanging from the yard-arm, which affected Collingwood so much as the cause of punishment. He felt less for the victim's agony and indignity than at the thought of the flaws and sins inherent in human nature. The fact argues an assurance that justice was done at sea, and that it was indeed the guilty who paid retribution. Certainly, where he himself was concerned, trials would have been conducted with scrupulous fairness, in so far as he could ensure this. But such a state of affairs could not have been so everywhere. If one thing is more certain than another, it is that Collingwood was incapable of the cruelties which at times (though surprisingly rarely, considering the centuries during which almost unbearable incarceration and iron subordination continued) drove men beyond endurance, while as he grew older and wiser, so did his compassion.

Ambitious to serve his country in the highest rank to which his capabilities entitled him, Collingwood wrote to his sister while at Bantry Bay to tell her: 'They talk of a naval promotion by way of a concluding reward for our hard service and I hope they will make me a Vice Admiral.' Collingwood had been a Rear-Admiral of the Red since New Year's Day 1801, but he had to wait over three years for his next step in rank.

[1] H., Letter 72.   [2] Add. MSS. 52780.

Peace preliminaries had at last restored certain alleviations, including the old style of socialities among fellow officers.

We dine with each other when the weather will allow boats to pass, and indeed the young men find ladies even among these rocks [of Bantry Bay] to make a dance now and then. I mean all those who have shoes and stockings and a bit of blue ribbon to adorn their black heads. They can all dance, and while they hold their tongues, are very decent behaved people.[1]

Another consolation was that it was Collingwood's considered view that the purpose of the war had been attained:

it was to resist principles of revolution which the enemy disseminated in our country [he wrote to Mrs. Stead], and which threatened our existence as a nation, but when those principles are become the object of universal abhorrence, and their dire effects fully exemplified, as they have been, they lose their danger, and the price of peace can scarce be rated too high . . . Now it remains to be proved whether the French are equally sincere and whether the Republican government is more disposed to live in amity with the world than their monarchs were. The experiment is a fair one to make.

Collingwood qualified this view a little later in a letter to Sir Edward Blackett, when he remarked about Bonaparte, then the master in France: 'A Frenchman is such a ticklish animal that I cannot consider him but with suspicion, and a Corsican has given proof that he can out-trick a Frenchman.'[2]

By the end of January 1802 the news about the Morpeth house was proving satisfactory: 'they tell me it is good and strong built, and will be a good house after our time,' Collingwood told Sir Edward, and his words were true, for the building outlasted the century in which he wrote.

In April, all was nearly over, and on the 20th he wrote to his sister from Torbay:[3] 'Today, six are going to the different ports and then there will only remain the Commander-in-Chief, and myself, with six ships and the frigates, which I think in a week or ten days will also go off to their resting places. I am

[1] H., Letter 71.   [2] H., Letter 73.   [3] H., Letter 74.

sure I have had my share of the war. I begun it early and see the last of it, and I hope it is the last we shall ever see.'

On Friday 7 May, Collingwood was able to conclude his Journal[1] with the satisfactory entry: 'At sunset struck my Flag by order.'

[1] Col., 13a/0310.

7 *Interlude At Home*

The state of peace which was introduced by the Treaty of
Amiens lasted, in a formal sense, one week short of a year
(25 May 1802 to 18 May 1803)—though in practicalities somewhat longer. Not many shared Collingwood's opinion that, as
the 'object' of the war had been 'fully obtained', matters could
be regarded as satisfactory. What in fact had occurred was
that Bonaparte required a breathing-space before a gigantic
new outburst of energy which would be applied to conquest
and aggression. He made every use of his time: but Britain
acted differently. Numbers of tourists, deprived for so long of
any chance to visit or re-visit the Continent, flocked across the
Channel, many of them to be caught and remorselessly interned
when the moment came for the French to reopen hostilities.
This was sad enough, but what was far more serious was the
effect of St. Vincent's drive to purge corruption in the dockyards, and of his laying up most of the ships in the interests of
economy. The dockyards, from that state of age-long waste and
peculation which at least had produced some internal harmony
based on custom, became chaotic. As a result, when war was
resumed, the Navy had insufficient ships in good repair for its
needs, or to support an aggressive policy.

It was long before such weighty matters concerned Collingwood. He proceeded from Portsmouth to Thorpe Lee, Egham,
where he spent a day or two with Sir Edward and Lady
Blackett. Then he went to London, and so to the north. He
wrote on 9 May from Thorpe Lee to Mrs. Stead, who was living
in Berkshire but was threatened with the re-occupation of her
house by the landlord, since, like Collingwood's at Morpeth, it
had been rented. 'I should recommend Northumberland for

your residence,' Collingwood suggested,'[1] a fine healthy air; in winter, a comfortable fire and friends about you that would be made happy by your neighbourhood.' He reported the Blacketts as being well, 'but,' he added, 'I observed old age had made considerable advances since I saw them last, they are both very deaf, but in cheerful good spirits.'

In his next surviving letter, which was written on 25 June from Morpeth, Collingwood gave Dr. Carlyle an exact account both of his sources of happiness, and of the inroads which the passing of the decades, and hard service, were making on himself. He was then two months short of fifty-four, a much more advanced landmark towards old age than it is today.

> I have great gratisfaction in the improvement of my children [he wrote], and am full of thankfulness to God that they, and their beloved mother, enjoy such perfect health that it is hardly known in our family what an ail or an ache is. I never knew Mr Blackett better than he is now. He is cheerful and far less deaf than he was formerly. When he is not obliged to be in Newcastle about his business he comes to us, and as the children are with us for the holidays we are a merry family, and I do not wish that this state of our domestics may be interrupted by any public employment.
>
> Lord St. Vincent was kind enough to offer me command immediately, but as I believe this proposal was made in kindness to me I have no idea of his being offended at my declining it, or that it shou'd at all interfere with my employment in the event of a war. And until that happens, which I hope is very distant, I am not desirous of being engag'd in the sort of service that peace offers.[2]

One of the happier of Collingwood's reunions must have been with Bounce, the second and more famous dog with which he was associated. How long the creature he had taken with him in the *Mermaid*, years before, lasted there is no means of telling, but Bounce was to become a well-loved character. He had been dispatched north in a collier the previous January,[3] 'amongst the valuables', together with some heavy gear, no doubt in charge of a servant. While he lived, he was never again to be long parted from his master.

[1] H., Letter 75.   [2] H., Letter 76.   [3] H., Letter 72.

Like most sailors ashore, and all property owners, Collingwood was concerned with 'improvements', and wished to transform his place at Morpeth nearer to what he thought desirable.

> I have workmen opening out the back part of our premises, [he told Carlyle] by pulling down the old crazy walls and dog houses, and building a low wall to separate the garden. When we get the ground opposite to us, we intend to throw it into a little field which will be convenient, and improve the prospect from our house. But this must remain with the tenant until February next, and I believe I shall do little more this summer than is now in hand.

There followed one of those references to the state of his physical well-being which do much to make clear successive stages in Collingwood's life.

> I do not hear as I did formerly. I am not short sighted, but I do not see as I did formerly, and sometimes can scarce read without spectacles. In ten years I think I shall be as old a man as you are now,[1] but this is a subject I contemplate with pleasure rather than regret. To live a good life has been my care, ever since I had care: to live a long one has never given me a thought.

A brief undated note to his sister, probably written in July, spoke of heat, accompanied by rain storms. The family had been on a visit to Newcastle and had returned 'all very well, myself only well wet, for the heat obliged me to pull off my coat. Of two evils I chose the cool and refreshing drops.'[2]

At the end of August, Collingwood wrote to Carlyle to tell him:

> We have been jaunting about a good deal which has wearied Sarah, and she has become languid and relaxed, so that the sea bathing, she thinks, is quite necessary to set her up before the winter pinches her, and in about ten days we go down to Newbiggin.[3]

He included an account of the progress of the work at Morpeth.

---

[1] Carlyle was then eighty.   [2] H., Letter 77.   [3] H., Letter 80.

I have been very busy with the ground about our house, very much to its improvement. The old cottages that were opposite to us are removed, not a vestige of them left. In their place is a low parapet wall, with iron rails on it which opens our view to what will be a very pretty little field, at the end of which is the river [Wansbeck] and the high banks covered with wood. On the other side our house we have done a great deal but there is yet as much to do, and next summer we purpose making some alterations within, which altogether will make it a very comfortable dwelling. My wife likes it, which makes me take much pleasure in improving it. It is very expensive, but then we in the mean time avoid the expenses as much as possible, which makes that matter easy.

Perhaps what was the happiest of all peace-time letters was sent to Mrs. Stead from Newcastle on 11 October. This began:

My dear Sister

It is always a great satisfaction to me when I have any thing to communicate to you that will please you, and now all I have to say to you is comfortable. Here we are a set of happy creatures. The bathing at Newbiggen has given your sister health and strength and spirits that brightens all the objects round her. Mary Pat is quite recovered from the meazles which have been of the most favourable kind, and Sarah is very desirous that her turn should come soon; from little appearances I do not think she will have long to wait. Your father is as well as can be. We came from Morpeth on Saturday that we might be here to celebrate your birthday, my dear sister, on Wednesday, when we shall join in wishing you to see many in health and happiness, and we came for a few days before, that Ingham [surgeon] might stiffen my limbs a little which have been rather infirm lately with rheumatism, but are better. No creature was ever more carefully nursed than I have been while home, by your dear sister. Her kind attentions have contributed much to my cure and was a sweet source of comfort to *me*.[1]

Collingwood had been really unwell, for Sarah included a note

[1] H., Letter 81.

within the letter which told of a violent attack, and that it was only because her husband had had a good night, that she was enabled to write at all. The family would be at Newcastle for about ten days, and then return home.

Only two letters from Morpeth have survived from 1803, and after that year Collingwood never saw the place again. On 13 March he wrote to Carlyle that he was once more disturbed at the world situation.

We are again threatened with war, and all its miseries. I have little hope that it can be avoided and, in that case, I suppose I shall be employed immediately. I received a letter five days since from Sir Evan Nepean [Secretary of the Admiralty] to know if I was ready (in the event of being wanted) to go on service at very short notice. I answered 'To be sure I was' and packed up my trunk and my signal book and am now waiting for a summons to take my station wherever it may be. I have only to hope, if we are compelled to resist, by arms, the ambition of that arch enemy to the peace and happiness of mankind [Bonaparte] that all will feel in their hearts that detestation of his character and that zeal for the preservation and honour of our country which fills mine, that when the day of trial comes we may strike hard, and with God's help, punish the injustice that would invade its happiness.[1]

Sarah, so her husband reported, was showing her usual fortitude. He told Carlyle: 'Sarah is bearing this event like a British lady, who far prefers her husband's honour to her own comforts.'

The last note of all was to the Newcastle sisters. It was undated, but was almost certainly sent at the end of April. Collingwood hoped that the two elder sisters, at least, might 'change their air' and go to Morpeth for a little. 'I think it would do you good,' he added, 'and establish your health.' For a time at least, the alarm seemed over. 'I have never heard more from the Admiralty,' he added. 'Indeed, I did not look for further notice until war was positively determined. And now I hope affairs will be so accomodated that peace will stand on a greater certainty than hitherto. But the best security we can have for

<hr>

[1] H., Letter 82.

it is not great while France continues to be governed as it is.'[1]

It was during May that the summons came, and in that month Collingwood travelled south for the last time. On 2 June he was at Portsmouth, whence he wrote to the Admiralty to say: 'My baggage, including my charts, instruments etc, necessary to sea service will arrive on Sunday evening. I would request that their Lordships would be pleased to permit me to stay at Spithead a day or two in order to receive them.'[2]

Next day, a Friday, Collingwood reopened his journal with the words: 'P.M. I hoisted my flag on board H.M.S. *Diamond* and saluted Admiral Lord Gardner.'[3] Almost at once, he sailed in the frigate to join Cornwallis off Brest. By the end of July he was in command of the inshore squadron, anchored in 27 fathoms, not far from the enemy port. He had actually been appointed to the two-decker *Venerable*, which had been Duncan's flagship at the battle of Camperdown, but she was not then ready for service, and for more than two months Collingwood had to put up with cramped quarters. Nelson had had much the same experience during May in the *Amphion*, as he made his way out to the Mediterranean as Commander-in-Chief.

When Collingwood reached the blockading force, Cornwallis remarked: 'Here comes my old friend Coll, the last that left and the first to join me.'[4] Cornwallis had no warmer admirer than Collingwood, and they were two of a kind. The waters off the Atlantic coast of France had grown as familiar to them as their native shore, for to watch hostile ports was the main business of their lives. Where Collingwood was more fortunate than his Commander-in-Chief, who was renowned in the Navy for his skill in defence when opposed by overwhelming numbers, was in the fact that three times in his career he took a notable part in fleet actions. The long train of events which led to the last of these was about to open.

[1] H., Letter 83.
[2] Admiralty Correspondence, 112, f. 60; quoted Hughes, 147*n*.
[3] Col., 13a/0310.
[4] Quoted in J. Ralfe, *Naval Biography of Great Britain* (1828), ii. 340.

8 *The Campaign of Trafalgar*

By early in August 1803 Collingwood was quartered, though scarcely settled, in the *Venerable*, for he was to have the undesirable experience, in the earlier days of the resumption of blockading, of having frequently to shift about at short notice. It was a matter to which he objected, not so much on personal grounds as because it involved changes in subordinates, and led to at least some preliminary uncertainties as to the qualities and defects of the ship which happened to be wearing his flag. Only protracted experience of any given vessel could yield full knowledge of her capabilities.

It was from the *Venerable* that on 9 August, from 'off Brest' he wrote to his father-in-law:

> . . . we know they have four or five and twenty great ships, which makes it necessary to be alert, and keep our eyes open at all times. I therefore bid adieu to snug beds and comfortable naps at night, never lying down but in my clothes. Sarah's account of our improved house pleases me very much: I hope she will make it as comfortable as possible, and enjoy peace and happiness there, whatever may happen in the world abroad. It will cost a good deal of money, but I have provided for it, as I reckon the comforts of my wife among my chief luxuries; it is, indeed, the only one which my present situation will allow me to gratify. We hear no news here, and cannot be in more complete seclusion from the world, with only one object in view, that of preventing the French from doing harm.
>
> The Admiral sends all the ships to me, and cruises off

Ushant by himself; but with a westerly wind, it is impossible with one squadron to prevent ships getting into Brest Harbour; for it has two entrances, very distant from each other, one to the south of the Saints, but which, off Ushant, where we are, is entirely out of view. I take the utmost pains to prevent all access, and an anxious time I have of it, what with tides and rocks, which have more of danger in them than a battle once a week . . .

I have this moment received orders to send the *Venerable* in to replenish, and shall go myself on board the *Minotaur* till she returns, for I do not expect to go into port until the conclusion of the war.[1]

Collingwood was not long in the *Minotaur*, and on 10 October, once more from the *Venerable* 'off Ushant', he wrote a further long letter to James Erasmus Blackett,[2] relieved that at last he had been able to give charge of the inshore squadron to another officer. Being so close in to Brest, he reported,

. . . was a station of great anxiety and required a constant care and look out, so that I have often been a week without taking my clothes off, and sometimes up on deck the whole night. I was there longer than was intended for want of a proper successor, and saw all my squadron relieved more than once.

This time he was able to report well of the Newcastle volunteers who had been sent to him. 'They are a set of stout young men and a great addition to my strength, my ship being now very well manned, and so many are ill manned that I cannot say I have any anxiety to change her at present.'

There were worries about Spain, which country was once more being drawn into the French orbit. Supplies were being sent from Spain to the French ports for the use of the enemy's navy. 'But certainly,' said Collingwood, 'we shall not allow this friendly aid to be given . . . while they will not permit us to take a little sand off the beach to scour our decks. Is this being in amity with us?'

Bonaparte had resumed preparations on a grand scale for the

---

[1] N.C., 92–93.
[2] H., Letter 85; the transcription in N.C. 93–94 is attenuated and imperfect.

invasion of the British Isles, a threat which was to continue for many months to come. Collingwood hoped that the menace would 'not be held too lightly; in that consists the only danger. They should not only be repulsed, but it should be with such exemplary vengeance as may deter them from any future attempt to subjugate our country. We should give an example to all nations how to preserve their independence.'

There were frequent nuisance raids by naval units on enemy ports, and beaches where the invasion fleet was assembling or practising. Such activities he disliked. 'I do not know that this firing and bombing upon their coast is of any essential benefit, or rather whether it does not harm, by accustoming them to a great fire which does them little injury.' He gave Blackett an exact description of how he thought beach defences should be constructed, which affords an idea of how closely Collingwood went into every detail of amphibious warfare.

I would strongly recommend that on all the points of Bays where there is a probability of their landing should be thrown up close redoubts, two of them in front, towards the beach, 350 yards apart, one in the rear and forming an equilateral triangle, with the two others: those towards the beach should have a 32 pd carronade and an 18 pounder, that in the rear two 18 pounders mounted on barbet or slides; the ditch 12 feet deep and 16 wide, a hut in the middle for a barrack for twenty men, which would be a sufficient garrison for them. They are to be entered by a ladder, which must be taken into the work. No work would give such annoyance to the enemy, such protection to our assembling troops, and could not be carried in a short time; they should be well supplied with hand grenades, fire balls, to fill the ditch with fire when they are assailed. From their situation, each redoubt is a defence to the other two, and can be constructed by country-men in forty-eight hours without the help of an engineer.

There was some point in sending such careful directions to Blackett, for as a former mayor of Newcastle, and a prominent local citizen, his advice might well be taken in the preparation of seaward defences for his native county. Collingwood ended his autumn letter on a personal note.

I have been eighteen weeks at sea, and in this time, except two or three sore legs, have not a sick man in my ship. But now that the cold weather is beginning I am afraid we shall feel the want of warm clothing: I am sure I shall, for I have only two coats, and one of them is very old. When I sailed I had not time to make a coat, and did not suspect I should have been so long without the means of getting one.

In December, Collingwood wrote from Cawsand Bay, not very cheerfully about the *Venerable*.[1]

Now for my miseries, of which I have a good store just now. I came in from sea with orders from the Admiral to refresh my ship's company, and, poor creatures, they have been almost worked to death ever since. We began by discovering slight defects . . . and the further we went in the examination, the more important they appeared, until at last she was discovered to be so completely rotten as to be unfit for sea. We have been sailing for the last six months with only a sheet of copper between us and eternity.

I have written to Lord St. Vincent to ask him for a sounder ship; but it deranges me exceedingly to be thus for ever changing.

In point of fact, St. Vincent was shortly to leave the Admiralty in favour of Lord Melville. Kind though the earl had been to Collingwood, he was to find Melville even more considerate.

Collingwood was ashore at Plymouth over Christmas, and for a few weeks afterwards, while the *Culloden* was fitting out for his reception. This 74-gun ship, although then twenty years old, had a distinguished record, for she had been present at the Glorious First of June, at St. Vincent, and at Nelson's attempt on Tenerife. Troubridge, who was long her captain, also received the gold medal for the Nile, though in fact when the battle was in progress the ship was ashore off Aboukir Island. It was while in the *Culloden* that Collingwood heard two items of sad news. The first was the death, early in 1804, of Sir Edward Blackett, one of the most assiduous of his correspondents, and the second was the loss of Mrs. Carlyle, which grieved Sarah.

Collingwood was much helped in the *Culloden* by one of his

[1] N.C., 95.

lieutenants, John Clavell, an officer on whom he had come to rely more than any flag-captain who ever served with him. 'I was miserable when I first came into this ship,' he wrote to Blackett off Ushant on 28 February 1804, 'but things are now much mended, and in an orderly state. It has been a laborious job for poor Clavell, but he has done it well.'[1]

Clavell was a parson's son, and twenty-five years old. He had been entered on the ship's books of the *Centurion* when still in the cradle, but did not go to sea until he was thirteen. Since that time he had seen much service. He had been in the *Victory* as a midshipman in Lord Hood's time in the Mediterranean, had shared the ardours of the land campaign in Corsica, and been present at the battle of St. Vincent. Collingwood seldom commented favourably on his flag-captains, who must sometimes have thought their status superfluous, if not resented, and this in spite of the fact that Collingwood himself, from his time with Bowyer in the *Barfleur*, knew just how tricky was their situation. Clavell, on the other hand, could do no wrong, and indeed his whole career showed him to have been an exceptional officer. Newnham Collingwood recorded that in the close blockade of Brest Collingwood would sometimes say to Clavell that they must not leave the deck that night. Clavell would then try to persuade the admiral that there was a good look-out kept, and that he was almost exhausted. Collingwood would reply: 'I fear *you* are. You have need of rest, so go to bed, Clavell, and I will watch by myself.' The account concluded: 'Very frequently have they slept together on a gun, from which Admiral Collingwood would rise from time to time, to sweep the horizon with his night-glass, lest the enemy should escape in the dark.'[2]

In June, Collingwood had a spell in the slow-sailing though spacious *Prince*, well remembered from days with Howe's fleet. On the 17th of the month, from sea, he wrote to Carlyle to give him his view of Pitt, who had taken over the reins of government the previous month from Addington.

Mr. Pitt [wrote Collingwood], has shewn himself the greatest statesman in Europe. During the late war, when Europe presented a new state of things, when no rule of conduct could be drawn from the example of former times, he extricated the country from dangers at home and abroad which would have overwhelmed any country whose councils were not directed by profound wisdom. [Later he added:] Mr Addington was a sensible man, and an honourable man, he was industrious and had the best intentions in the world. But the times require talents, which fall to the lot of few men. Perhaps Pitt is the only man in England who can find resources against all the evils we have to encounter.[1]

Collingwood thought well of Melville as a choice for First Lord of the Admiralty, but he deplored the dearth of ships, a legacy from a regimen of investigation and economy which would continue in its effects.

We have seldom been able to muster more than fourteen or fifteen ships here [he told Carlyle], while the French have twenty complete in all things; Now if they were to come out and we even got the advantage of them with this fleet, it is not likely to be such a victory as is necessary to the country at this time. Nothing short of exterminating them whenever they appear should be in idea, and we should have a force equal to it.

Collingwood's last sentence was a striking parallel to one written by Nelson to George Rose the following year, not more than a fortnight before Trafalgar. 'It is,' wrote Nelson, 'as Mr. Pitt knows, annihilation that the country wants, and not merely a splendid victory of twenty-three to thirty-six, honourable to the parties concerned, but absolutely useless in the extended scale to bring Bonaparte to his marrow-bones: numbers can only annihilate.'[2] Bonaparte (now crowned as Emperor of the French) was teaching his enemies the meaning of total war.

It seemed more certain than ever that Spain would soon be actively engaged in hostilities. 'The Spaniards,' said Collingwood, 'will soon join their Imperial friends; the aids they give them in money is little short of hostility now. I think I should like to go off Cadiz, because I know that coast well.' In fact, Spain declared war on Great Britain before the end of the year,

[1] H., Letter 88.
[2] Nic. vii. 80; generally misquoted as 'only numbers can annihilate'.
10

and Collingwood had not long to wait for the opportunity he wanted.

A final item of news, added to the letter in a postscript, said: 'I have been told Lord Melville found at the Admiralty an order recalling Lord Nelson from the Mediterranean, which he put in the fire.'

In July, Collingwood returned to the *Culloden*, from which ship he wrote to Blackett on the 20th:

> Admiral Cornwallis left us the day before yesterday, and is gone to Spithead . . . I dare say he is heartily tired of this cruising, as every body must be of such a life. Nothing but a sense of its being necessary for the safety of the Country could make us support such a deprivation of everything which is pleasurable. I have had a good share of it; and whenever we are blessed with peace, I shall go ashore with extreme satisfaction, never to embark again.
>
> My chief anxiety now is to see my daughters well and virtuously educated, and I shall never think anything too good for them if they are wise and good-tempered. Tell them, with my blessing, that I am much obliged to them for weeding my oaks. I have got a nurseryman here from Wrighton. It is a great pity that they should press such a man because when he was young he went to sea for a short time. They have broken up his good business at home, distressed his family, and sent him here, where he is of little or no service. I grieve for him, poor man![1]

Collingwood seldom had out of his remembrance the chronic shortage of suitable ship-timber which had endured for generations. Early in the following year he wrote to Blackett: 'You will be surprised to hear that most of the knees which were used in the *Hibernia*[2] were taken from the Spanish ships captured on the 14th February [1797]; and that what they could not furnish was supplied by iron. I wish everybody thought on this subject as I do; they would not walk through their farms without a pocket-full of acorns to drop in the hedge-sides, and then let them take their chance.'[3]

[1] N.C., 96.
[2] A first-rate then just completed. She survived until the present century.
[3] N.C., 100.

On 27 August Collingwood addressed Dr. Carlyle from the three-decker *Dreadnought*,[1] which was then only four years old. Though she was 'a very fine ship', in Collingwood's opinion, she had 'been ill fitted out, for it was part of Lord St. Vincent's economy to employ convicts to fit out the ships, instead of the men and officers who were to sail in them. The consequence is, that they are wanting in every kind of arrangement that skilful men would have made, and most of them have been obliged to be docked since, at very great expense.'[2]

Collingwood told Carlyle he had been much cheered by news from Northumberland received by way of one of the *Dreadnought*'s lieutenants, William Landless, who like Clavell followed the admiral from ship to ship, whenever this was practicable. Landless had been at home in the north on leave.

All agree [Collingwood wrote], that Mr Blackett grows younger, and I really think his trips to Morpeth, out of the heat of Newcastle, conduces much to his good health. Mr Landless, when he joined me here, said in passing through Morpeth he had seen my daughters and my brother, who I found on further enquiry was no other than grandpappa, who was with the girls.

Carlyle, as was his habit from time to time, had enlisted the aid of his friend in sending a lad to sea.

The little Claudius [wrote Collingwood], arrived here about a fortnight since and was more acceptable to me for having brought to me so good an account of your health and well being. I will take the best care of him, and I hope he will turn out a good boy. He is in my cabin every morning soon after six, to read, and after breakfast goes to the school master who, I believe, is an able mathematician and would take pains with the young sirs, but in general they are so abominably fine, and in their own conceit so wise, that they think nothing wanting to their perfection but a larger hat and a pair of boots and tassels.

Collingwood had heard a tit-bit of news from the Admiralty which had caused him a wry smile. It was said that when Lord

---

[1] H., Letter 89.　　[2] N.C., 98.

Hood had been proposed in place of St. Vincent, he had replied 'that the paralysed state to which the navy was reduced required superior abilities to his to restore it'. Collingwood's comment was: 'Such was the opinion of men capable of judging its condition.'

With Lord Melville he remained pleased. He had complained to Their Lordships about having had to move from ship to ship, and above all of their having given the *Culloden* to Sir Edward Pellew with no advance warning to himself. 'But on my stating the circumstance,' he told Carlyle, 'they have done every[thing] I wished, and, in return (if ever the occasion arises) I will do everything they wish, to the extent of my power and ability.'

Collingwood told his correspondent that four deserters from the French fleet had joined the British in a small boat, giving news of poor conditions, ill discipline and dissention at Brest. Collingwood was sceptical.

It may be so [he wrote], but I would not put much faith in such fellows, who I rather suspect had robbed a shop, by the number of goods they had with them, and ran away from the gallows. But Sir Thomas Graves is so satisfied of the truth of all they say that he thinks it possible to overwhelm Brest, burn the arsenal and take all their fleet. I think he could not have given a stronger proof of his want of a cool judgement. His zeal is unbridled and wou'd run away with him if there was not discretion somewhere.

Graves, a kinsman of the admiral second-in-command at the Glorious First of June, was an officer with many exploits to his credit, among them the support he had given Nelson in the critical circumstances of the battle of Copenhagen; but Collingwood could not help recalling that the only time he had himself met the French in a full-scale action, he had been impressed by their strength and unity.

The day after he had written to Carlyle, Collingwood wrote to Blackett:

It seems odd, when you consider, that I have not seen a green leaf on a tree since I left Mrs Hughes's, at Portsmouth, in June 1803, except indeed those of my own creation, in the drawing which I sent you some time ago, and which I hope you received. The want of exercise makes me very languid and low in spirits; but I hope we shall come into port this winter, and not be torn to tatters as we were last year. I wish Admiral Cornwallis were here again. A good deal has been said about his having it in contemplation to leave the fleet, and that Lord Duncan is coming to the command; but, in my opinion, there is no officer on the list who has the skill of Lord Gardner, and it seems to me very strange that he is not appointed to any situation of importance.[1]

Collingwood's allusion to his drawing may have indicated the fact that he was trying to grow plants in the great cabin of the *Dreadnought*, or he may have used his ability as an artist to recall what he loved to see at home. As for Lord Gardner, Collingwood well remembered the splendid handling of the *Queen* in Howe's battle, all the more remarkable because of the fact that in day-to-day life, Gardner was of a highly nervous disposition. St. Vincent once said of him: 'He is a zealous and brave man, with the worst nerves possible, and full of doubts as to the precision of other men.'[2]

On 4 November 1804, when Collingwood was watching Rochefort, where a French squadron was preparing, he gave Blackett this view of the situation at large:

Of peace with France, I see no prospect [he wrote], nothing less than a revolution in that country can rescue Europe from the tyranny of a military despot; but God knows whether even that would be more than changing one tyrant for another. The army in that country is everything—the people nothing, but as they are necessary to the support of that army, which is a complete subversion of order, and the most melancholy state to which society can be reduced. This dilatory war they carry on with us looks like design to continue it for a term of years; and there is no power in Europe now of consequence enough to say that the peace of mankind shall no longer be disturbed. Russia cannot; Prussia will not; Austria dare not. All the rest must do as they are ordered.[3]

[1] N.C., 97.
[2] *Spencer Papers*, ed. H. W. Richmond (1924), iii. 295.
[3] N.C., 98–99.

Added to his concern over Cornwallis's health, Collingwood was not altogether happy over Nelson's, for his friend was then enduring the long watch on Toulon. The previous month he had written to Captain Thomas Byam Martin to say: 'I do not wonder that the constant anxiety attached to such a command . . . should have worn out his body, which was always but a flimsy case for his Herculean soul.'[1] On 13 December, when the *Dreadnought* had put in to Cawsand Bay, Collingwood wrote to Nelson in a relieved way to tell him that he had just had more cheerful news from Captain Sutton, lately from the Mediterranean. By the time of this letter, Cornwallis was temporarily back, and Collingwood told Nelson he thought they would soon be joined by Gardner.

In a letter to Admiral Braithwaite, in which, as one seaman to another, he described how difficult it sometimes was to keep the great three-deckers off the land, particularly during the strong gales the Fleet had encountered that winter, Collingwood wrote:

> I think some of our ingenious citizens should apply their wits in inventing a sort of patent admiral, a machine that would rub on a length of time without wearing out; for this incessant cruising seems to me beyond the powers of human nature. Calder is worn to a shadow, quite broken down, and I am told Sir Thomas Graves is not much better.[2]

Early in April 1805 Gardner made his appearance with the Fleet, but Collingwood found him poorly. On the 9th he wrote to Blackett:

> Lord Gardner joined us a week ago, to command the fleet in the absence of Admiral Cornwallis. I saw him yesterday for an hour or two, and was sorry to find him altered for the worse—old and out of spirits; yet, I think, if he were established he would recover again, and be as active as ever, for there is no officer a more perfect master of the discipline of the fleet than he is.[3]

Collingwood's letter ended by expressing a wish concerning his

[1] *Letters and Papers of Sir Thomas Byam Martin*, ed. Sir R. V. Hamilton, i. 305.

[2] N.C. (Additional letter, 1837 edition.)

[3] N.C., 101–2.

daughters (then aged twelve and eleven respectively) which reflects their father's very decided tastes.

> I am delighted with your account of my children's improvement, for it is a subject of the greatest anxiety to me. Above all things, keep novels out of their reach. They are the corrupters of tender minds: they exercise the imagination instead of the judgement; make them all desire to become the Julias and Cecilias of romance; and turn their heads before they are enabled to distinguish truth from fictions devised merely for entertainment. When they have passed their climacteric it will be time enough to begin novels.[1]

Collingwood could not have suspected that Jane Austen, the sister of two officers then in the Navy (one of them, Captain Francis Austen, much approved by Nelson), would within a few years have helped to transform at least one type of novel into a channel for wit and observation which might well have won his approbation.

II

By the time that Collingwood's letter about his children's reading had gone off to Blackett, the chain of events which led directly to Trafalgar had begun. The initiative was Napoleon's. Ordering his fleets about as if they were armies, his immediate plan was for Villeneuve to leave Toulon, pick up Spanish ships at Cartagena, sail through the Strait of Gibraltar, release more Spaniards watched by a force off Cadiz, and then proceed to the West Indies. There, so the Emperor intended, Villeneuve would be joined by the squadrons of Brest and Rochefort. With a vast armada, the admiral would re-cross the Atlantic, sweeping all before him, make a strong diversion in Ireland, and enable the flotillas of Boulogne and elsewhere to cross to the English coast under cover of the main force. His Grand Army, once landed, would overcome such military formations as his enemy could assemble, and the British government would thereupon capitulate.

In essentials the design was at once grand and simple, but it was based on assumptions which no sea officer could have

[1] N.C., 101–2.

accepted. First, it assumed that all the main fleets, those of Toulon and Brest pre-eminently, would be able to evade the blockaders within a reasonable time of one another, and afterwards that winds would serve to carry them to their rendezvous and onwards unhindered. It next assumed that Villeneuve would be pursued, but that the chase would fail. It assumed that Cornwallis's western fleet, in whatever numbers it might be met with, would be signally defeated. Lastly, it assumed that the invasion flotillas, supported by a victorious main fleet, would overwhelm the British inshore squadrons so completely as to ensure a safe passage for the troops. Once landed, Napoleon took it for granted that his military capacity would accomplish the rest. A diversion in Ireland would spread general alarm and would, in Napoleon's belief, meet with strong local support.

Although hindsight has made nonsense of the plans, so much so that some historians have wondered whether it was not all a huge bluff, Napoleon was in fact never more in earnest about any project, and he had recollections of heartening experiences to fortify him. One of his own earliest successes had been in helping to drive Hood from Toulon in 1793. Five years later, with a huge armada, he had made an unhindered passage right through the Mediterranean, had landed in Egypt, and conquered the country. Even though Nelson had destroyed his battle-fleet at the Nile, Villeneuve, his 'lucky' flag-officer, survived that holocaust, while Napoleon himself had later returned safely to France in a Venetian-built frigate, eluding the forces which, since the Nile, had been paramount in the Middle Sea.

Part of the French plan did succeed. Villeneuve, at the end of March 1805, evaded the force watching Toulon, as he had done once before, and would have picked up the ships from Cartagena if the Spaniards had been more active. Joined by some ships from Cadiz, after a successful passage of the Strait of Gibraltar, he then got clear away to the West Indies before Nelson could learn for certain his destination and strength. If the fortunes of the Brest fleet had been comparable, a formidable force indeed would have gathered for the return passage, and to face 'Billy Blue' Cornwallis. Even so, recollecting the qualities shown in the past by Cornwallis when faced with heavy odds, it was doubtful whether Villeneuve, after meeting him in battle, would have been in any state to support an invasion.

By early in May Nelson, having reinforced the escort of a convoy which was carrying an army under General Craig destined
for the Mediterranean, was in hot pursuit of Villeneuve to the
West Indies, where he would have met and fought the Combined
Fleet but for false information—supplied by a military officer—
which sent him south to Trinidad. Villeneuve did some damage
to the trade in the Caribbean, but the moment he knew that
Nelson was on his track, he returned post-haste to Europe
without waiting for the expected ships from France. Nelson
followed, and when he anchored at Gibraltar on 18 July he was
able to go ashore from the *Victory* for the first time in nearly
two years, a disappointed though not a disheartened man.

Collingwood's adventures during this tense period were described in a letter written on 2 July from off Cadiz, a place, he
said, which 'has the advantage of the finest climate in the
world'. It was the last he ever wrote to Musselburgh, for Carlyle
died during the following month.

I must tell you by what chance I came here [he wrote]. In
the beginning of March I was ordered to prepare with a small
squadron for prize service, the number was increased to the
time of my sailing, but I apprehend no certain destination
was then determined for me, but merely a measure of precaution to have a force ready for anything.

The sailing of the Toulon Squadron and their joining the
Spaniards here put me in motion: my ships were increased to
14 sail, to pursue them, unless I received certain information
that Lord Nelson had, and then I was to be directed in my
conduct by the intelligence I could get of the enemy. Lord
Nelson was at this time supposed to have taken a station
west of Ireland, convinced from the stile of their preparations
that the enemy were destined for that quarter.

In my way south I met Sir Richard Bickerton who first
informed me of the real state of things, when finding the
Spaniards here and at Carthagena had a considerable force
ready to sail I determined to come here, where I found them
on the eve of departing, waiting only for the Carthagenians,
who actually did sail on the very day I arrived here, but
hearing of us on their way down, returned back to their Port.
I sent two ships to strengthen my friend in the West Indies,

and the rest are divided between the two Ports here. Such is my employment at present, without means of giving much annoyance to the Spaniards, while they keep snug, and little expectation of their coming out. But I think it is not improbable that I shall have all those fellows coming from the West Indies again, before the Hurricane months, unless they sail from thence directly for Ireland, which I have always had an idea was their plan, for this Bonaparte has as many tricks as a monkey. I believe their object in the West Indies to be less conquest, than to draw our forces from home.[1]

In London, there had been sad trouble at the Admiralty. Melville had been impeached for irregular conduct of his office, involving public funds. Collingwood was sympathetic. 'Nothing could have happened to any person to whom I am unknown,' he wrote, 'that would have given me so much concern as Lord Melville's affair has done.' He thought, rightly, that it was in great measure a party matter, aimed to discomfort Pitt, which it did:

> . . . all other subjects seem to be of no consideration [Collingwood wrote bitterly]. Invasion by the most wily enemy England ever had to contend with is scarce a matter for a moment's discussion, and I really think he is making a progress more alarming now, than at any former period. His fleet is become numerous and increase like mushrooms; they are ill manned I believe, but they will avoid a battle at sea for some time, and for all the purposes of carrying an army, they are enough. I hope notwithstanding all this, that I shall live to spend some cheerful days with you in peace; & happy days they will be, for once landed again, I never more will embark, I think so now.

It was fortunate for the country that in Sir Charles Middleton, raised to the peerage as Lord Barham, there was a man of unrivalled knowledge of the Admiralty who could and did step into the breach caused by Melville's trouble. Barham was nearly eighty, and his supervision of the strategy of the Trafalgar campaign was his last and one of his greatest services.

From Gibraltar, Nelson wrote to Collingwood on 18 July:

[1] H., Letter 91.

I am, as you may imagine, miserable at not having fallen in with the enemy's fleet; but for false information, the battle would have been fought where Rodney fought his,[1] on June the 6th . . . The moment the fleet is watered, and has got some refreshments, of which we are in great want, I shall come out and make you a visit—not, my dear friend, to take your command from you, (for I may probably add mine to you) but to consult how we can best serve our Country by detaching a part of this large force. God bless you, my dear friend, and believe me ever most affectionately yours,

NELSON AND BRONTË.[2]

Collingwood replied from the *Dreadnought* on 21 July:

We approached, my dear Lord, with caution, not knowing whether we were to expect you or the Frenchmen first. I have always had an idea that Ireland alone was the object they have in view, and still believe that to be their ultimate destination. They will now liberate the Ferrol squadron from Calder, make the round of the bay, and, taking the Rochefort people with them, appear off Ushant, perhaps with thirty-four sail, there to be joined by twenty more.

This appears a probable plan; for unless it be to bring their powerful fleets and armies to some great point of service—some rash attempt at conquest—they have only been subjecting them to chance of loss, which I do not believe the Corsican would do without the hope of an adequate reward. The French Government never aim at little things while great objects are in view. I have considered the invasion of Ireland as the real mark and butt of all their operations. Their flight to the West Indies was to take off the naval force, which proved a great impediment to their undertaking. The summer is big with events; we may all perhaps have an active share in them; and I sincerely wish your Lordship strength of body to go through with it, and to all others your strength of mind.[3]

Nelson hoped that he and Collingwood might meet and

---

[1] The allusion was to Rodney's victory off Dominica on 12 April 1782.
[2] N.C., 105.   [3] N.C., 107–8.

exchange news, but this was not to be, for the present. On 25 July Nelson sent word from the *Victory*:[1]

We are in a fresh levanter, you have a westerly wind—therefore I must forego the pleasure of taking you by the hand until October next, when, if I am well enough, I shall (if the Admiralty please) resume my command . . . I feel disappointed, my dear friend, at not seeing you, so does Admiral Murray, and many, I am sure, in this fleet. May God bless you, and send you alongside of the *Santissima Trinidada*, and let me see you in perfect health . . .

On 9 August, Collingwood wrote to Blackett:

I have just time to tell you that I am as well as can be, and in great expectation that we shall have a rattling day of it very soon. The Spaniards are completely ready here; they have 4000 troops embarked: at Carthegena they have many more, and a strong squadron. Whenever they come, Sir R. Bickerton is to join me with his ships, and then there will be two to one; but we must beat them, or—never come home; and yet I intend it fully. A dull superiority creates languor; it is a state like this that rouses the spirits, and makes us feel as if the welfare of all England depended on us alone. You shall not be disappointed.[2]

On 21 August Collingwood wrote to his wife to tell her about one of the most skilful actions of his professional life.

I have very little time to write to you, but must tell you what a squeeze we had like to have got yesterday. While we were cruizing off the town, down came the combined fleet of thirty-six sail of men-of-war: we only three poor things, with a frigate and a bomb, and drew off towards the Straits, not very ambitious, as you may suppose, to try our strength against such odds.

They followed us as we retired, with sixteen large ships; but on our approaching the Straits they left us, and joined their friends in Cadiz, where they are fitting and replenishing their provisions. We, in our turn, followed them back, and today have been looking into Cadiz, where their fleet is now as thick as a wood. I hope I shall have somebody come to

[1] N.C., 108.   [2] N.C., 109–10.

me soon, and in the mean time I must take the best care of myself I can. This is a comfortless station, on which it is difficult to procure refreshment, except the grapes which the Portuguese bring us. But this being for ever at sea wears me down; and if I did not have Clavell with me I should be ten times worse, for he is the person in whom my confidence is principally placed.

Pray tell me all you can think about our family and about the beauties of your domain—the oaks, the woodlands and the verdant meads.[1]

As was so often his way, Collingwood went into considerable detail about his adventure in a letter to his sister begun on 26 August, when he had had more time to reflect on what had been done.

To be sure we had a squeak for it [he wrote], but the winds were favourable to us, and I believe the enemy did not believe us to be English when they first saw us, for the *Thunder* bomb, being far to the North, I lay with a short sail to enable her to join us.

We were close to the light house at Cadiz when at 6 o'clock in the morning we discovered first 6 sail, and soon after 26. I soon made out what they were, and called in any detached ships—jogging off slowly as people do when they are sullen. For as the Spaniards had eight sail in the port, 4 of them ready to come in a moment, and I was exactly between the two, I did not chuse to shew any alarm which might rouse their activity. The Combined Fleet had run down about 2 hours when 16 sail of them parted from the rest and gave chase to us. I gave the bomb all the time I could to join us, but she sailed heavily as we do.

I had only 3 ships, *Dreadnought*, *Colossus* and *Achille*, with the *Niger* frigate. We ran until we had the gut of Gibraltar open and then put an impudent face on our shabby weak state. We shortened sail, and I sent the *Colossus* (an excellent sailer) to reconnoitre them more closely, which she did most masterly, and when they made a push at her we tacked and stood towards her as long as it was prudent. Whether they suspected by these movements that we had discovered a

[1] N.C., 109-10.

reinforcement or were afraid of being drawn through the Streights and separated from the body of their fleet, I do not know, but soon after, they all hauled off and made the best of their way to Cadiz. Two chased the *Thunder*, and certainly they might have taken her in half an hour, but with great good management she ran so near the shoals that they did not like to follow, and they all seemed careful to secure a retreat to Cadiz.

While they were in chase of us I sent the frigate off to put Sr Richd Bickerton on his guard, but he was sick and gone ashore. The *Mars* joined me the next morning, and the *Euryalus* came a day after the [af]fair, to give me intelligence of them. I had sent off to England by the way of Lisbon the same night and the *Euryalus* enabled me to send home direct. I returned immediately to Cadiz and it falling calm, we were a great part of two days in sight of them. They entered Cadiz with 36 sail—twenty seven, or twenty eight of the line, and are in the port like a forest. I reckon them now to be 36 sail of the line and plenty of frigates. What can I do with such a host? But I hope I shall get a reinforcement, suited to the occasion and, if I do, well betide us.

The Mediterranean ships came to me three days after; they are only four sail, and perhaps had better staid where they were, for I reckon they were a check upon 8 sailing from Carthegena which may now join their friends and I cannot help it, when they will be 44 sail of the line. They are embarking troops in great numbers: this is either for England or Naples—I rather think the former, and wish it . . .

I think my stay abroad will not be long because if those fellows move northwards I shall stick to their skirts and I rather wish it, for I am exceedingly worn with fatigue. I have a diligent young man for my secretary [Cosway] and Clavell, my lieutenant, is the spirit of the ship; but such a captain, such a stick, I wonder very much how such people get forward. I should (I firmly believe) with his nautical ability and knowledge and exertion, have been a bad lieutenant at this day. Was he brought up in the Navy? For he has very much the stile of the Coal trade about him, except that they are good seamen.[1]

[1] H., Letter 92.

Collingwood's inquiry of his sister about Edward Rotheram, his flag-captain, argues an extraordinary state of distance and formality, which can scarcely have increased Rotheram's confidence in himself. Collingwood knew that he was a Northumbrian, no more. A little inquiry would have elicited the information that Rotheram, who was the son of a doctor, had been born at Hexham in 1752 and had indeed started his sea life in a collier. He had transferred to the Navy and had been senior lieutenant in the *Culloden* at the Glorious First of June. Writing many years later, Hercules Robinson, who as a youth got to know Collingwood as well as any midshipman may know a vice-admiral, reported as follows of an incident of this time.

Collingwood's dry, caustic mind lives before me in the recollection of his calling across the deck his fat, stupid captain— long since dead—when he had seen him commit some monstrous blunder, and after the usual bowing and formality— which the excellent old chief never omitted—he said: 'Captain, I have been thinking, whilst I looked at you, how strange it is that a man should *grow* so big and *know* so little. That's all, sir; that's all.' Hats off; low bows.[1]

The letter to the sister-hood at Newcastle told them that an attentive brother had placed '2000£ in 3 pr Cents' at their disposal 'as a mark how true an interest I have in your comforts'. Lastly Collingwood gave news of William Ireland, his former servant.

Did William come to see you when he was at Newcastle? [he asked]. I found as he grew rich he was less usefull to me and he often got drunk which I abhor. But our being ordered abroad determined him and the moment he mentioned his wish I acceded to it and now have a quiet sober young man who has been well educated and whose parents are respectable people in London, and am very glad of the change, for servants may live so long with one that they think themselves entitled to take liberties.

Collingwood wrote two postscripts to his letter, which did not go off to Newcastle until the end of the month. In the first of them he said: 'I have not yet seen any account of Sir R.

[1] *Sea Drift*, by Rear-Admiral Hercules Robinson (1858), 43.

Calder's fight, but hear it was rather a puzzled affair which I am sorry for.'

What in fact had happened was that Calder, detached by Cornwallis, had met Villeneuve and fought an indecisive action a month earlier, on 22 July, in which he had taken two Spanish prizes. He had not resumed the action on the following day, and Villeneuve had put into Vigo. On 9 August, when the Combined Fleet first re-emerged, Calder had had to fall back on Cornwallis, while Villeneuve, his heart failing him at the thought of meeting a strong western squadron, had later turned south for Cadiz, where Collingwood had encountered him. The moment Napoleon knew what had happened, he realized that his stroke against England had been parried, and in a storm of memoranda traced the pattern of a campaign against Austria. The Emperor still had a use for Villeneuve's fleet, which was ordered to the Mediterranean to threaten Naples.

In his final postscript Collingwood wrote: '31st August. I have a reinforcement of 18 sail, making me 26 of the line and now a fig for their Combinations.' The enemy could not get through the Strait of Gibraltar without a battle, and Collingwood was as eager for this as any officer in the Fleet.

How happy should I be [he wrote to Blackett on 21 September] could I but hear from home, and know how my dear girls are getting on! Bounce is my only pet now, and he is indeed a good fellow: he sleeps by the side of my cot, whenever I lie in one, until near the time of tacking, and then marches off, to be out of the hearing of the guns, for he is not reconciled to them yet.

I am fully determined, if I can get home and manage it properly, to go on shore next spring for the rest of my life; for I am very weary. There is no end to my business: I am at work from morning till even; but I dare say Lord Nelson will be out next month. He told me he should; and then what will become of me I do not know. I should wish to go home, but I must go or stay as the exigencies of the times require. This, with all its labour, is a most unprofitable station; but that is not a consideration of much moment to me. What I look to as the first and great object, is to defeat the projects of this combined fleet, of whom I can get little information;

but I watch them narrowly, and if they come out will fight
them merrily; for on their discomfiture depends the safety of
England, and it shall not fail in my hands if I can help it.[1]

III

Nelson was indeed on his way. After exchanging messages with
Collingwood off Cadiz, he had sailed home in the *Victory* for a
few weeks' leave. When the news of the advent of the Combined
Fleet at Cadiz reached him by way of Captain Blackwood of
the *Euryalus*, he expected a summons from Lord Barham to
resume his station. It came; and very soon he was off. He wrote
a brief note from the Admiralty to Collingwood, beginning in
his old familiar way:

                                              September 7, 1805
My dear Coll,
   I shall be with you in a very few days, and I hope you will
remain second in command. You will change the *Dreadnought*
for the *Royal Sovereign*, which I hope you will like . . .[2]

Collingwood may have been glad enough that Nelson was to
join him, but his heart must have sunk at the thought of yet
another change of ship, particularly as the *Royal Sovereign*,
built at Plymouth in 1786, was so slow a sailer that she was
known as the 'West Country waggon'. What Collingwood could
not foresee was that, newly coppered, she had become trans-
formed. Had he remained in the *Dreadnought* he would have
been handicapped by a slow ship, whose bottom had become
foul through her long period at sea, 'her only fault', he told
Nelson later.[3]
   Nelson sailed on 15 September with the *Euryalus* in company.
On the 25th he sent Captain Blackwood forward with a note
to Collingwood to ask that no salute be fired by the Fleet to
greet his arrival, and no colours hoisted. 'It is well,' he said,
'not to proclaim to the enemy every ship which may join the
fleet.'[4]
   Collingwood was not the only officer before Cadiz who was
glad of Nelson's presence, for discipline had been kept taut,

[1] N.C., 112.   [2] N.C., 113.   [3] Nic. vii. 115*n.*   [4] N.C., 113.
11

and many captains were becoming restive, bored by the lack of socialities of which Collingwood had himself once complained. Captain Fremantle, for instance, in the three-decker *Neptune*, had written to his wife on 6 September:

> . . . since I wrote last we have been standing off and on without being offered the means of sending a letter even to the next Ship, our Admiral is an humble follower of Cornwallis, and I have not yet seen him or any body else, I am entirely confined on board and know no more what is going on than you do. We see the French and Spanish Fleets daily and what adds more to this cursed deprivation of Society is that the Weather has been remarkably fine and the Sea as smooth as in the Lake at Stow[e]. I wish and hope either Lord Gardner or Lord Nelson will soon be here as I confess I do not bear patiently from Collingwood what I should do more with a man of better pretensions to such severity . . .[1]

Nelson was in sight of Collingwood by 28 September, when tension eased, and visiting was resumed. On 6 October Nelson sent his friend a trunk, with a duplicate key. 'I shall send you despatches &c, occasionally, to read,' he wrote, 'and it will save the trouble of packets. Put your letter in it, and send it back with my letters, when read. Telegraph upon all occasions without ceremony. We are one, and I hope ever shall be.'[2] After Trafalgar, when Dr. William Beatty, the *Victory*'s surgeon, produced an account of Nelson's last days, he miscopied a word in Nelson's private diary in which the admiral appeared to have written, under the date of 9 October: 'Sent Admiral Collingwood the Nelson *truth*', as if Nelson possessed some magic secret which he wished his second in command to know. Beatty sent a copy of his work to Collingwood, who wrote against the sentence: 'it was the Nelson *trunk*—which passed with Papers and letters between us each having a key.'[3]

In one of the first notes to Collingwood which he put into

---

[1] *The Wynne Diaries*, ed. Anne Fremantle (World's Classics selection, 1952), 410.

[2] N.C. 114: Nelson was inviting Collingwood to semaphore freely, as well as to write.

[3] William Beatty, *Authentic Narrative of the Death of Lord Nelson* (1807); Collingwood's annotated copy is in the library of the National Maritime Museum, Greenwich.

the trunk, Nelson praised the handling of the situation on
20 August: '. . . twenty six sail of the line were not to be left
to chance,' he wrote, 'and if you had, for want of such precaution, been forced to quit the vicinity of Cadiz, England
would not have forgiven you.' When, some few days later, the
Commander-in-Chief had learnt more about the details of the
episode, he added: 'The Admiralty could not do less than call
your conduct judicious. Everybody in England admired your
adroitness in not being forced unnecessarily into the Straits.'[1]

Answering the note of 6 October on the same day it was
received, Collingwood wrote to Nelson:

> We shall have these fellows out at last, my dear Lord. I
> firmly believe that they cannot be subsisted in Cadiz: their
> supply from France is completely cut off. And now, my Lord,
> I will give you my ideas. If the enemy are to sail with an
> easterly wind, they are not bound to the Mediterranean; and
> your Lordship may depend on it the Carthagena squadron
> is intended to join them. If they effect that, and with a
> strong easterly wind they may, they will present themselves
> to us with forty sail. Should Louis, by any good fortune, fall
> in with the Carthagena squadron I am sure he would turn
> them to leeward; for they would expect the whole fleet was
> after them. Whenever the Carthagena people were expected,
> they opened the light-house.[2]

Collingwood had it in mind that, despite the lateness of the
season, the invasion project had not yet been abandoned.
Nelson, with the advantage of later news from home, and hence
from Europe, was sure that Villeneuve's orders, if he came out,
were to make for the Mediterranean.[3] He intended to give him
every chance to attempt the passage. He kept most of his force
far out of sight of land, and took advantage of the wait to get
to know such of his officers as he did not know well already,
and to explain his mode of attack. This was the subject of a
well-known tactical memorandum, which was circulated in the
Fleet,[4] the gist of which was given in a conversation with

[1] Nic. vii. 114.
[2] N.C., 114: Rear-Admiral Louis had been detached to provision.
[3] Nic. vii. 109.
[4] Add. MSS. 33963, f. 104.

Captain Keats of the *Superb*, who had been on the chase to the West Indies.

One morning [so Keats told Edward Hawke Locker, at one time Commissioner of Greenwich Hospital, and the son of Nelson's and Collingwood's old captain], walking with Lord Nelson in the grounds at Merton, talking on Naval matters, he said to me, 'No day can be long enough to arrange a couple of Fleets, and fight a decisive Battle, according to the old system. When *we* meet them,' (I was to have been with him,) 'for meet them we shall, I'll tell you how I shall fight them. I shall form the Fleet into three Divisions in three Lines. One Division shall be composed of twelve or fourteen of the fastest two-decked Ships, which I shall keep always to windward, or in a situation of advantage; and I shall put them under an Officer who, I am sure, will employ them in the manner I wish, if possible. I consider it will always be in my power to throw them into Battle in any part I may choose; but if circumstances prevent their being carried against the Enemy where I desire, I shall feel certain he will employ them effectually, and, perhaps, in a more advantageous manner than if he could have followed my orders.' (He never mentioned, or gave any hint by which I could understand who it was he intended for this distinguished service.) He continued—'With the remaining part of the Fleet formed in two Lines, I shall go at them at once, if I can, about one-third of their Line from their leading Ship.' He then said, 'What do you think of it?' Such a question I felt required consideration. I paused. Seeing it, he said, 'but I'll tell you what *I* think of it. I think it will surprise and confound the Enemy. They won't know what I am about. It will bring forward a pell-mell Battle, and that is what I want.'[1]

In sending a copy of his plan to Collingwood on 9 October, Nelson said it was:

. . . as far as a man dare venture to guess at the very uncertain position the Enemy may be found in. But, my dear friend, it is to place you perfectly at ease respecting my

[1] Nic. vii. 241*n*.

intentions, and to give full scope to your judgment for carrying them into effect. We can, my dear Coll, have no little jealousies. We have only one great object in view, that of annihilating our Enemies, and getting a glorious Peace for our Country. No man has more confidence in another than I have in you: and no man will render your services more justice than your very old friend,

NELSON AND BRONTË.[1]

In the event, Nelson's force was not large enough to provide the line of fast ships which were to play such an enterprising part in battle, and the 'two Lines' which he spoke about in the final part of his conversation with Keats, formed the whole attack. In his tactical memorandum Nelson wrote:

The second in command will in all possible things direct the movement of his line, by keeping them as compact as the nature of the circumstances will admit. Captains are to look to their particular line as their rallying point, but in case signals cannot be seen, no captain can do very wrong if he places his ship alongside that of an enemy.

As a further assurance that Collingwood would be allowed the initiative fitting to his skill and experience, Nelson added:

. . . the entire management of the Lee Line after the intentions of the commander in chief are signified is intended to be left to the Admiral commanding that Line.

The remainder of the Enemy's fleet . . . are to be left to the management of the commander in chief, who will endeavour to take care that the movements of the second in command are as little interrupted as possible.[2]

Nelson had given a splendid expression of his wish for freedom of action for trusted and intelligent subordinates—this within a general pattern which could readily be understood. The method had proved astoundingly successful at the Nile, and it was directly opposed to the principles of Howe, for whose rigidity of direction, and suspicion of the abilities of those he commanded, Nelson had no sympathy whatever, ready as he was to agree that Howe was himself a master of naval war.

---

[1] Nic. vii. 95.   [2] Add. MSS. 33963 f.104.

When Nelson first joined Collingwood, there were three other flag-officers with the Fleet, but on 3 October Rear-Admiral Louis was detached with five ships of the line and a frigate to replenish. The senior of the two remaining was Sir Robert Calder who, astonished that his brush with Villeneuve on 22 July had not met with general approbation, wished for an inquiry into his conduct. This wish had been anticipated by Lord Barham, who was angered that Calder had not clung to Villeneuve like a leech, mauling him as much as he could at any cost to himself: that was what he had been detached to do.

Barham told Nelson to send Calder home in the *Dreadnought*, overdue for docking, but Nelson, though he had no reason to like this rich, opiniated, and jealous-minded officer, disobeyed, and out of kindness of heart, let Calder sail home in his own flagship, the *Prince of Wales*. If it was wrong of Nelson to weaken his force by this powerful unit, his motive was generous. Calder should have declined the gesture, and any particle of sympathy which might have been felt for him was removed by the knowledge that, shortly after Trafalgar, Collingwood had word that Calder intended to claim prize money.[1] Even before Calder left the Fleet (unconvinced, as were several other responsible officers, that the enemy would come out), Collingwood wrote to Nelson: 'I am grieved whenever I think of Sir Robert Calder's case. I think he must be aware of his situation, and feels more about it than he chooses should appear. I wish he was in England, because I think he wants a calm adviser.'[2]

The remaining flag-officer, the seventh Earl of Northesk, who was the same age as Nelson, had learnt his seamanship under Rodney, but had had no chance to distinguish himself in a major fleet action. He flew his flag in the *Britannia*, known as 'Old Ironsides', and the veteran before Cadiz. This ship had been launched in 1762 and had been Vice-Admiral Charles Thompson's flagship at the battle of Cape St. Vincent. Both Nelson and Collingwood liked Northesk, though they knew him but little, and after Trafalgar, Collingwood greatly relied on him until Northesk went home in 1806.

In due course, and without any inconvenience that Nelson could spare him, Collingwood transferred from the *Dreadnought* to the *Royal Sovereign*, taking with him such officers as he

[1] H., Letter 98.   [2] Nic. vii. 115*n*.

particularly wished for, including the invaluable Clavell and
Gilliland, his signal lieutenant. He kept Captain Rotheram with
him, despite shortcomings, but left Landless in his old ship as
his eyes were giving him trouble. Calder sailed in the *Prince of
Wales* for Spithead on 13 October, an ominous day, as it proved
to be, for he was duly censured for what was deemed to be an
error of judgement in not resuming battle on 23 July. Next day
Nelson invited Collingwood over to the *Victory* for a talk, 'that
I may tell you all I know, and my intentions', so the Commander-in-Chief explained. He added: 'I am glad Sir Robert
Calder is gone; and from my heart I hope he will get home safe,
and end his enquiry well. I endeavoured to give him all the
caution in my power respecting the cry against him; but he
seemed *too wise*.'[1] It was to be Collingwood's third visit to
Nelson within ten days.

Everyone in the Fleet was becoming restive, for the enemy as
yet made no move, and on 18 October Collingwood wrote to
Nelson: 'It is very extraordinary the people in Cadiz do not
make some movement; if they allow the War to begin in Italy,
they cannot hereafter make up for the want of the assistance
they might give in the first instance.' He had been converted
to Nelson's view of Villeneuve's destination. The letter concluded with one of Collingwood's postscripts, this time about
some reading-matter he had borrowed. 'I return your Lordship
three books. I should suspect Mr. Twist has got a *twist* in his
head.'[2] Collingwood was well known for punning, but it is not
a form of humour which often survives.

On 19 October, Nelson wrote:[3] 'What a beautiful day! Will
you be tempted out of your ship? If you will, hoist the Assent
and *Victory*'s pendants. I had a letter from Sir James Saumarez
yesterday, of October 1st. He sent me some papers; I take it
very kind of him.'

On this letter Collingwood wrote: 'Before the answer . . .
had got to the *Victory*, the signal was made that the Enemy's
Fleet was coming out of Cadiz, and we chased immediately.'[4]
The pair had met for the last time, and now the guns would
speak.

---

[1] Nic. vii. 121.   [2] Nic. vii. 127n.   [3] N.C., 118.   [4] Nic. vii. 130n.

IV

There was neither eagerness nor boredom within Cadiz: only contention, indecision, and dejection. The once allegedly lucky Villeneuve had received his sovereign's orders for the Mediterranean, but would willingly have disobeyed them had there been a reasonable excuse, staying snug under the land batteries while Collingwood and Nelson tossed outside in the Atlantic. Gravina, the Spanish admiral, requested a Council of War, and this was held on 8 October. The vote was for the Fleet to remain at anchor for the present.

Naval disobedience had been anticipated by Napoleon, who dispatched Admiral Rosily to supersede Villeneuve. Rosily reached Madrid on 12 October, and a few days later, Villeneuve learnt of his coming. Anxious to attempt something before he could be replaced, he ordered an attack on the British inshore squadron, then, learning that Nelson had detached some ships to the Strait he realized that now, if ever, he must seize his chance. He prepared for sea in the manner of one for whom victory was out of the question, but escape a success in itself.

A collation of the signal logs for the time immediately before the two fleets clashed tells the story, from the victor's side, in its own telegraphic way.[1] At six o'clock on the morning of 20 October Captain Duff of the *Mars*, who had been acting as link between Blackwood's frigates and the body of Nelson's ships, signalled to the *Victory*: 'I have discovered a strange fleet', which was almost a code message, though everyone knew its purport. At 6.30 Blackwood signalled from the *Euryalus*: '13 of the enemy's ships have put to sea.' At 6.59 Nelson put his Memorandum into practice: 'Form the order of sailing in two columns,' a signal repeated at 9.10 and again at 10.30 and yet again next day at 6.10 a.m.

At 7.03 Nelson signalled to Collingwood to 'Close nearer the Admiral.' At 7.30 Blackwood signalled that '22 of the enemy's ships have put to sea.' At 8.32 Captain Capel of the frigate *Phoebe* signalled, 'The enemy's ships have put to sea' (signifying the greater number of them), a message which was repeated by

---

[1] *Report of a Committee Appointed by the Admiralty to Examine and Consider the Evidence Relating to the Tactics Employed by Nelson at the Battle of Trafalgar* [Cd. 7120] (1913), 92–103.

the *Mars*, when there could be no question of their turning back, at 1.50. Detailed signals continued throughout the 20th, the last of note being made by Nelson to Blackwood, just before daylight failed: 'I rely on your keeping sight of the enemy', meaning that the *Euryalus* was to be in visual touch throughout the hours of darkness.

By 21 October, the day of battle, it had become clear to Nelson that Villeneuve would reverse his fleet and, instead of making his run for the Strait, would seek the shelter of Cadiz without an encounter, if he had skill enough to avoid it. At 6.13 Nelson made a general signal to 'Bear up and sail large on E.N.E. course', followed nine minutes later by 'Prepare for battle.' Course was altered to East at 6.46, and between 7.05 and 7.20 Nelson signalled to the slow three-deckers *Britannia*, *Prince*, and *Dreadnought* to 'Take station as convenient without regard to the established order of sailing.' At 7.35 he summoned the frigate captains on board the *Victory*, to give them his final instructions.

The *Royal Sovereign*'s bunting began to flutter at 8.45 when Collingwood ordered his 'Larboard Division'—which would actually come into action to starboard of the *Victory*'s line—to 'Keep on the larboard line of bearing though on the starboard tack,' and at 8.50 for all his ships to 'Make more sail, leading ship first.' He signalled for the *Tonnant* and *Belleisle* to change places at 9.15 and later to the *Dreadnought*, *Belleisle*, and *Revenge* to make more sail, since it was evidently his opinion they were being slow over his earlier order.

By 9.41 Nelson had perceived that the *Mars*, with the eager Duff in command, was close behind Collingwood, and, not wishing that Collingwood should expose himself first to the enemy fire without strong support, actually signalled direct to Duff to take station astern of the *Royal Sovereign*, which Collingwood could well have construed as an unwarrantable interference with the disposition of his line. At 10 o'clock Nelson went still further and ordered Duff to 'Head the larboard column', and he repeated the instruction at 10.45. Collingwood's answer was to crowd on more sail, which was precisely Nelson's own reaction when at 12.15, after action had begun in Collingwood's division, he ordered Captain Harvey of the *Témeraire* to keep in his station astern of the *Victory*.

At 11 o'clock Nelson signalled: 'Prepare to anchor at close of day' and at about 11.30 he notified Collingwood 'I intend to go through the enemy's line to prevent them getting into Cadiz.' This was followed by a general signal 'Make all sail possible with safety to the masts.' At 11.48 came the well-known hoist: 'England Expects that every man will do his Duty,' the message which so impressed Napoleon, but which was regarded as superfluous by many in the Fleet, Collingwood being heard to say, when he saw more flags go up in the *Victory*, that he wished Nelson would stop signalling, since they all knew well enough what they had to do: 'but', wrote Newnham Collingwood, 'when the purport of it was conveyed to him, he expressed delight and admiration, and made it known to his officers and ship's company.'[1]

Nelson's last general signal was made at 12.15, 'Engage the enemy more closely', which was once again superfluous, since not a ship which could bring guns to bear was by that time showing the slightest indication of what used to be described as 'shyness'. By that time, too, Collingwood was in close action, and in so splendid a manner that Nelson exclaimed: 'See how that noble fellow Collingwood takes his ship into action. How I envy him!' Almost simultaneously, Collingwood said to Captain Rotheram (a tiger in battle, for all his stupidity): 'What would Nelson give to be here!' Collingwood was well and truly first, but the rest had not long to wait.

Young Mr. Smith, who had succeeded William Ireland as Collingwood's servant, gave Newnham Collingwood an account[2] of how his master began the day.

I entered the Admiral's cabin about daylight [he said], and found him already up and dressing. He asked if I had seen the French fleet; and on my replying that I had not, he told me to look out at them, adding that, in a very short time, we should see a great deal more of them. I then observed a crowd of ships to leeward; but I could not help looking with still greater interest at the Admiral, who, during all this time, was shaving himself with a composure which quite astonished me.

Admiral Collingwood dressed himself that morning with

[1] N.C., 123-7.   [2] N.C., 126-31.

peculiar care; and soon after, meeting Lieutenant Clavell, advised him to pull off his boots. 'You had better,' he said, 'put on silk stockings, as I have done: for if one should get a shot in the leg, they would be so much more manageable for the surgeon.' He then proceeded to visit the decks, encouraged the men to the discharge of their duty, and addressing the officers, said to them: 'Now, gentlemen, let us do something today which the world may talk of hereafter.'

Smith also supplied some details of the action itself.

The *Royal Sovereign* [he said] was far in advance when Lieutenant Clavell observed that the *Victory* was setting her studding-sails, and with that spirit of honourable emulation which prevailed between the squadrons, and particularly between these two ships, he pointed it out to Admiral Collingwood, and requested his permission to do the same. 'The ships of our line,' replied the Admiral, 'are not yet sufficiently up for us to do so now; but you may be getting ready.' The studding-sail and royal halliards were accordingly manned, and in about ten minutes the Admiral, observing Lieutenant Clavell's eyes fixed upon him with a look of expectation, gave him a nod; on which that officer went to Captain Rotheram and told him that the Admiral desired him to make all sail. The order was then given to rig out and hoist away, and in one instant the ship was under a crowd of sail.

The Admiral then directed the officers to see that all the men lay down on the decks, and were kept quiet. At this time the *Fougueux*, the ship astern of the *Santa Anna*, had closed up, with the intention of preventing the *Royal Sovereign* from going through the line; and when Admiral Collingwood observed it, he desired Captain Rotheram to steer immediately for the Frenchman and carry away his bowsprit. To avoid this, the *Fougueux* backed her main top-sail, and suffered the *Royal Sovereign* to pass, at the same time beginning her fire; when the Admiral ordered a gun to be occasionally fired at her, to cover his ship with smoke.

As Collingwood intended, the *Royal Sovereign* had her main duel with a Spanish Admiral's flagship, and the *Santa Anna*, as he later told a friend, was 'a Spanish perfection . . . she towered over the *Royal Sovereign* like a castle'.[1]

In about a quarter of an hour [ran Newnham Collingwood's account], and before any other English ship had been enabled to take part in the action, Captain Rotheram, whose bravery on this occasion was remarkable even among the instances of courage which the day displayed, came up to the Admiral, and shaking him by the hand, said, 'I congratulate you, Sir: she is slackening her fire, and must soon strike.' It was, indeed, expected on board the *Royal Sovereign* that they would have had the gratification of capturing the Spanish admiral in the midst of a fleet of thirty three sail, before the arrival of another English ship; but the *Santa Anna*, though exposed to a tremendous loss from the unremitting fire of the *Sovereign*, and unable to do more than to return a gun at intervals, maintained the conflict in the most determined manner, relying on the assistance of the neighbouring ships, which now crowded round the English vessel, hoping, doubtless, to destroy her before she could be supported by her friends. The *Fougueux* placed herself on the *Sovereign*'s lee quarter, and another two-decked French ship across her bow; while two Spanish ships were also on her bow: a number probably greater than could fire at a single ship without injuring each other.

The Admiral now directed Captain Vallack, of the Marines, an officer of the greatest gallantry, to take his men from off the poop, that they might not be unnecessarily exposed; but he remained there himself much longer. At length, descending to the quarter-deck, he visited the men, enjoining them not to fire a shot in waste, looking himself along the guns to see that they were properly pointed, and commending the sailors, particularly a black man, who was afterwards killed, but who, while he stood beside him, fired ten times directly into the port-hole of the *Santa Anna*. The *Fougueux* at one time got so much on the quarter of the *Sovereign* that she almost touched, when the English quarter-deck carronades were brought to bear upon her, and after receiving several double-shotted guns directly into her forecastle, she dropped

[1] N.C., 165.

a little astern. Being there out of the *Royal Sovereign*'s reach, she kept up a destructive, raking fire, till the *Tonnant* arrived and drove her away.

The account continued:

The *Santa Anna* struck at half-past two o'clock, about the time when the news of Lord Nelson's wound was communicated to Admiral Collingwood; but the *Royal Sovereign* had been so much injured in her masts and yards by the ships that lay on her bow and quarter, that she was unable to alter her position. Admiral Collingwood accordingly called the *Euryalus* to take her in tow, and make the necessary signals. He despatched Captain Blackwood to convey the Spanish Admiral on board the *Euryalus*, but he was stated to be at the point of death, and Captain Blackwood returned with the Spanish Captain. That officer had already been to the *Royal Sovereign* to deliver his sword, and on entering, had asked one of the English sailors the name of the ship. When he was told that it was the *Royal Sovereign*, he replied, in broken English, while patting one of the guns, 'I think she should be called the "Royal Devil".'

The action was still general, when Captain Blackwood, to whom Admiral Collingwood had communicated the intelligence of Lord Nelson's wound, and who was anxious to fulfil his promise of revisiting his friend, proceeded to the *Victory*. On his arrival, he saw the boat alongside which had carried the news to Admiral Collingwood, and on inquiry, was told that Lord Nelson was still alive; but, on hastening below, he found that the hero had just expired.

Months later, on 28 March 1806, Collingwood wrote to his wife to give her some circumstances of the death of the *Royal Sovereign*'s master, Mr. William Chalmers, who had been mortally wounded by a great shot as close to Collingwood as Bowyer had been when he lost his leg at the Glorious First of June.[1]

. . . he laid his head upon my shoulder [wrote Collingwood] and told me he was slain. I supported him till two men carried him off. He could say nothing to me, but to bless me; but as they carried him down, he wished he could but live to read the account of the action in a newspaper . . .

[1] N.C., 204–5.

Did I not tell you how my leg was hurt? It was by a splinter—a pretty severe blow. I had a good many thumps, one way or the other: one in the back, which I think was the wind of a great shot, for I never saw any thing that did it. You know nearly all were killed or wounded on the quarter-deck and poop but myself, my Captain, and Secretary, Mr Cosway, who was of more use to me than any officer, after Clavell.

The first enquiry of the Spaniards was about my wound, and exceedingly surprised they were when I made light of it; for when the Captain of the *Santa Anna* was brought on board, it was bleeding and swelled, and tied up with a handkerchief.[1]

Collingwood was seen to munch an apple as he walked up and down during the battle, cheering everybody on, oblivious of the shot.

By the time of Nelson's death, about four o'clock in the afternoon, some twenty enemy vessels had apparently struck their colours, but the sea was rising, many ships were in no condition to anchor because their tackle had been destroyed, prizes were not secured, and although an annihilating victory had been achieved on a scale greater than anything known hitherto, there was still almost everything to do, and Collingwood would have to do it alone.

With nightfall, such a burden descended upon him as had rarely been placed on any single man.

V

Nelson's fleet had been a heterogeneous body, and not a high proportion of the captains had served with him before. Still fewer knew Collingwood, except perhaps by reputation as one to whom duty was indeed, as Wordsworth called her, 'Stern

[1] Sarah Collingwood had her own alarms about the battle. She was in a Newcastle shop when the Mail arrived covered with ribbands, but the coachman with a black hat-band. He announced the great victory, adding that Nelson and 'all the admirals' had been killed. Sarah Collingwood fainted. *The Letter Bag of Lady Elizabeth Spencer-Stanhope*, by A. M. W. Stirling (1913), Vol. i. 69.

Lawgiver', and one who looked for a higher degree of efficiency in his officers than most men.

Blackwood's reaction to Collingwood, and his general impression of the battle, was probably typical. It was expressed in a letter he wrote to his wife within twenty-four hours of the event.

> I hope it is not injustice to the Second in Command, who is now on board the *Euryalus*, and who fought like a hero, to say that the Fleet under any other, never would have performed what they did under Lord N. But under Lord N. it seemed like inspiration to most of them . . .
>
> Admiral Collingwood, who came to hoist his flag here for a week or so, because his own ship was dismasted, and unfit for him, is a very reserved, though a very pleasing good man; and as he fought like an angel I take the more to him.[1]

'A very reserved, though a very pleasing good man . . .'—the phrase is exactly right, so different from Nelson's free-flowing, colourful, and imperfect character. One quality the two men had in common which Blackwood could scarcely have been expected to perceive on earliest acquaintance—an exceptional generosity of mind. Nelson seldom blamed subordinates, and never, except in very private letters, did he censure. He worked by encouragement, so that officers and men found themselves acting, while under his command, better than their best. Collingwood (with bitter experience of how past actions had been reported and spoken of) would not only snap off the head of anyone who even suggested that a single officer or man had not done well in the battle, but he composed a General Order, on board the *Euryalus*, which could have served as a pattern of its kind.[2]

> The ever-to-be-lamented death of Lord Viscount Nelson, Duke of Brontë, the Commander-in-Chief, who fell in the action of the 21st, in the arms of Victory, covered with glory, —whose name will be ever dear to the British Navy and the British Nation, whose zeal for the honour of his King, and for the interest of his Country, will be ever held up as a shining example for a British seaman—leaves me a duty to return my thanks to the Right Honourable Rear-Admiral,

[1] Nic. vii. 225–6.   [2] N.C., 131–2.

the Captains, Officers, Seamen and Detachments of Royal Marines, serving on board His Majesty's squadron, now under my command, for their conduct on that day. But where can I find language to express my sentiments of the valour and skill which were displayed by the Officers, the Seamen, and Marines, in the battle with the enemy, where every individual appeared a hero on whom the glory of his country depended? The attack was irresistible, and the issue of it adds to the page of naval annals a brilliant instance of what Britons can do, when their King and Country need their service.

To the Right Honourable Rear Admiral the Earl of Northesk, to the Captains, Officers and Seamen, and to the Officers, non-commissioned Officers and Privates of the Royal Marines, I beg to give my sincere and hearty thanks for their highly meritorious conduct, both in the action, and in their zeal and activity in bringing the captured ships out from the perilous situation in which they were, after their surrender, among the shoals of Trafalgar, in boisterous weather. And I desire that the respective Captains will be pleased to communicate to the Officers, Seamen and Royal Marines, this public testimony of my high approbation of their conduct, and my thanks for it.

Collingwood wrote many accounts of the battle, including a public dispatch in the form of letters to the Admiralty which received general applause. Every one of them is fresh, and they are all the more astonishing when it is recalled that the earlier were composed in the cramped quarters of a frigate, the ship herself tossing about in the swell, with reports continually coming in, vital decisions needing to be made on still imperfect information, signals having to be sent off, and all this by a man not far short of sixty who had been on watch in all weathers for months on end, who had fought a great battle, lost the greatest friend of his Service life, and had the whole complication of Mediterranean strategy and diplomacy suddenly thrust upon him, without a day's warning. As for a staff, apart from a secretary and a new signal lieutenant (Gilliland had been killed), Collingwood had nothing. Many quite unimportant documents of the time, and all the personal letters which survive, were written in his own clear hand, with scarcely a sign of erasure or haste. Every attribute of his conduct after Trafalgar shows Collingwood worthy to have succeeded his brilliant friend.

As the result of a bullet fired from a French ship, Collingwood had been thrust into a position of responsibility which he had not sought, and for which he had no training. For although he had long shown himself perfect master of the business of a fleet, his experience of the world in general was extremely limited. It is a measure of their serene confidence in his capacity not merely as admiral but as ambassador-at-large, that the government in London assumed, without hesitation or after-thought, that this hitherto obscure sea officer was fully capable of managing his country's affairs from Cadiz in the west to Turkey in the east, and this in time of general war. There is no record that George III had any particular knowledge of Collingwood whatever, no record that they ever met, apart from the celebrations after Howe's battle, but the King, who knew a man when he saw one, and who was an admirable judge of naval and military capacity, placed unwavering confidence in Collingwood for the rest of his life. Hardly had he digested the Trafalgar dispatch than he commanded Colonel Taylor, his private Secretary, to address a letter to the Secretary of the Admiralty which not only became Collingwood's proudest possession, but which kept him at work on his sovereign's behalf long after most others would have failed from sheer weariness.

The letter ran as follows:

Windsor, Nov. 7, 1805.

His Majesty has commanded me to express, in the strongest terms, his feelings of approbation of every part of the conduct of his gallant Fleet, whose glorious and meritorious exertions are made yet more conspicuous, if possible, by the details of the opposition and difficulties which it had to encounter, both during and subsequent to the glorious action, and by the intrepidity and skill with which they were overcome.

Every tribute of praise appears to His Majesty due to Lord Nelson, whose loss he can never sufficiently regret; but His Majesty considers it very fortunate that the command, under circumstances so critical, should have devolved upon an officer of such consummate valour, judgment and skill, as Admiral Collingwood has proved himself to be, every part of whose conduct he considers deserving his entire approbation and admiration. The feeling manner in which he has described the events of that great day and those subsequent,[1] and the modesty with which he speaks of himself, whilst he does justice, in terms so elegant and so ample, to the meritorious exertions of the gallant officers and men under his command, have also proved extremely satisfactory to the King.[2]

This was one gentleman of sensibility to another, and it is scarcely surprising that, during all the difficulties, frustrations, and loneliness of his last few years, Collingwood should have felt his sovereign's words to be his highest consolation. 'Shew it to any body,' Collingwood wrote later to his sister 'that it may be publickly known what His Majesty's opinion of my services is, but allow none to have a copy of it, lest it should get into a newspaper, which would give me great concern.'[3] 'It is there,' Collingwood wrote to Sarah on Christmas Day, 'I feel the object of my life attained',[4] and next to the letter was 'the praise of every officer in the fleet'.[5] 'Many of the Captains here,' he wrote, 'have expressed a desire that I would give them a general notice whenever I go to court; and if they are within 500 miles they will come up to attend me.'[6]

A long way first with news of the battle was the *Gibraltar Chronicle*, whose editor was handed a scoop of the first magnitude. The issue of 24 October printed a brief letter from Collingwood to Governor Fox, and an account, in parallel columns in English and French, of such information, much of it inaccurate, as the master of the vessel which brought word to Fox had been able to pick up.

As a clearer picture of the results of the action began to unfold, the wonder grew rather than diminished. Of the 33 enemy ships of the line present, 18 French and 15 Spanish, four (three Spanish and one French) were brought to Gibraltar as prizes. Sixteen ships were sunk (including, at last, the great *Santissima Trinidada*), or burnt, or wrecked beyond recovery. Nelson had hoped for twenty, and his wish was granted with precision. In the end, nine ships returned to Cadiz, including the battered *Santa Anna*, which was re-captured during a sortie.

---

[1] Collingwood's original letter-dispatches are printed as an Appendix. The details were considerably amended in the light of later information.
[2] N.C., 157.   [3] H., Letter 96.   [4] N.C., 168.   [5] N.C., 160.   [6] N.C., 166.

Six of these were badly damaged, three were serviceable. Four escaped south, to be snapped up on 4 November by Sir Richard Strachan, who from the exuberance of his dispatch became known as 'the delighted Sir Dicky'.

Collingwood had a courteous correspondence with d'Alava, who he considered had surrendered to him, but who had not been removed from his ship on account of a very severe head wound. Two firm men could not agree, and d'Alava continued to refuse to surrender himself as prisoner of war. Otherwise, relations between the British and the Spanish were extremely cordial, as they had been after Nelson's repulse from Tenerife seven years earlier.

> To alleviate the miseries of the wounded as much as in my power [wrote Collingwood to Blackett on 2 November], I sent a flag to the Marquis Solana, to offer him his wounded. Nothing can exceed the gratitude expressed by him for this act of humanity: all this part of Spain is in an uproar of praise and thankfulness to the English.
>
> Solana sent me a present of a cask of wine; and we have a free intercourse with the shore. Judge of the footing we are on, when I tell you he offered me his hospitals, and pledged his Spanish honour for the care and cure of our wounded men. Our officers and men who were wrecked in some of the prize ships were most kindly treated: all the country was on the beach to receive them; the priests and women distributing wine, and bread, and fruit, amongst them. The soldiers turned out of their barracks to make lodgings for them; whilst their allies the French, were left to shift for themselves, with a guard over them to prevent their doing mischief . . .
>
> All the Spaniards speak of us in terms of adoration; and Villeneuve, whom I had in the frigate with me, acknowledges that they cannot contend with us at sea. I do not know what will be thought of it in England, but the effect here is highly advantageous to the British name.[1]

The letter of Collingwood's which George III most admired was written on 1 November from the *Queen*, the splendid old ship into which Collingwood exchanged from the *Euryalus*. It was addressed to Admiral Sir Peter Parker, the man who had

[1] N.C., 137–8.

given both Nelson and Collingwood their first great chance, a quarter of a century before.

You will have seen from the public accounts that we have fought a great Battle, and had it not been for the fall of our noble friend, who was indeed the glory of England, and the admiration of all who ever saw him in Battle, your pleasure would have been perfect—that two of your own pupils, raised under your eye, and cherished by your kindness, should render such service to their Country as I hope this Battle, in its effect, will be.

I am not going to give you a detail of our proceedings, which you will have seen in the public papers; but to tell you I have made advantage of our calamities, and having lost two excellent men, have endeavoured to replace them with those who will in due time, I hope, be as good. I have appointed Captain Parker to the *Melpomene*, which, I am sure, my dear Nelson would have done had he lived. His own merit entitles him to it, and it is highly gratifying to me to give you such a token of my affection for you.[1]

It was a severe Action, no dodging or manœuvring. They formed their line with nicety, and waited our attack with great composure; nor did they fire a gun until we were close to them, and we began first. Our Ships were fought with a degree of gallantry that would have warmed your heart. Every body exerted themselves, and a glorious day they made of it. People who cannot comprehend how complicated an affair a Battle at sea is, and who judge of an Officer's conduct by the number of sufferers in his Ship, often do him a wrong. Though

---

[1] Gratitude was a marked trait in both Collingwood and Nelson, and Collingwood was repaying Parker for making him a post captain in 1780, and thus giving him a chance for distinction, by appointing Parker's grandson to that rank, even though he had not been present at the battle. (The attention was justified, though Parker was killed in action before the end of the war.) The other promotion Collingwood made was that of Thomas, who had served long with him, gained his thorough approval, and had recently saved the *Eurydice*, which had gone ashore after taking a French privateer. Collingwood later complained, with an uncommon degree of tartness, that his other recommendations were not attended to, but in fact this was due more to difficulties of communication, and to changes at the Admiralty, than to inattention. The two 'death vacancies' due to the deaths of Captain Duff of the *Mars* and Cooke of the *Bellerophon* at Trafalgar were undoubtedly in Collingwood's own gift.

there will appear great difference in the loss of men, all did admirably well; and the conclusion was grand beyond description; eighteen hulks of the Enemy lying amongst the British Fleet without a stick standing, and the French *Achille* burning. But we were close to the rocks of Trafalgar, and when I made the signal for anchoring, many Ships had their cables shot, and not an anchor was ready. Providence did for us what no human effort could have done; the wind shifted a few points, and we drifted off the land.

The storm being violent, and many of our own Ships in most perilous situations, I found it necessary to order the captures, all without masts, some without rudders, to be destroyed, and many half full of water, to be destroyed, except such as were in better plight; for my object was their ruin, and not what might be made of them.

God bless you, my dear Sir Peter! May you ever be happy. Your affectionate and faithful servant,

C. COLLINGWOOD.[1]

The King was so impressed with this letter that he asked for a copy, when Sir Peter showed it to him, so Collingwood told his sister.[2]

Collingwood was able to summarize his considered view of Nelson in three letters, one to Blackett, one to Admiral Sir Thomas Pasley, who had been so attentive to Sarah during her stay at Plymouth, and one to W. Spencer-Stanhope, the latter having only recently came to light.

To Blackett he wrote:

When my dear friend received his wound, he immediately sent an officer to me to tell me of it, and give his love to me. Though the officer was directed to say the wound was not dangerous, I read in his countenance what I had to fear; and before the action was over, Captain Hardy came to inform me of his death. I cannot tell you how deeply I was affected; my friendship for him was unlike any thing I have left in the Navy—a brotherhood of more than thirty years. In this affair he did nothing without my counsel, we made our line of battle together, and concerted the mode of attack, which was put in execution in the most admirable style.[3]

[1] Nic. vii. 233-4.   [2] H., Letter 159.   [3] N.C., 136.

To Pasley, Collingwood wrote:

A happy day it would have been indeed had my dear friend survived it—but I cannot separate from the glory of such a day, the irreparable loss of such a Hero. He possessed the zeal of an enthusiast, directed by talents which nature had very bountifully bestowed upon him, and everything seemed as if by enchantment to prosper under his direction: but it was the effect of system, and nice combination, not of chance. We must endeavour to follow his example, but it is the lot of very few to attain to his perfection.[1]

Spencer-Stanhope was told:

. . . since the year 73 we have been on the terms of the greatest intimacy; chance has thrown us very much together in service, and on many occasions we have acted in concert; there is scarce a naval subject that has not been the subject of our discussion, so that his opinions were familiar to me, and so firmly founded on principles of honour, of justice, of attachment to his Country, at the same time so entirely divested of every thing interested to himself, that it was impossible to consider him, but with admiration. He liked fame, and was open to flattery, so that people sometimes got about him who were unworthy of him: he is a loss to his country that cannot easily be replaced.[2]

As for rewards, the Nelson family, in the person of the admiral's elder brother William, were given an earldom splendidly endowed, while Collingwood was raised to the peerage as Baron Collingwood of Caldburne and Hethpool, after two properties brought to him by his wife. He received the thanks of both Houses of Parliament, and an honourable augmentation was made to his arms, by the introduction in chief of one of the lions of England, navally crowned, and surmounted by the word Trafalgar. An additional crest was granted to him, representing the stern of the *Royal Sovereign*. He received the Freedom of many cities, and a pension was granted by Parliament of £2,000 per annum for his own life, and, in the event of his death, of £1,000 to Lady Collingwood, and of £500 per annum to each of his two daughters; but his request that the

[1] H., Letter 97.   [2] Add. MSS. 52780.

peerage should descend through his daughter's children was never attended to, and caused him much sadness.

Collingwood told Sarah that he had dreamed many details of Trafalgar while at home, years before the battle,[1] and to her father he described his immediate losses with that touch of humour which was so characteristic: 'I have had a great destruction of my furniture and stock; I have hardly a chair that has not a shot in it, and many have lost both arms and legs, without hope of pension. My wine broke in moving, and my pigs were slain in battle; and these are heavy losses where they cannot be replaced.'[2]

Among his rewards, Collingwood was promoted, becoming a Vice-Admiral of the Red on 9 November 1805, a rank which took him past that held by Nelson, who had died as a Vice-Admiral of the White. This general promotion (the last in which Collingwood ever partook), brought his old friend Admiral Roddam to the highest rank in the Navy, for he found himself an Admiral of the Red, 'which,' as Collingwood remarked, 'he did not expect.'[3] Sarah's uncle, the Rev. Henry Blackett, wrote[4] from Bolden on 24 November to say that he had met the old warrior at a celebratory party. 'Was you a dear son of his own,' said Blackett, 'he could not enjoy more apparent happiness than he does in our just applauses, and says no Rewards are equal to your Services.'[5]

One of the surprises of the aftermath of the battle was a letter from Sir Roger Curtis, about whom Collingwood had said such harsh things after the Glorious First of June. It is probable that Collingwood and Curtis had grown warmer in the days they had spent together under St. Vincent; certainly there was nothing reserved or artificial in Curtis's praise. He wrote from the Admiralty on 10 November, opening in a most familiar way:[6]

I hope, my dear Cuddie, it will not be unacceptable to you, to receive from me, as an old mess-mate and friend, my most sincere congratulations on the great and unparalleled Victory, to the obtaining of which, you so conspicuously contributed by your highly distinguished conduct, and also on the most honourable rank His Majesty has been pleased to bestow on

[1] N.C., 161.   [2] N.C., 170.   [3] H., Letter 96.   [4] H., Letter 95.
[5] H., Letter 95.   [6] Col. 15.

you, as a mark of the sense he entertains of the important
services you have rendered to the State . . . There is nothing
more creditable to you, nor spoken of with more admiration,
than the dignified modesty with which your publick letters
are composed . . .

Collingwood wrote on this letter: 'Answered Decr. 21st'; and
it would have been in character to have been as cordial as the
occasion seemed to warrant.

As for Bounce, Collingwood told his wife that he was out of
all patience with him.

> The consequential airs he gives himself since he became a
> right honourable dog are insufferable. He considers it
> beneath his dignity to play with commoner's dogs, and
> truly thinks that he does them grace when he condescends to
> lift up his leg against them. This, I think, is carrying the
> insolence of rank to the extreme, but he is a dog that does it.[1]

Collingwood specialized in postscripts, and one of the
happiest of the campaign related to a decision which came
hard upon the battle. Learning that the French squadron at
Rochefort had got to sea, Vice-Admiral Duckworth went in
chase. After a long interval of silence and speculation, Collingwood at last had news that Duckworth had come up with a
squadron of the enemy at San Domingo, in the West Indies,
and destroyed it.

One of the more consoling sides of this episode was that a
number of officers who had been almost heart-broken at missing
Trafalgar, including Rear-Admiral Louis, his flag-captain
Francis Austen, Captain Keats of the *Superb*, and Pulteney
Malcolm of the *Donegal*, were afforded another chance to win
distinction and gold medals. One of the less consoling was that,
as so often with actions resulting from detached service, it led
to a dispute about the prize-money to which Collingwood had
an undoubted claim, a view contested by Duckworth and
Louis. 'How very oddly men are swayed by their interest from
all true bearings', wrote Collingwood to Lord Northesk;[2] but
no disagreement of this sort could lessen his praise of Duckworth's attack or his consideration for his personal as well as
his Service requirements.

[1] N.C., 167–8.   [2] N.C. (Additional letter, 1837 edition.)

9 *Commander-in-Chief, Mediterranean*

George III indeed showed judgement in supporting Collingwood, and in approving his appointment as Commander-in-Chief, Mediterranean, in succession to Nelson, and with the same powers as his predecessor. The King had need of all the ability he could discover, for, soon after Trafalgar, affairs both at home and abroad took a turn which would have taxed the qualities of the most gifted. Pitt did not long survive Nelson, dying on 23 January 1806, and a 'Ministry of all the Talents,' headed by Lord Grenville, which succeeded Pitt's final administration, included Charles James Fox as Foreign Secretary. Fox would have come to terms with Napoleon, had he been able, but he failed, and he himself had not long to live.

Lord Barham's spell at the Admiralty had always been regarded as temporary, and his successor, Charles Grey, who was created Lord Howick, though an able man, had had no earlier experience of naval business. It was therefore scarcely surprising that for months Collingwood heard little from Their Lordships. Although his desk was piled high with congratulatory letters from all quarters, and his wife at home was blossoming into Society, he was given few official directions, and these mainly on foreign affairs.

The European scene was becoming excessively complicated, as much so in the Mediterranean as anywhere else, and while it was Collingwood's first duty to exercise that general superiority at sea which had been so magnificently won, it was also necessary for him to perceive, and so far as possible anticipate, the main trends of current movements, and to implement and support the policy of his masters in London. When, owing to changes in ministers, long and vexing delays in communications, some accidental, some avoidable, and those uncertainties which seem inseparable from diplomacy, such support required personal initiative, and the shouldering of great responsibility, he was expected to supply what was necessary. Although Collingwood never failed to respond to circumstances of difficulty or crisis, such a characteristic could not reasonably have been looked for in a man bred to the sea who was, and who would always remain, a stranger to the corridors of power. 'The business of the fleet,' he wrote to Blackett,[1] 'appears trifling and easy when compared with the many important things I have to settle.' The situation was indeed extraordinary when a flag-officer on active service, who sometimes did not anchor for months at a time, who rarely saw anyone but fellow officers, and who came to be wary of professional diplomatists, was yet increasingly turned to for advice by those in London who had every facility and personal contact to aid them in making their decisions. London, and not only London, relied on Collingwood, but the cost to him was heavy and, in the course of a few years, fatal. Ministers had found a willing horse, and they proceeded, quietly but inexorably, to work him to death. 'When I err,' Collingwood wrote to his wife, 'it will be from my head, and not my heart. It is not every body that is so indulgent as you are in their judgment of my poor head, but there is no one by whose judgment I can be so much flattered.'[2] Sarah Collingwood, and those in authority, in this case judged the same.

II

Foiled in his scheme of subjugating Great Britain, Napoleon turned upon the Austrians and Russians, and defeated their armies at Austerlitz on 2 December 1805. In support of his dominating position on the Continent, he put his brother Louis on the throne of Holland, and—a matter which affected Collingwood more closely—another brother, Joseph, was given the crown of Naples. General Craig landed an army at Naples which, so it was agreed, should co-operate with the Russians in expelling the French from Bourbon territory, but it soon became clear that King Ferdinand would have to retire once more to

[1] N.C., 192.   [2] N.C. 200.

Sicily, as he and his Queen had done in the winter of 1798, after Nelson had become their protector. Craig and the Russians withdrew from Naples, and the security of Sicily thereupon became a main British pre-occupation, and so remained until the very end of the war.

Collingwood saw his immediate primary task as keeping the French fleet out of the Mediterranean, and while disposing a ship of the line, (his own old *Excellent*), to guard the Bourbons, with light forces acting in support of Craig's army, his duty, both in defence of Sicily as well as in preventing the junction of French squadrons with their allies further south, was to continue watching Cadiz, and to keep guard over the Spaniards at Cartagena. His worries never included meeting the enemy at sea—('another touch at them would just set me up,' he wrote to his sister on New Year's Day, 1806[1])—however inferior his numbers and foul his ships at any given time; but the thought of the harm which hostile detachments could do if they eluded him was an unceasing pre-occupation.

By mid-December 1805 Collingwood was already so hard pressed that he wrote to his wife:[2]

I labour from dawn till midnight, till I can hardly see; and as my hearing fails me too, you will have but a mass of infirmities in your poor Lord whenever he returns to you.

I suppose I must not be seen to work in my garden now; but tell old Scott that he need not be unhappy on that account. Though we shall never again be able to plant the Nelson potatoes, we will have them of some other sort, and right noble cabbages to boot, in great perfection.

A fortnight later he told Blackett:[3]

It was once full in the contemplation of my mind, considering that I am now far advanced in years, to have retired from sea service when my three years were up, in May next; but I am afraid that is now out of the question; and as long as I have health I must go on . . .

I hope my children are every day acquiring some knowledge . . . If there were an opportunity I should like them to be taught Spanish, which is the most elegant language in Europe, and very easy.

[1] H.. Letter 98.   [2] N.C., 165.   [3] N.C., 169–70.

In March 1806 Collingwood told his wife to make his children read to her, 'not trifles, but history, in the manner we used to do in the winter evenings: blessed evenings indeed! The human mind will improve itself if it be kept in action; but grows dull and torpid when left to slumber. I believe even stupidity itself may be cultivated.'[1]

On the 10th of that month he wrote to Lord Radstock, who as Vice-Admiral William Waldegrave had written to him so feelingly after the battle of St. Vincent:[2]

> I see the names of some very indifferent young men in the promotion, who never go to sea without meeting some mischief, for want of common knowledge and care. Every three brigs that come here, commanded by three boys, require a dock-yard. The ships of the line never have anything for artificers to do. I have sent some home, because they could not be maintained in this country, and their service amounted to nothing. Better to give them pensions, and let them stay on shore.

At the end of March, something of a trial appeared in the person of Rear-Admiral Sir Sidney Smith, newly promoted to flag rank. The 'Swedish knight', as his fellow officers sarcastically called him, was then enjoying a life of adventure which had already extended over many years. As a captain he had gained a title as naval adviser to Gustavus III of Sweden. Since then, his exploits had been many-sided. Collingwood among others had blamed him severely for not effectively destroying the French ships at Toulon in 1793 when he had the chance, and both St. Vincent and Nelson found him a roving nuisance in the Mediterranean in 1798, though his defence of Acre against Napoleon would ever be remembered to his credit.

It was Smith's way to talk big and act independently, and when Collingwood sent him on to Italy to support operations against the French, it was with considerable misgivings. The ardours and endurances of a dull blockade were not for such a man. Smith's enthusiasm was for the employment of 'explosion vessels and sky rockets' to annoy the enemy. Collingwood wrote about this idea to the First Lord:

---

[1] N.C., 192.   [2] N.C., 196.

Besides the written instructions which I gave to Sir Sidney Smith, I had much conversation with him on the service which would probably be required in Sicily, in which I endeavoured to impress on him the inefficacy of that mode of war which is carried on by explosion vessels and sky rockets. I know no instance of a favourable result from them. They serve merely to exasperate, to harass our own people, and, by reducing the companies of the ships, to render them unfit for real service when it is wanted.[1]

Sir Sidney took little notice of what he considered to be a reactionary attitude on the part of the Commander-in-Chief. In the end, he enjoyed various successes against the French, but he remained without that balance, or sense of selfless responsibility, which would have made him a tolerable fleet commander. Moreover, when in Sicily he extracted from the active and highly political Queen Maria Carolina such a grandiloquent sounding extension of the normal powers of a Rear-Admiral of the Royal Navy on detached duty that when Collingwood came to hear about it, he was as perturbed as he had every right to be. The Queen was a born intriguer, known to have French advisers in addition to others better disposed, and in a letter to Lord Radstock, Collingwood remarked that although he had heard that King Ferdinand had expressed concern lest the morals of his people should be corrupted by communication with the French, 'God bless him, honest King! He might have begun his correction nearer home.'[2] The mischief which the Queen and her 'Schmidt' as she called him might between them do to affairs in Italy caused Collingwood more than a little unease.[3] Within six months he wrote to his brother John:[4] 'I am sadly off with this Sir S. Smith in Sicily: the man's head is full of strange vapours and I am convinced that Lord Barham sent him here to be clear of a tormentor, but he annoys me more than French or Spanish fleet and the squadron he has is going to ruin.' History was repeating itself, for Lord Spencer, whilst at the Admiralty eight years earlier, had done much the same as Barham.

It was doubly fortunate that Collingwood was shortly to be joined by a flag-officer of his own choice in Rear-Admiral John

[1] N.C., 205. [2] N.C., 261. [3] N.C., 246. [4] H., Letter 116.

Purvis, a steady disciplinarian and a thorough seaman, to whom he could safely leave the watch on Cadiz when he himself was needed elsewhere. 'Admiral Knight at Gibraltar,' he wrote to Purvis at the end of April, 'is rather worse than having nobody there.'[1] Further north, the Earl of St. Vincent, on his last spell of active service, later took over the Channel and Tagus-based squadrons from Cornwallis, living for a short time in a house at Lisbon from which he wrote kindly and helpfully to Collingwood, though unable, owing to ill-health to be much at sea. 'He is endeavouring,' wrote Collingwood to his wife, 'to inspire a decayed Government with vigour, and to give strength to a nerveless arm.'[2]

So far as his personal life was concerned, the next event which affected Collingwood was the unexpectedly sudden death of his cousin of Chirton, who bequeathed him his estate for life, after which it was to go to John. This led Collingwood into a great deal of somewhat complicated business correspondence with his family, and with the Duke of Northumberland, regarding rights of access to a colliery in which he had now become interested. The Duke was a military veteran of the Seven Years War and the War of American Independence who was soon highly impressed by Collingwood's perspicacity over foreign affairs, and who, with his Duchess, was not only gracious to Sarah, but accommodating over a colliery way-leave. The Duke provided Collingwood with a wide ranging and free speaking commentary from home, which also had its advantages,[3] though he was no different from so many other correspondents in that he hoped Collingwood might show favour to various young friends of his in the Navy.

On 5 April 1806, Collingwood wrote to his wife to tell her: 'Every thing makes me nervous; and constant labour and pre-occupation weary me exceedingly', but he was glad to hear she was going to London, and hoped she would be presented at Court as soon as possible.

I wish [he continued], that in these journeys the education of our children may not stop; but that, even on the road, they may study the geography of that part of England through which they travel, and keep a regular journal, not of what

[1] H., Letter 105.   [2] N.C., 241.   [3] H., Appendix B: Letters 1–13.

they eat and drink, but of the nature of the country, its appearance, its produce, and some gay description of the manners of the inhabitants. I hope you will take your time in town, and show my girls everything curious. I am sure you will visit the tomb of my dear friend. Alas! the day that he had a tomb.[1]

Collingwood was referring to the splendid sarcophagus, in the crypt directly beneath the centre of the dome of St. Pauls, which had been prepared for Nelson. He ended: 'I need not tell you, my dear, to be very kind to Mr. Collingwood's dog; for I am sure you will, and so will I whenever I come home.' He had been greatly irritated at the thought that the pension granted to him might have been taken to imply some degree of indigence, which was far from the case. He esteemed it, so he told Lord Barham,[2] 'as it is the approbation of me from the Parliament, which, with his Majesty's, is the highest honour that can be conferred on a faithful subject.'

In a letter of 17 April, written to his sister from the *Queen* off Cadiz, Collingwood told her that he was soon expecting to move into a new flagship.[3] Her name was the *Ocean*, and she was brand new. She had sailed past his squadron in the middle of the month with a convoy to Gibraltar. Then she returned, and the first surviving letter addressed from her was written to Sarah on 27 April, when Collingwood reported:[4] 'She is, I think, without exception the finest-looking one I ever saw; but, like all new ships, she wants every thing to be done to her, to fit her for war. The ships are now put into very indifferent hands, at a time when all the exertion of the most skilful is wanted.'

Collingwood deplored the fact that so many people wished to send their sons to him. 'When I was Captain of a frigate,' he said, 'I took good care of them; now I cannot and have not time to know any thing about them.' He seemed more isolated than ever, with only Bounce to talk to in the late evenings. 'I wish I could collect something in the fleet to amuse you,' he continued 'but we are all very grave. The only subject that gives a gleam of cheerfulness is the hope that the fleet in Cadiz may venture out again: they will soon be strong enough.' Sir John Duckworth, so he told his sister at the end of the month[5] had recently

[1] N.C. 206-7.   [2] N.C., 210.   [3] H., Letter 103.
[4] N.C., 218-19.   [5] H., Letter 106.

joined him, fresh from his triumph in the West Indies off San Domingo, but he had been authorized by the Admiralty to give Duckworth leave to return home, as his son had fallen from his horse and was believed to be in danger. Duckworth duly went off, and made good use of his time in England, as Collingwood was not long in discovering. He reported that Collingwood seemed in indifferent health, and as he himself was of the necessary seniority to succeed to the chief command, the implication soon became clear enough. Such intrigue, for it seemed scarcely less,[1] merely fortified Collingwood in his belief that it was his duty to stay where he was, if the Admiralty, under successive First Lords, continued to approve his conduct, as he had every evidence they did.

At this time the affairs of three foreign countries in particular were beginning to preoccupy Collingwood. The first of them was Portugal, where the facilities long enjoyed by the British Fleet seemed in danger of curtailment. The second was Morocco, which supplied his ships with beef. It was essential to keep the people friendly, despite the drawbacks of their ramshackle administration and their piratical tendencies at sea. The third was Turkey. Every indication served to show that the Sublime Porte was increasingly being drawn within the French orbit, and was hardening its attitude to the traditional enemy, Russia, largely owing to Russian activities in Greece.

The Tsar Alexander was still allied with Great Britain, although the amount of active help which his troops and squadrons in the Mediterranean theatre had been able to render towards the prosecution of the war against France had always been small. As Alexander felt the same about Britain's efforts in the joint cause, and resented Britain's assertion of power in areas where he himself had aspirations, a re-orientation of policy was looked for by those best able to judge the climate of opinion in the circles where ultimate power lay.

Concerned as he always had to be with what affected the vast range and ramification of his command, Collingwood at no time neglected his own affairs, difficult as it sometimes was to piece together a coherent story from letters and other communications which always reached him late, often came in the wrong order, and from time to time were lost altogether, their

[1] H., Letter 118.

purport having to be deduced from copies, or from still more belated successors.

On 16 June, the 15th anniversary of his wedding, Collingwood wrote to Sarah telling her that being with his family was the only sort of happiness he could enjoy. He feared, rightly, that his wife would want to change from Morpeth, no doubt to Chirton, despite the proximity of collieries, with their noise, pumping engines, and smoke, 'but then,' he continued, 'I should be for ever regretting those beautiful views which are nowhere to be exceeded; and even the rattling of that old waggon that used to pass our door at 6 o'clock in a winter's morning had its charms.'

The fact is [he continued], whenever I think how I am to be happy again, my thoughts carry me back to Morpeth, where, out of the fuss and parade of the world, surrounded by those I loved most dearly and who loved me, I enjoyed as much happiness as my nature is capable of.

Many things that I see in the world give me a distaste to the finery of it. The great knaves are not like those poor unfortunates, who, driven perhaps to distress from accidents which they could not prevent or at least not educated in principles of honour and honesty, are hanged for some little thievery; while a knave of education and breeding, who brandishes his honour in the eyes of the world, would rob a state to its ruin. For the first I feel pity and compassion; for the latter, abhorrence and contempt: they are the tenfold vicious.[1]

How he longed to be merry again! 'Is your sister with you, and is she well and happy?' he asked. 'Tell her—God bless her!—I wish I were with you, that we might have a good laugh. God bless me! I have scarcely laughed these three years.'

Almost inevitably, Collingwood proceeded next to his hobby-horses, his children's education and his planting. He wanted the girls taught geometry ('of all sciences in the world the most entertaining'), and mathematics and astronomy would give them an idea of 'the beauty and wonders of creation . . . I would have my girls gain such knowledge of the works of the creation, that they may have a fixed idea of the nature of that

[1] N.C., 233-5.

Being who could be the author of such a world. Whenever they have that, nothing on this side the moon will give them much uneasiness of mind.'

As for the planting, he hoped Sarah would let him know how the trees thrived. 'Is there shade under the three oaks for a comfortable summer seat? Do the poplars grow at the walk, and does the wall of the terrace stand firm?' Sarah did not answer these questions, for by the time the letter reached her, her mind was elsewhere. The house at Morpeth, however happy its associations, was no place for a peer of the realm, and in his heart Collingwood knew it. Not that he, for all his high estate and power at sea, lived anything but simply. Ever since Trafalgar he had had to eat his meals with scarcely a sound utensil, after 'losses, movings and breakings'. Since then, Sarah had sent him 'knives, forks, teapot' and he was more or less comfortable again, though as he was suffering from lack of those walks which had done him so much good in Northumberland he had become weak, and his limbs 'lady-like'.[1]

On 5 July Collingwood wrote a letter to Lord Radstock which must have given him special pleasure.[2] So many of the young people recommended to his care were dull, or difficult, or had ill health, or were incompetent and therefore disappointing both to him and to those who sent them to sea. But Radstock's son was after his own heart, and he could say so without reserve.

I have the pleasure to tell you [he said], that Captain Waldegrave is very well; he is upon my advanced post just now, for I can trust any thing to his zeal. Did he tell you what a lecture I gave him? I thought it proper to do so, though I was very much pleased with him. He fell in with a gun-boat convoy, and knocked them all to pieces, killed a great many men, and destroyed several boats; but in doing it he got ashore, and was very near losing his ship. In the lecture I gave him, I wished to impress on his mind that he should never risk beyond the value of the object; and meant by it to temper his zeal with a little discretion.

In September, Collingwood had the belated news of the death of Admiral Richard Braithwaite, with whom he had spent so

[1] N.C., 227.   [2] N.C., 238.

much of his earlier time at sea, and for whom, so he wrote to the admiral's daughter Georgina, 'I ever felt the affection for, of a respected and beloved friend.' On the 12th of that month he sent word to his brother to say:[1]

> My sister says she never hears Chirton named by any of my family. The fact is they know not of my determination respecting it. It is a place I should dislike exceedingly as a residence. I could never bring my mind to be at home there. Yet it has conveniences that Morpeth has not, and is more like a gentleman's house. Had I been fortunate in prizes I would have bought a suitable residence, but as it is I fancy I must make Chirton my home, in a neighbourhood very disagreeable and in the smoke of coal engines and every kind of filth. I think in the letting there should be a condition that no engine should be erected within a certain distance of the house, nor small coals burnt for the repair of waggon ways or roads . . .'

A few weeks later he wrote to Mrs. Stead:[2]

> How you delight me, my sister, when you speak of the comforts of my house and the beauties of my garden etc. I may say they are all the work of my own hands. I planned every thing and planted almost every tree, every honey suckle and rose bush; the sturdy oak and poplar tall owe their stations to me. But how are the sturdy oaks? For since Sarah resolved for Chirton, she very cunningly has left off talking of those old beauties of Morpeth . . . As for being in the town, I never was in the town, nor know any thing about it, but if I had been fortunate enough to have got money here, I would have bought a residence where my family might have called themselves at home.

Longing as he was to renew his pleasure in the sights and sounds of Morpeth, Collingwood was not going home. He wrote to his sister on 13 November:[3]

> It is so long since I heard from you that I think you must have been deceived by the current report which I have heard was circulated with great industry in England 'that I was

[1] H., Letter 116.   [2] H., Letter 117.   [3] H., Letter 119.

coming home.' I have not yet thought of such a thing, but I suppose it originated with those who wished to succeed to my command. I came here, not of my own solicitation, or to answer my own private purposes, but because I was ordered as a proper person to conduct the service, and I have such a contempt for every thing like chicanery that I will certainly disappoint the authors.

One great inconvenience I suffer from it, that the people I employ at Portsm'th and Plym'th to send me occasional supplies, expecting me in England, have discontinued to send them. The state of the war will not allow me to think of retiring from it while my health continues good . . . It is not that I delight in war, am ambitious of high office, or insensible to the comforts of a peaceful, quiet home, but that I consider the war such that every man capable of serving is bound to render his best services.

To Lord Radstock he wrote, four days after Christmas:[1] 'I have heard from all quarters that I was going home, except from the Admiralty: there I had every reason to believe my proceedings met with full approbation. Lord Howick, on leaving that office, wrote to me a letter, which was very flattering to me, inviting me to continue my correspondence in matters relating to the political state of affairs here.' Howick was replaced in September 1806 by Thomas Grenville, who was in office only a few months. His successor was Lord Mulgrave, the last First Lord to whose ways Collingwood needed to become accustomed, for Mulgrave saw the admiral out.

'This is my second Christmas at sea,' Collingwood wrote to Sarah from off Cadiz on 20 December 1806,[2] 'and, unless it shall please God to take the Corsican out of this world, I see no prospect of a change.' This perpetual motion of the flagship may seem strange, and even misguided, to modern notions, but it was not so. Collingwood and his 800 or so fellow-prisoners on board the *Ocean*, who never even had the satisfaction of seeing themselves as others saw them, a towering, smartly-manned three-decker wearing a flag which was emblematic of the country's domination at sea, were in fact an extremely healthy community, and the very fact that the ship never

---

[1] N.C., 260.   [2] N.C., 257.

anchored was in itself a threat to the enemy. Napoleon was for ever denied what would have been the priceless knowledge of what Britain considered to be the point of greatest threat at any given time.

Although there was no great fleet action after Trafalgar, this does not alter the fact that to Admiralty and admirals alike it appeared so probable that there would be, that the best available officers were always given what Collingwood described as 'the dullest life that can be conceived, and nothing but the utmost patience can endure it'.[1] Nor was it possible that he could have exercised effective command ashore. Gibraltar was too far west. Malta was uncomfortably far from Toulon and Cartagena. Palermo had proved fatal even to Nelson's activity, and in the last span of his life, when he held the Command-in-Chief, he was invariably afloat. As he was ten years younger than his friend, the strain on him was correspondingly less; even so, it was severe enough, and so were his complaints. Collingwood's grew tedious, but they sprang from a loneliness and endurance of a kind which it requires an effort to conceive. And whereas Nelson was in his nature gay and spontaneous and resilient, Collingwood found that it was only in the bosom of his family that he could be amused, amusing, and always his freer self. That he had been able to relax with Nelson as with no other fellow officer made his loss truly irreparable. In his later years, no fellow admiral even began to take his place.

Although Collingwood's tremendous assiduity was in itself remarkable, illustrating not only that iron sense of duty which was one of his chief characteristics, but a determination to have complete control, in matters both large and small, over everything which concerned not only the supply, maintenance and disposition of the Fleet, but over matters of policy and sea appointments, it also emphasized a defect. He could not delegate. He must see to every detail himself. This was noted, and commented upon unfavourably, both before and after Trafalgar, by such experienced captains as Fremantle of the *Neptune* and Codrington of the *Orion*, and the trait did not grow weaker with age.

From the nature and consequence of his appointment, Collingwood was entitled to a First Captain, or Captain of the

[1] N.C., 242.

Fleet (in addition to the flag-captain of the ship in which he sailed), an officer who would correspond to a present-day Chief of Staff. Some of the best and most senior captains would have been glad to have been offered the post, and it was singular that Collingwood never chose one. It was true that Nelson, immediately before Trafalgar, made do with the services of his flag-captain, Thomas Masterman Hardy, but only as a temporary measure. He had had a Captain of the Fleet in earlier days as Commander-in-Chief, Mediterranean, and, although astonishing in the range of his interests, he never over-burdened himself with detail if he could help it.

Collingwood went on an opposite principle, for having promoted his former signal lieutenant, Richard Thomas, whom he had brought up under his own eye in the *Excellent*, into the post captain's vacancy caused by the death in action of Cooke of the *Bellerophon*, Collingwood kept this young officer as his flag-captain for the rest of his life. It was a great honour and responsibility for a newly promoted captain to be given charge of a three-decked ship, and a great burden undoubtedly fell on him and on Cosway, Collingwood's secretary, particularly when Collingwood grew progressively more ill. It emphasized the admiral's self-imposed isolation. The fact that, year after year, there is scarcely a mention of Thomas in his private correspondence implies at once a distance, and a reliance on his captain's competence in matters of mere routine, which were unusual. During the years he later spent as a retired admiral, Thomas never put pen to paper to give posterity the benefit of his reminiscences. This was sad, for he was a favourite with Nelson as well as with Collingwood, and he knew Collingwood, during the last fifteen years of his life, better than any other officer of his rank.

Collingwood's insistence on and continuance of absolute control and responsibility not only over his fleet but his flagship argued an immense self-confidence which was, in fact, entirely justified. It also argued at least some distrust of the value of any help. In the event, a succession of Boards of Admiralty not only approved of his actions and advice, but came to rely on him as much as he did upon himself. So did Foreign Ministers and other members of Government with whom he corresponded. Isolation, it seemed, provided that detachment which, accompanied as it was by common sense so massive as to deserve the name of wisdom, justified his manner of control. It is conceivable that, had the ideal Captain of the Fleet become available, Collingwood might have employed his services, but such a paragon did not present himself, and Collingwood carried on alone, until the time came when any other course would have seemed intolerable. The cost was high. It was paid, not ungrudgingly, but with steady acceptance.[1]

Above all else, Collingwood had for years realized and emphasized in his letters home that his country was engaged in a different *kind* of war from anything in the past, a fact which he, Nelson, and a number of others, grasped in the opening phase of the conflict, and when they were together under St. Vincent. If they had found St. Vincent difficult, they had learnt much from him in the way of discipline, and of the need for its application from the top.

'It is not as it was in former wars,' Collingwood wrote to Blackett at the end of the year,[2] 'when France was to be subdued in her colonies. Her Ruler acts on very different principles; his force is collected; he sends no armies to succour or defend colonies; his object is to strike at the heart, and not at the extremities; and he would, I dare say, see with great satisfaction half the troops in England employed, even successfully, in conquering Mexico itself.'

III

The year 1806 had seen one success by British arms at Maida, in Calabria, where Sir John Stuart had beaten the French and proved, in Collingwood's view, 'the superiority of British troops; but as we could not keep an army there, I am afraid the sufferings of the Calabrians will be increased by our having made them take a part against their enemy, which they were not in a condition to maintain.'[3] 1807 was to be a year of increasing

---

[1] For a short time in 1806, until he went home at the end of April, Collingwood had the 'comfort' of Captain Richard Grindall, who had commanded the *Prince* at Trafalgar, and who had since been promoted Rear-Admiral, on board his flagship. Even so, it would seem that Collingwood regarded Grindall more as a companion than as a staff officer. (N.C., Additional letter to Mrs. Grindall; 1837 edition.)

[2] N.C., 256.   [3] N.C., 243.

crisis, but as a New Year's Day letter was not to be made a matter of solemnity, Collingwood gave his family, through Blackett, a glimpse of Bounce. This dog, though he did so much in his canine way to relieve the tedium of Collingwood's life, was by now himself suffering from that boredom inseparable from the life that he and his master led.

Tell the children [wrote Collingwood][1], that Bounce is very well and very fat, yet he seems not to be content, and sighs so piteously these long evenings that I am obliged to sing him to sleep, and have sent them the song:

> Sigh no more, Bouncey, sigh no more,
> Dogs were deceivers never;
> Though ne'er you put one foot on shore,
> True to your master ever.
>
> Then sigh not so, but let us go,
> Where dinner's daily ready,
> Converting all the sounds of woe
> To heigh phiddy diddy.

There was at least one evening in the week when there was no need for Collingwood to sing Bounce to sleep. Thursdays were reserved for matters at once gayer and less private.

This is a queer world we live in [Collingwood wrote to his wife on 22 January],[2] or rather that you live in; for I reckon that I have been out of it for some time past, except the mere ceremony of shaking off mortality, which we do with great facility here. The only thing we have in common with you, are our assemblies, concerts and plays.

We have an exceedingly good company of comedians, some dancers that might exhibit at an opera, and probably have done so at Sadlers Wells, and a band consisting of twelve very fine performers. Every Thursday is a play night, and they act as well as your Newcastle company. A Moorish officer, who was sent to me by . . . the Governor of the province of Tetuan, was carried to the play. The astonish-

---

[1] N.C., 262: Collingwood's little parody was of Balthasar's song: *Much Ado*: II. iii.

[2] N.C., 269-70.

ment which this man expressed at the assembly of people, and their order, was itself a comedy.

When the music began, he was enchanted; but during the acting, he was so transported with delight, that he could not keep his seat. His admiration of the ladies was quite ridiculous; and he is gone to his Prince fully convinced that we carry players to sea for the entertainment of the sailors: for though he could not find the ladies after the entertainment, he is not convinced tnat they are not put up in some snug place till the next play-night.

Collingwood had always encouraged entertainments among the sailors, not least when in command of the *Excellent*, in the same area, nearly ten years before. He had need of every distraction to disengage his attention, at least from time to time, from those intricate problems, not always connected with the management of the Fleet, which crowded upon him.

During the previous autumn Napoleon, after he had soundly beaten the Prussians, who had ventured to declare war on him without first assuring the close support of those best able to help them, at Jena and Auerstädt, issued decrees from Berlin establishing what became known as the 'Continental System'. The British Isles were declared to be blockaded. This invited counter-measures from London in the form of 'Orders in Council' forbidding trade with France. Collingwood was soon inquiring amusedly of Blackett how he liked being blockaded, and from the start the system failed egregiously. It invited wholesale smuggling, which was already a well-established side of life, and it was so ineffective that at one stage French troops were at least partially equipped with items made in England, while delicacies derived from the British colonies were rarely absent from the French Imperial table. It was chiefly the northern countries which suffered. In the Mediterranean, thanks to the security provided by Collingwood's naval dispositions, trade flowed regularly to and from Britain, and continued so to do all through the war years. On the other hand, countries within Napoleon's orbit found it excessively difficult, and often impossible, to conduct any sea-borne trade whatever. On the subject in general, Louis Bonaparte of Holland once remarked that you might just as well try to stop the skin from sweating as to prevent trade.[1] Collingwood came to be persuaded of the truth of this observation when it was necessary for him to try to prevent supplies reaching the Turks.

The need even to consider measures against Turkey, which since Napoleon's invasion of Egypt in 1798 had been benevolently inclined towards Britain, and since 1799 formally allied with her, arose partly from the menacing power of Napoleonic France, and from the Anglo-Russian alliance. Turkey was becoming increasingly hostile towards Russia, which had appropriated the Ionian islands, and her influence in Greece was resented. France had at this time an exceptionally able young ambassador at Constantinople, Horace Sébastiani, at whose instance the Turks not only refused to renew their alliance with Britain, but threatened to prevent Russian ships from passing the Bosphorus.

In December 1806 the Russians, in an act of open war, defeated a Turkish army at Groda, afterwards entering Bucharest. Charles Arbuthnot, who was in charge of Britain's affairs at the Porte, kept Collingwood informed of events, and as soon as Collingwood realized the turn which events had taken, he sent Rear-Admiral Louis, by now a baronet, with three sail of the line, to the danger area. Louis himself proceeded to Constantinople in the *Canopus*, leaving the *Thunderer* and the *Standard* off the Dardanelles. The appearance of this force had such an effect that difficulties were composed, only to start afresh when news arrived of Napoleon's victory at Jena, when Sébastiani indicated the sort of pressure which his master was now likely to apply to the Russians. 'The detaching of the squadron under Sir Thomas Louis,' wrote the First Lord,[2] on receiving word of Collingwood's initial dispositions, 'had in a great measure anticipated the wishes of the King's Government, and . . . the promptitude and judgement with which that step had been taken could not but be highly satisfactory to His Majesty.' It soon became necessary to augment Louis's ships, and to plan measures to occupy Egypt, if the French were to be forestalled. Had the Russian admiral shown even a fraction of the necessary initiative in support of measures taken by an ally on the Tsar's behalf, events would have taken a happier course than they did.

[1] *The Continental System*, E. F. Heckscher (1922) 38. 367.   [2] N.C., 264.

The Admiralty took the unusual though not unprecedented step of nominating Duckworth to reinforce Louis in Turkish waters, without leaving the choice to Collingwood's discretion. They gave as their reason the sound one that the Commander-in-Chief was needed off Cadiz, and there was probably another. Duckworth had 'made interest' in his own cause. He had seen, from Nelson's career, what glory might accrue from detached service in the Mediterranean, and if he were to be spectacularly successful in his mission, any good was within the bounds of possibility. Unfortunately, like Sir Sidney Smith, he could never hold his tongue, and his destination was soon known to the enemy, much to Collingwood's annoyance.

Duckworth had been chagrined not to have joined Nelson in September 1805 as second-in-command,[1] and still more so to have missed Trafalgar narrowly. Collingwood had afforded him his chance on detached duty, and his victory at San Domingo had been creditable to him, but he was hopeful of still better things. He had already held one command-in-chief, that of Jamaica. Another, and at sea, would suit his book. He once told Collingwood all about a difference he had had with the Earl of St. Vincent, but Collingwood must have been bored, or more than usually deaf, or both, for when he tried to tell his sister something about it, the gist had escaped him, as it never did, even in the smallest detail, where he was truly interested.[2]

Collingwood behaved in a generous way to Duckworth, and sent him more ships than the Admiralty themselves suggested, which weakened his own force to such an extent that he would have been blamed if the enemy had made a successful sortie. Yet he would not have it said that he did not give ample backing to a flag-officer on a highly important mission. He also lent Duckworth the services of Sir Sidney Smith, who had had previous experience of dealing with the Turk. No possible ground for failure could be laid at Collingwood's door.

Collingwood had been asked by the Admiralty to leave as much discretion in his orders to Duckworth as possible, a piece of advice which he might well have resented. His instructions could not have been clearer. When the force reached Constantinople, so ran the order:

[1] Nic. vii. 44n.   [2] H., Letter 128: a typical postscript.

. . . should Mr Arbuthnot inform you that it is his opinion that hostilities should commence, having previously taken all possible precautions for the safety of that Minister and the persons attached to his mission, and having disposed the squadron under your orders in such stations as may compel compliance, you are to demand the surrender of the Turkish fleet, together with a supply of naval stores from the arsenal sufficient for its complete equipment, which demand you are to accompany with a menace of immediate destruction to the town.

At this crisis, should any negotiation on the subject be proposed by the Turkish Government, as such proposal will probably be to gain time for preparing their assistance, or securing their ships, I would recommend that no negotiation should be continued for more than half an hour: and in the event of an absolute refusal, you are either to cannonade the town, or attack the fleet, wherever it may be . . .

The force which is appointed for this service is greater than was originally intended, as it was expected that the Russians from Corfu would be ready to co-operate with you: but as its success depends upon the promptitude with which it is executed, I have judged it proper (that no delay may arise from their squadron not joining) to increase your force by two ships. I have, however, written to Admiral Siniavin, to request him to detach four ships, with orders to put themselves under your command; and that you may be possessed of all the force that can be supplied to the important service, and your immediate direction, you are hereby authorized to call from the coast of Sicily whatever can be spared, as well as the despatch-vessels at Malta; but as little more naval force is at Sicily than is absolutely necessary for its defence, and for the convoy which may be wanted for the troops, a strict regard must be had that that island be not left in a weak state of defence.[1]

From the outset, matters went badly. The first misfortune was that the *Ajax*, a ship of the line commanded by Captain Blackwood, once of the *Euryalus*, accidentally caught fire and was destroyed, with the loss of many of her company, 'the

[1] N.C., 266–7.

most dreadful scene I ever witnessed,' wrote Arbuthnot, who
was present in the flagship. Even before Duckworth had
achieved the passage of the Dardanelles, on 19 March, Arbuthnot was giving it as his view:

> As everything has been fully obtained by negotiation from
> the Porte it was in my opinion unjust and unwise of Russia
> to go to war at all. At any rate, if this Empire was to be
> attacked it ought to have been a measure so combined with
> us, that the Porte should not have been put upon her guard
> before we were prepared to act. Had this been done, Turkey
> must necessarily have been completely at our mercy and
> nothing then but the appearance of Bonaparte before Con-
> stantinople could have revived French influence.[1]

Duckworth's squadron had some fighting on their way towards Constantinople, and destroyed a few Turkish vessels.
When the ships anchored, some miles short of the city, envoy
and admiral lost no time in presenting their demands, which
were: acceptance of British mediation in the quarrel with
Russia; renewal by the Porte of the Anglo-Turkish treaty; a
British guarantee of the integrity of the Ottoman Empire; and
the removal of the French ambassador. After some days of
tension, it had become apparent that the Turks did not intend
to negotiate seriously, and on the other hand they were hourly
strengthening the defences of their capital. Arbuthnot fell ill
with rheumatic fever, and Duckworth, with no military force
to exploit any success which he might have had as the result of
a bombardment, was forced to return, having achieved nothing
but the destruction of some ships of war in the Sea of Marmora.

Even before he knew the result of the expedition, Collingwood was writing to his very old friend Alexander Ball, then
in charge at Malta, with what proved to be exceptional perspicacity:

> We are identifying ourselves at Constantinople with the
> Russians; an excess of friendship that I do not think they
> are disposed to show to us. If they have beaten or effectually
> resisted the French armies, as it is said they have, Buona-
> parte will cajole the Emperor Alexander, and make peace

---

[1] Add. MSS. 40098, f. 114.

with him upon any terms that relate to the Continent; for anarchy and impotence are sufficiently established there for all his purposes. They will then dispose of Turkey as they please, and the Russian squadron may find a welcome reception in Brest before the year has expired. I may be thought to hold the Russian friendship light; indeed I do not, but I believe that if Buonaparte can convince Russia that her interest goes another way than ours, her friendship will soon follow.[1]

Collingwood summed the whole sad matter up in a letter to Lord Radstock written on 13 April:[2]

The attempt at Constantinople has not succeeded at all; and yet, as far as depended on me, we were well prepared. Sir John Duckworth, you will have heard, passed the Dardanelles, and burned the ships which lay above them. The squadron stopped at Prince's Island; the winds, the currents, and every thing, being unfavourable for their getting up to the town. The ten days they were there were spent in an attempt, by negotiation, to prevent the war, and detach the Turks from the French.

On our part it was faithful; on theirs, it was an expedient to gain time, until their defences were completed, and their fleet secured in the Bosphorus. When they had fully accomplished this, they dropped all further intercourse, and the squadron returned.

Constantinople appears to be more difficult to attack than has generally been thought: the strong current from the Black Sea prevents access to it with a light wind; and then between it and Scutari, both sides of which are well fortified, it is like going into Portsmouth harbour. The French have established their interest completely; or rather, the Russians did that for them, by their premature attack on the Turkish territory. How they are to profit by it, I am not politician enough to discover; but we have increased the number of our enemies most unfortunately. I say so because I believe the Turks esteem the English nation as much as they detest the Russian.

[1] N.C., 277.   [2] N.C., 284, 285.

Duckworth retreated only just in time. His return passage through the Dardanelles was opposed, and he suffered more than double the number of casualties that he had sustained on his way up.

Whatever his private feelings about his subordinate, Collingwood confined his criticism to the letter to his sister in which he told her of Duckworth's loquacity, charging her that 'what I say . . . is to you alone, and must not go out of the walls of your house'.[1] In public, even to a correspondent so little known to him personally as the Duke of Northumberland, Collingwood wrote:[2]

> I assure your Grace I have suffered much uneasiness on Sir Jn Duckworth's account, who is an able and zealous officer. That all was not performed which was expected is attributable to difficulties which could not be surmounted, and if they baffled his skill, I do not know where to look for the officer to whom they would have yielded.

Collingwood could not have been more loyal to a brother officer, however much he may have mistrusted his ambition.

IV

Duckworth's abortive mission was not the only failure of the time, in areas far distant from the home country. In South Africa two officers who had been jointly successful in recapturing the Cape of Good Hope, which had been relinquished at the Peace of Amiens, decided on their own initiative to cross the Atlantic and mount an attack on the Spaniards at Buenos Ayres. After an initial success, the town was recaptured by local forces, and the general, William Beresford, taken prisoner. This unauthorized operation affected Collingwood because the naval officer concerned, Sir Home Popham, was exposed to attack from any French or Spanish squadron which might elude the watch on the western ports. There were also indications of a Franco-Spanish move into the Mediterranean, possibly with the aim of an attack on Sicily, and certainly with the idea of a menacing concentration at Toulon, where new ships were making ready.

[1] H., Letter 128.   [2] H., Letter 138.

There were cardinal difficulties in the watch both on the Atlantic ports and on Toulon. Under Napoleon, the French had established a swift and efficient system of coastal signals which helped in the co-ordination of ship movements or attempts at such, while Collingwood never put the problem of Toulon more succinctly than in a letter to the First Lord written from off Cadiz on 27 February:[1]

I am told their Lordships are very anxious that the Port of Toulon should be blockaded; and could it be done without reducing the force which is absolutely necessary in other quarters, it would be very desirable. I have hitherto considered Sicily, the Adriatic and Egypt, to be more securely covered and protected from the Navy of the enemy, by a well-appointed squadron on the coast of Sicily, than if that squadron were off Toulon. Seldom a fortnight will pass without an opportunity offering for them to escape even the most vigilant watch, particularly in the winter.

Experience has shewn that they have always done it; and if I remember rightly the letter which Admiral Richery wrote to the Directory, he assigns as the reason for his not having sailed, the doubt which he had of the position of the English fleet; but he adds, 'they have now come in view: I have seen from the hills the direction in which they are, and will sail tonight.'

The geographical situation of Toulon, with high ground behind the port from which movements could be observed far out to sea, gave the French every advantage. It was to the interest of the British to keep as far as possible out of sight with their main body, a practice which Nelson had adopted on his long watch, and which Collingwood followed. Nelson always made the point that Toulon was never truly blockaded, and that this indeed was the last thing he wanted, since he hoped the French would be tempted to sea, where he could beat them. Neither he nor Collingwood at any time feared battle; what kept them on the stretch was to guess where the French might go, once they had put to sea and driven off the shadowing frigates. Then their problem was to discover the true object of

[1] N.C., 274.

VII. The *Santissima Trinidada* dismasted after Trafalgar.
Collingwood attacked this ship off St. Vincent in 1797; she was captured at Trafalgar but afterwards foundered. An unknown artist shows her flying the white ensign above the flag of Spain. *Collection of Mr. H. Sjögren, Stockholm*

VIII. Admiral Sir John Duckworth, by Sir William Beechey. Duckworth served under Collingwood in the Atlantic and Mediterranean theatres of war. He wears the Star of the Bath and gold medals for the Glorious First of June, and for San Domingo, 1806. *National Maritime Museum, Greenwich Hospital Collection.*

the enemy, and to dispose themselves in the likeliest area to meet them.

By the summer of 1807 Collingwood told Blackett that he was worn to a thread. 'I am so in health—not ill. My labour is unceasing, and my vexations many; but I cannot help them. My eyes are weak, my body swollen, and my legs shrunk to tapers; but they serve my turn, for I have not much walking. I hardly ever see the face of an officer, except when they dine with me, and am seldom on deck above an hour in the day, when I go in the twilight to breathe the fresh air.[1]

On 1 July Collingwood wrote to Mrs. Stead[2] telling her of his dread of an education of a 'fine lady' for his daughters, 'Filling their poor little heads with Tiffany and Gew Gaws, and neglecting the happy impulses of nature which might be cultivated with ease and profit. To force upon them that which is repugnant to their nature 'tis like teaching a rook to sing, or Bounce to play upon the fiddle—long labour lost—for though Bounce is a dog of talents, I suspect he wou'd make but a discordant fiddler.'

My days [he continued], are days of constant labour, and with such a compound of subjects that really my head is sometimes giddy with them. The only thing I have like pleasure is the consciousness that I have spared nothing to execute my trust faithfully, and the first joy I shall feel will be when I am relieved from it. I am now going on a service that I doubt the practicability of, but without having difficulties to surmount the mind would soften to effeminacy.

Weak as he might be on his legs, and feeling in every other respect like a rapidly ageing man, Collingwood's mind still retained its fine edge, and he was even capable of curious asides in otherwise sober letters home, as when he wrote to John Davidson, who was managing his colliery business at Chirton, to tell him, apropos of affairs in Egypt, the method employed by the Bedouin Arabs in taking prisoners. 'They are well mounted,' he wrote, 'gallop in upon those they would surprise, and hooking them with a hook rope, tow them off at full speed; if they fall they are killed by the hook. They carried off two

---

[1] N.C., 287–8. [2] H., Letter 133.

officers of Marines and some sailors who were employed water-
ing and a woman who, poor body, was gone to the stream to
wash her smock. The day after she was found: she had lost her
head; did not tow well I suppose.'[1]

The 'service' which Collingwood mentioned to Mrs. Stead was
to take him to Malta and to the Dardanelles, a respite from the
incessant cruising which had occupied him since Trafalgar. The
news from Continental Europe was momentous, though not
very different from what he himself had long expected. The
Emperors of France and Russia, who had met at Tilsit, had
decided to parcel the world between them. Napoleon hoped to
induce the Tsar to take an effective part in his 'Continental
System', and, with a friendly east assured, he intended to turn
his attention to Portugal, which had so far held out against his
embargo on trade with Britain, and also obtain more complete
control of Spain. As a maritime and colonial Power Spain would,
so he was convinced, be useful to him to a far greater extent
heretofore in the war against Britain, that most obdurate
enemy.

Collingwood's own immediate object was to ensure that as
little benefit should come to France through the assistance of
Turkey, even if he could not induce her, any better than
Arbuthnot and Duckworth had done, to become once again an
open friend. To forestall any possible moves from France, he
had already sent an able officer to Egypt—Benjamin Hallowell,
one of the stalwarts of the Battle of the Nile, a captain held in
the highest esteem by both Nelson and Collingwood.[2] Had the
military force under General Fraser which went with Hallowell
confined itself to objects within the attainment of a force of
some 4,000 men, all might have been well. But expeditions were
undertaken with insufficient knowledge of the difficulties, and
a series of reverses resulted which were as humiliating as they
were unnecessary. Fraser re-embarked, having achieved nothing, though the Navy was able to continue to exercise control
in Egyptian waters. 'There are seasons,' wrote Collingwood
sagaciously to Hallowell, 'when a dilatory war is most expedient,
and it seems in this instance that the defence of Alexandria,
and entering into amicable engagements with the natives, who

[1] H., Letter 129.
[2] He replaced Admiral Louis, who died at sea on 17 May 1807.

have suffered from the oppression of the Turks, was all the small army was equal to.'[1]

Collingwood was at Malta in July 1807 and was off the Dardanelles during August. There he smoked a pipe and took coffee and sherbet with a Turkish representative, but he soon decided that his talks would get him nowhere: Sébastiani had done his work too well, and with Russia and France in amity, it was to Turkish interest to do nothing which might annoy these powerful countries. Collingwood also found that control of traffic through the Dardanelles would have no appreciable effect on the city of Constantinople. He wrote to Lord Mulgrave on 19 August, from Turkish waters:[2]

It was hoped that by a rigorous blockade the capital would be reduced to a state of want, as would urge them to a speedy treaty; but, by the best information which I can get here, the supply of Constantinople depends very little on the navigation of the Dardanelles; and indeed, it would appear that it ought not to do so even in times of profound peace, as the strong N.E. winds which prevail during the summer months, and strong current which runs out, as effectually prevent vessels from entering any blockade. The supplies are said to go by caravans to Gallipoli or other shipping places on the Sea of Marmora, and it is the Greek islanders who suffer most from the interruption of trade. Those islands draw most of their supplies of corn from the Continent; so that there appears little reason to expect that an insurrection in the Capital from scarcity will urge them to treat; and there is not the smallest attempt made by vessels of any kind to enter the Straits.

During the autumn and early winter, Collingwood was off Toulon. His ships were badly buffeted by Gulf of Lions gales, and suffered so much strain that on 6 December the admiral put in to Syracuse to re-fit. He was well entertained, and he even made time to visit the so-called Ear of Dionysius, a cavern celebrated for its echoes and reverberations. Two days before Christmas, he was suddenly called away with the news that the French were out. On 26 December, 'from the Sea' he wrote to

---

[1] Add. MSS. 37425, f. 79. [2] N.C., 296.

his children, in answer to one of their increasingly frequent letters:[1]

I am now . . . looking for some Frenchmen whom I have heard of; but I was lately at Syracuse, in Sicily. It was once a place of great note, where all the magnificence and arts known in the world flourished: but it was governed by tyrants; and a city which was twenty-two miles in circumference, is now inconsiderable.

Its inhabitants have great natural civility; I never was treated with so much in my life. The Nobility, who live far from the Court, are not contaminated by its vices: they are more truly polite, with less ostentation and show. On my arrival there, the Nobility and Senate waited on me in my ship. Another day came all the military; the next, the Vicar-General, for the Bishop was absent, and all the clergy. I had a levee of thirty priests—all fat, portly-looking gentlemen. In short, nothing was wanting to shew their great respect and regard for the English.

The nobles gave me and the officers of the fleet a ball and supper, the most elegant thing I ever saw, and the best conducted. The ladies were as attentive to us as their lords, and there were two or three little Marquisinas who were most delightful creatures. I have heard men talk of the *dieux de la dance*, but no goddesses ever moved with the grace that distinguished the sisters of the Baron Bono.—God bless you! my dear girls.

[1] N.C., 328-9.

10 *Wild Goose Chase*

Nelson once at least referred to his ships of the line as his 'wild geese', and in the early months of the year 1808 there occurred a wild goose chase such as illustrated the difficulties inherent in sail warfare. These were emphasized because by this time the British, by their dominance of the Mediterranean sea-routes, had driven unconvoyed shipping, from which information could often be obtained, from the area. An enemy design came to nothing, but it might well have led to Collingwood's fourth fleet action, and to his first in chief command. It certainly gave him the chance to explain to his captains the way in which he intended to fight a battle, and it was characteristic that this was done in the form of a memorandum, without that additional and personal explanation which so invigorated admirals and captains on the eve of Trafalgar. The circumstances were totally different from those before Cadiz in 1805; nevertheless, had there been similarities, it is doubtful whether Collingwood would have expatiated so fully and thoroughly as Nelson about the tactics he intended to employ. It was not his way. He was much nearer to Howe than to Nelson in his attitude to his subordinates, but he drew upon his personal experience of both these great officers.

In his customary New Year letter to Blackett, written on this occasion from 'off Cephalonia', Collingwood told his father-in-law that his visit to Syracuse had been cut short by 'an express from the Sicilian Minister, to inform me that the French were at sea'.[1] The news was premature, but it showed that, though French intrigue was rife at Palermo, this did not prevent information of vital consequence being passed on to Collingwood. Although it was only a rumour, it had some basis in

[1] N.C., 332.

fact. Napoleon was planning an attack on Sicily, which he later altered to an expedition to replenish Corfu, which the Russians had by then agreed should fall within the French sphere of influence.

Collingwood soon had a message saying that the news of the French being at sea was false, and he returned to Syracuse, whence, on 11 January, he wrote to the First Lord:[1]

On a report of the French squadron having put to sea, I sailed from hence, with a view to intercept them in their way to the Adriatic, whither I had no doubt they were going. The information was founded in a mistake; and on my return I was relieved from much anxiety by the receipt of their Lordships' order to act against the Russians.

Mr. Adair, at Vienna, had prepared me for such an event; but a subject of such importance required that the necessity of acting hostilely should be most clearly ascertained.

The Russian ships sailed from Corfu on the 26th last, when they were probably informed of the war; yet they passed our squadron without showing the least disposition to annoy them, though there was only the *Standard* with two frigates. I now propose to proceed into the Adriatic; and if I find them in any situation where they may be assailed, I shall be glad of it. Your Lordship may trust I will spare no pains to get at them.

The state of Sicily is becoming exceedingly critical. The French are marching a large body of forces into the south of Calabria, which have already approached so near to Scylla as to skirmish with the Massi quartered near it. I think it probable that a great effort will be made against this island, when I believe the principal, perhaps the only resistance, will be by the British forces.

The want of frigates on the coast, to bring and convey intelligence to all quarters, is very great; and I entreat your Lordship to reinforce me with ships of that class. I should be glad that Captain Hoste, of the *Amphion*, should come, for he is active, vigilant, and knows the coast; and more depends upon the man than the ship.

William Hoste was perhaps Nelson's most brilliant pupil. He

[1] N.C., 334–5.

was on his way, and he later made himself master of the
Adriatic. It was one more instance of where Nelson and Collingwood thought alike in their assessment of an officer, and one
more instance of where that same officer made a name under
both admirals.

Napoleon's original orders, as for the campaign which resulted
in Trafalgar, were for various blockaded squadrons to escape
and unite. This time, they were to embark troops from Joseph's
army at Naples, secure the Strait of Messina, across which the
Sicilians and British had lodgements at Reggio and Scylla, and
invade Sicily, which the Emperor was confident would fall without much resistance. As usual, he took little account of possible
British movements at sea, which he deemed the province of his
admirals. Brest, Rochefort, Cadiz, and Toulon all held ships
ready for the projected expedition, but at Brest and Cadiz the
respective admirals saw little hope of evading the watch: nor
did they do so.

On 17 January 1808, Admiral Allemand, always an enterprising officer, found Rochefort uncovered. He put to sea with five
sail of the line, chased off the British cruisers, and steered for
Gibraltar. Instantly Ganteaume was ordered to hoist his flag
at Toulon, and to prepare to sail when Allemand joined him.
On 24 January the Emperor sent detailed instructions for the
Sicilian expedition to Joseph, but within a week he had changed
his mind. Ganteaume should proceed to Corfu with three transports, and deliver artillery, ammunition, and troops to the
island. Joseph was told to press the preparations for the assault
on Sicily by a movement in Calabria, as if no change had been
made in the original plan. General Reynier did so with such
energy as to make the fall of the lightly-held defensive main-
land positions almost inevitable. Whatever the French Emperor's immediate intentions, Collingwood had been right to see
a continuing threat to Sicily.

One of the reasons for Napoleon's change of plan was that
he feared a British attack on Corfu, which he regarded as an
invaluable base and harbour for any future eastern enterprise,
such as was never altogether absent from his mind. One of the
best ways to defend it was to menace Sicily. The garrison at
Reggio actually capitulated to Reynier without a struggle, adding nine guns to the enemy train. The capture of some gunboats

a few days earlier had already made it certain that the British garrison at Scylla would have to face a formidable bombardment. The troops held out, creditably enough, until mid-February, when they were withdrawn across the Strait by the Navy at the cost of a single seaman killed and ten wounded. But as Joseph had no navy to speak of, and as Collingwood had ordered the 74-gun *Montagu* to Messina with four cruisers, there was no hope of the French making a successful crossing to Sicily unless Ganteaume defeated the British at sea. Nothing would have pleased and relieved Collingwood and his captains better than any attempt on his part to do so. It was what they had been waiting for, ever since Trafalgar.

Collingwood had the first firm news that the Rochefort ships were at sea on 7 February, when the *Surinam*, sloop of war, sailed into Syracuse with a message from Purvis. The reason for their escape was that Sir Richard Strachan had left his station to provision. On 23 January he learnt from one of his frigates that Allemand was at sea, and although bad weather held him up, he joined Purvis with seven of the line on 9 February. Purvis had reason to believe that the French were by that time inside the Mediterranean, and Strachan followed the trail, joining a force under Thornbrough off Palermo on 21 February, and considerably strengthening Collingwood's resources. The Commander-in-Chief concentrated his fleet off Marittimo, just to the west of Sicily, leaving a single 74 at Syracuse in case the ships off Corfu should be driven from their station and require support. When his concentration had been made, on 2 March, Collingwood had fifteen ships of the line with which to engage the enemy. Thornbrough told him he had had news that the Toulon ships were at sea. In fact, Allemand and Ganteaume had joined forces by 10 February, though Collingwood did not learn this until much later. In any case, he was ready for anything, or so he believed.

In fact, the French were already to the east of Sicily. Ganteaume had put to sea on 10 February to find Allemand, who had passed Gibraltar in darkness and storm, waiting for him inshore. Captain Fellowes of the *Apollo*, who had been watching Toulon, had been blown off the port by the gales, though not before he had made certain that the French were about to sail. Ganteaume's combined force was made up of ten ships of the line, of which two were larger than anything in Collingwood's fleet, and none of less than 80 guns.

Once at sea, little had gone right for Ganteaume. Almost at once, his ships were scattered by the heavy weather, and Rear-Admiral Cosmao, a survivor of Trafalgar, saw only one sail in sight on the morning of the 11th. This turned out to be the *Génois*. Two days later he fell in with the *Annibal*, standing by a rudderless transport. After three attempts to tow, Cosmao ran before the wind to the shelter of the African coast. Of the three transports loaded for Corfu, one never left Toulon, a second was now crippled and abandoned, and only the *Var* remained.

Sighting Cape Bon on 15 February, Cosmao ran down the African coast, keeping well clear of Malta, and reached the appointed rendezvous at the mouth of the Adriatic on the 19th, where he came upon another ship of the line and two sloops. Two days later the *Var* joined up. Cosmao now had a respectable force, quite enough to drive off the *Standard* and any cruisers watching Corfu. But his orders forbade him to approach the island independently, and he knew that his ships had been sighted as they skirted the Barbary coast. He feared to wait long in the open sea, and after three days summoned a conference of his captains. Their advice was to seek safety at Taranto. By the 25th the squadron lay under the batteries of the port.

A few days later, when Ganteaume searched the rendezvous, he found no trace of his subordinate. He himself had gone straight to Corfu, where he could repair his flagship, which had been dismasted. Cosmao, after appealing for orders to Joseph, who could not give him any, took the resolution, on 8 March, to weigh for Corfu, where he arrived on the 12th. Next day, Ganteaume returned to the island, his fleet at last reunited.

On 6 March, while cruising west of Sicily, Collingwood had belated news, by way of the *Standard*, that she had been chased by four unknown ships at the mouth of the Adriatic, first on 17 February and again three days later. Captain Harvey thought they might have been Russians from Trieste, but in the light of information which he had had from the *Ambuscade* that a French force had passed Pantelleria on 15 February, Collingwood's own belief was that the ships belonged to Ganteaume's force, as indeed they did. Yet if this was so, six French ships of the line were as yet unaccounted for, and so unlikely did it seem that Ganteaume would bring his whole force to the eastward, only to divide it, that Collingwood concluded that only four of the line had passed Pantelleria.

Preparations were being made at Naples to receive a fleet, and from Tunis came a report that there was a French squadron at Elba. The naval threat to Sicily thus seemed to be a double one, from both Naples and the Adriatic. Leaving a force at Palermo, Collingwood sailed to search the bay of Naples. There were no French ships there, but word was had that an enemy squadron was at Taranto, preparing to invade Sicily. Collingwood rounded the west of the island to reconnoitre, putting into Syracuse later. There at last, on 21 March, Collingwood at last had news that both the enemy squadrons were to the eastward. Harvey had reported that a three-decker had joined the enemy, and Collingwood guessed that this was Allemand's flagship from Rochefort. Battle now seemed certain.

So certain, that on 23 March Collingwood issued the tactical memorandum to his captains which described how he intended to engage the French. As his ships proceeded towards the Adriatic, keeping near the coastline of Italy, which was the course most likely to intercept a fleet of small transports, his subordinates had time to consider how this experienced man proposed to act in the clash which everyone expected.

II

The memorandum, or 'General Order', ran as follows:[1]

From every account received of the enemy, it is expected they may very soon be met with, in their way from Corfu and Tarentum, and success depends on a prompt and immediate attack on them. In order to which it will be necessary, that the greatest care be taken to keep the closest order in the respective columns during the night, which the state of the weather will allow, and that the columns be kept at such a sufficient distance apart, as will leave room for tacking or other movements; so that, in the event of calm or shift of wind, no embarrassment may be caused.

[1] N.C., 359–62.

Should the enemy be found formed in order of battle with his whole force, I shall, notwithstanding, probably not make the signal to form the line of battle; but, keeping the closest order, with the van squadron attack the van of the enemy, while the Commander of the lee division takes the proper measures, and makes to the ships of his division the necessary signals for commencing the action with the enemy's rear, as nearly as possible at the same time that the van begins: of his signals, therefore, the Captains of that division will be particularly watchful.

If the squadron has run to leeward to close with the enemy, the signal will be made to alter the course together; the van division keeping a point or two more away than the lee, the latter carrying less sail; and when the fleet draws near the enemy, both columns are to preserve a line as nearly parallel to the hostile fleet as they can.

In standing up to the enemy from the leeward upon a contrary tack, the lee line is to press sail, so that the leading ship of that line may be two or three points before the beam of the leading ship of the weather line, which will bring them to action nearly at the same period.

The leading ship of the weather column will endeavour to pass through the enemy's line, should the weather be such as to make that practicable, at one-fourth from the van, whatever number of ships their line may be composed of. The lee division will pass through at a ship or two astern of their centre; and whenever a ship has weathered the enemy, it will be found necessary to shorten sail as much as possible, for the second astern to close with her, and to keep away, steering in a line parallel to the enemy's, and engaging them on their weather side.

A movement of this kind may be necessary; but, considering the difficulty of altering the position of the fleet during the time of combat, every endeavour will be made to commence battle with the enemy on the same tack they are; and I have only to recommend and direct, that they be fought with at the nearest distance possible, in which getting on board of them may be avoided, which is always disadvantageous to us, except when they are flying.

The enemy will probably have a convoy of ships carrying

troops which must be disabled by the frigates, or whatever ships are not engaged, or whose signals may be made to attack the convoy, by cutting their masts away, and rendering them incapable of escaping during the contest with their fleet.

In fine weather the watch are to bring their hammocks on deck with them in the night, which are to be stowed in the nettings; so that on any sudden discovery of the enemy, they will have only to attend to the duty on deck, while the watch below clear the ship for action.

If any ship be observed by her second ahead to drop astern during the night to a greater distance than her station is, she is to notify it by shewing two lights, one over the other, lowered down the stern, so that it may not be seen by ships ahead; and should a ship not be able to keep her station, those astern of her are to pass her and occupy the place she should have been in.

A certain amount of misguided comment has been made on this well-known memorandum, arising from the fact that critics have attempted to discern some principle which Collingwood never intended to convey. His words referred to an attack designed for a particular occasion, and to suit a limited number of ships. If Collingwood met Ganteaume, as he hoped, he would have with him eleven or twelve sail of the line, hardly more, allowing for his detachments. If Ganteaume's force were concentrated, the enemy would have ten, but as they were powerful ships, Collingwood would have no nominal margin of strength. That did not matter, such was his confidence in the capabilities of the ships he had. He fully expected to annihilate the enemy.

In printing the memorandum, Newnham Collingwood had the good sense to consult some unnamed expert, who provided the following gloss:[1]

In the battle of Trafalgar Lord Collingwood's ship broke the enemy's line, without having sustained much damage during her approach; but Lord Nelson's ship, and many others in both squadrons, while running down, were greatly injured by the raking fire of the Combined Fleet. The Order is inserted ... to shew how Lord Collingwood proposed to guard against

[1] N.C., 359.

this, by making his ships, as they should draw near the enemy, keep a line as nearly parallel to the hostile fleet as they could, and by preserving, at the same time, that celerity of attack which the order of sailing in two columns presents.

That puts the matter well. Collingwood intended to have the benefit of using two manageable lines, and his purpose was to break through the enemy formation in the manner that Howe had wished all his captains to do in June 1794. The chief curiosity of the memorandum is that Collingwood seemed to envisage a much longer line than Ganteaume was likely to possess, but he was influenced by the knowledge that Russian and possibly even Turkish ships might be joined with the French to oppose him, a new sort of Combined Fleet, though not one to daunt him.[1]

Although the memorandum became a standing instruction in the Mediterranean command, Collingwood made amendments to it in the light of a possible increase in the force under his immediate command. Captain Hallowell's copy of an Order of Battle dated 12 December 1808 is preserved[2] in which as many as thirty ships of the line are provided for. To this Order of Battle are appended the following 'Observations'; they are in Cosway's writing, but are signed by the admiral:

> The respective Flag Officers will have the immediate direction of the Division in which their ships are placed, subject to the general direction of the Admiral commanding the squadron to which they belong.
>
> The ships in order of Battle and Sailing are to keep at the distance of two cables length from and in the wake of each other, increasing that distance according to the state of the weather; the leading ship of the starboard division is to keep the Admiral two points on her weather bow. The leading ship of the lee division is, when sailing on a wind, to keep the leader of the weather column, two points before her Beam, and when sailing large abreast of her.

Later still, on 4 January 1810, Collingwood made a further amendment:[2]

---

[1] Letter to Lord Castlereagh: N.C. 350.   [2] Add. MSS. 37405, f. 90.
[2] Add. MSS. 37405, f. 95.

When the signal No. 43 or 44 is made to form the Order of Battle the Fleet is to be formed in one line. If such signal should not be made, the Captains are referred to the General Order of 23rd March 1808.

This served to show that, with a large fleet, Collingwood was prepared to revert to the tactics of the Glorious First of June, if the particular conditions which had given rise to his memorandum of March 1808 did not apply when the enemy was actually encountered.

Collingwood was so careful to guard against straggling that, in this final instruction, he strengthened the clause applying to ships which got out of station.

The Captains are to be kept particularly careful that the Ships are kept in as close order as the state of the weather makes proper, particularly in the night time. If any ship drops astern from inattention and want of making sail in time, the ship stationed next is to pass her, and it is to be noted in the log book when such circumstance happens, and the name of the Lieutenant who had charge of the watch in such tardy ship.

When he drafted this instruction, from the *Ville de Paris*, his last flagship, Collingwood was visibly sinking, and had weeks, rather than months, to live. Yet there is no sign of any failure in elasticity of thought, and had he ever met the enemy again at sea, no one can doubt that the result would have been as decisive as in any naval battle ever fought. In his care for detail, he had not lost sight of the reason *why* his ships were at sea.

III

Armed with knowledge of their leader's intentions, the force off Italy sailed on. At Cape Rizzuto, near the mouth of the Gulf of Taranto, Collingwood had news, on 28 March, from the *Unité*, that a French squadron of eight or nine sail of the line had left Corfu with an easterly wind. Collingwood had the impression that they had gone to Taranto to join the expedition preparing there, and that they were now inside the Gulf at his mercy.

Many captains must have believed that a glorious day was before them, and the long search ended.

Yet even before he closed with the land, Collingwood was distracted by having to provide against another threat. The day before the *Unité* reported, he had had very belated word, via Purvis, that the Spanish squadron from Cartagena, six of the line, had sailed on 11 February for Majorca. In the intervening weeks they might well have gone to Naples and renewed a threat to Sicily. Collingwood strengthened his force at Palermo, and sent in his cruisers to look for the French. They found nothing.

Ganteaume had had no intention of allowing his squadron to be trapped and exposed to destruction for the sake of adding Sicily to Joseph's Neapolitan kingdom. On learning of the British concentration, he left the *Var* to discharge her cargo at Corfu, and sailed for France. His course brought him close to the British fleet, but he was never sighted, and by 10 April, after an escapade of two months, he was back at Toulon. When Collingwood reconnoitred the Balearics in mid-April, he found the Spaniards at Port Mahon, apparently unready for sea, and so the pattern of sea power in the Mediterranean re-asserted itself, as if it had never been disturbed.[1]

Collingwood told his wife, in the course of his vain chase:[2]

I am just now cruising with my fleet off Maritimo, and intend continuing here until I get information to lead me to the French, which I expect very soon, and then hope that God will bless me. Our Country requires that great exertions should be made to maintain its independence and its glory. You know, when I am in earnest on any subject, how truly I devote myself to it; and the first object of my life, and what my heart is most bent on, (I hope you will excuse me,) is the glory of my Country. To stand a barrier between the ambition of France and the independence of England, is the first wish of my life; and in my death, I would rather that my body, if it were possible, should be added to the rampart, than trailed in useless pomp through an idle throng.

[1] The most detailed study of Ganteaume's cruise is in *The War in the Mediterranean 1803–1810*: Piers Mackesy (1957): Ch. 9 and Appendices V, VI, which show earlier criticism of Collingwood's dispositions to have been misleading.

[2] N.C., 348–9.

. . . I have now as large a fleet as was ever employed from England, consisting of thirty sail of the line[1] and eighty ships of war of different sorts. You may easily conceive, that in the common occurrences of such a fleet, I have not much time to amuse myself. I have been rather unfortunate lately in not catching a small squadron of the enemy; but it was chance. I went to Corfu in January: the hard gales disabled my ships, and I found that, by continuing there, I should have no fleet when better weather came. A month after I left them, the enemy appeared there. Where they came from, is not well ascertained; but I hope, before it is long, we shall know a great deal more about them.

Even with all ships at his disposal, there were never enough frigates and scouts, nor were those that Collingwood had always in the right place. After all was over, he wrote to Purvis, on 24 April, from off Sicily:[2]

Ever since the 23rd Feb'y I have been in pursuit of the French squadron, and perhaps more than once have been near them, but until they are actually in sight there is no reckoning on them, not the least intelligence is to be obtained at sea for there is nothing on it but ourselves, and whatever accounts come from the land seem to be framed for deception. I went up to Corfu, where I knew they were, and found they were gone just before our arrival, pursued them to Minorca, where it was said they were to join the Spaniards, the Spaniards were there without them, and being apprehensive that they would return upon this island after having led us off, I returned to the rendez vous which I had appointed for all the frigates and vessels with despatches, and here I have been three days without having found one of them. I cannot conceive any thing more absurd than their having quitted this station, where alone they were directed to find me, all the despatches from England, which came from England a month since, are running about the sea every where but where I am.

The pursuit added years to a man already prematurely old.

[1] Collingwood was including his detached ships, and the squadron under Purvis off Cadiz.
[2] H., Letter 156.

IX. Collingwood in 1807, by Giuseppe Polite Sorcevani.
The last portrait from life, painted at Syracuse. *Collection of*
Mr. H. T. Simpson.

96

Ville de Paris Sunday 18th —

Dear Sir

I return you the Pamphlets and am much obliged to you for them — Mr Miles is a very good writer — and gives good advice — he thinks well of himself — and certainly has much knowledge of circumstances which have lead to unfortunate results — but politicks are so intricate in their nature, that they are much easier to discuss after events, than before them — If Mr Miles had an antidote for the prevailing Views of the age — and could make men reason independent of personal interest — he would restore Vigour to the Nation — and in making us good — would make us great — do you think he can do that? — I hope you keep well in health — and am Dear Sir your most faithfull serv

Capt Hallowell Tigre — Collingwood —

X. Letter from Collingwood to Captain Benjamin Hallowell.
Written on 18 April 1809 and referring to the work of W. A. Miles
(1753–1817), political writer. *British Museum* (Add. MSS.
37,425 f. 96).

Collingwood had had his portrait done in Syracuse, and sent it home to his sisters. Writing to them on 26 July[1] he added one of his postscripts two days later:

I wonder you did not think my picture like. Every body here thought it well done, and, for myself, I thought I saw myself in a glass. The painter was reckoned the best at Syracuse. Fashion on shore changes; mine does not, and my stock is worn as it used to be and the lumps under my chin is the slack skin that pulls down from age. I cannot always be young; in truth I am very old and feel it, in the weakness of my body.

Summing it all up to his wife, in the full tide of disappointment, Collingwood told her:[2] 'The only satisfaction that I have is, that they have done nothing, for when they found there was a probability of being overtaken, they quitted the place immediately . . . It has made me almost crazy, and if I had not a very good constitution, would have worn me quite out; for I know that in England success is the only criterion by which people judge, and to want that is always reckoned a great crime.'

[1] H., Letter 160.   [2] N.C., 355.

11 *Final Years*

Sicily being once again as secure as the Navy could make it, Collingwood could give more of his attention to that part of his command which lay beyond the Strait of Gibraltar. Change was taking place in the affairs of the Iberian peninsula, though at first more in the political than the naval sphere.

Writing to Lord Castlereagh from off Cadiz on 17 June[1] Collingwood informed him that, as was his way, he had stationed himself where he could make best use of any circumstances that might arise to the advantage of his country:

> Your lordship will probably have been informed [he stated], by my letters to the Admiralty, that on receiving intelligence from Sir Hew Dalrymple, when off Toulon, of the critical state of affairs in Spain, I left the squadron there under the orders of Vice Admiral Thornborough, on the 1st June, and repaired to this point of my station, where I arrived on the 11th.

Events were now taking place which were the result of moves made some months earlier, and General Dalrymple, who had been in command of the garrison at Gibraltar since 1806 had, both as a public servant and as a very old friend of Collingwood, kept the admiral fully informed of what was in train.

Napoleon's activities had begun in October 1807. He signed a treaty with Spain by which it was agreed that a joint attack should be made on Portugal, which was to be divided, part to go to Godoy, favourite of the Spanish Queen. One result of this arrangement was that the Portuguese Regent, and the nation's fleet, sailed for the safety of Brazil, protected by the British Navy. Napoleon then stirred up Prince Ferdinand against his

[1] N.C., 377.

father, King Charles IV, and, partly for the purpose of attack-
ing Portugal, partly to protect Ferdinand, sent an army into
Spain. Riots thereupon broke out in Madrid, and the king
abdicated in favour of his son. Charles soon repented, and both
he and Ferdinand appealed to Napoleon. The Emperor met the
pair at Bayonne, on French territory, and forced them both to
renounce the throne, making them prisoner. The Spanish people
rose in indignation, and when Napoleon put his own brother
Joseph on the Spanish throne (which was linked historically
with that of Naples, which Joseph already occupied)[1] he aroused
such feeling as to produce the 'Spanish ulcer' which did so much
to bring about the downfall of the French Empire.

In whatever contempt Napoleon held the power and resources
of Spain, by his interference in her internal affairs, insufferable
to a proud people, he had given Great Britain the opportunity
to offer help in what became a war for Spanish and Portuguese
independence. He also relieved the Royal Navy of the considerable burden of watching Cadiz and Cartagena, and provided it with a source of refreshment at Minorca, which so often
during the eighteenth century had been in British hands.

Although he had failed to advance his country's interests in
the eastern Mediterranean, through no fault of his own, Collingwood was now able to take an active part in encouraging Spain,
a chance which he seized at once. Owing to his personal prestige,
and to his chivalrous behaviour after Trafalgar, he was looked
upon as a hero at Cadiz, and he made it his business to visit in
person the town which for so many weary years had been the
object of his attention from the waters of the Atlantic. He was
received royally.

> I went on shore [wrote Collingwood to his elder daughter
> on 12 August],[2] a few days ago, and you cannot conceive how
> rejoiced the people were to see me. I was received with all
> military honours; but, besides this, all the inhabitants, at
> least forty thousand men and women, came to welcome me.
> I would gladly have staid longer with them, but I could not,
> as I had to return to my ship at night. I went, however, to
> visit Madame Apodaca whose husband is an Admiral, and

[1] Napoleon made his brother-in-law, Joachim Murat, King of Naples in
Joseph's place.
[2] N.C., 429.

one of the Deputies from the Supreme Junta of Seville to England, where they are gone to beg our Government will assist them in their war against the French. She is a genteel woman about 35, which is reckoned tolerably old here, and has two very fine girls, her daughters. I wished much to visit some other ladies, to whom I am in debt for civilities, but my time would not permit.

Collingwood had supper with the Governor, and altogether the visit was a gala occasion, though he told Purvis that getting away was something of a trial—'three hours in rowing off'.[1] He visited Cadiz without Bounce who, so he told his daughter, was 'growing very old. I once thought of having his picture taken, but he had the good fortune to escape that.'

The admiral's diagnosis of Spanish feeling was accurate, and it held good until, six years later, the kingdom was at last freed by the valour of British armies under Wellington. 'I learn,' so he told the Admiralty,[2] 'that the higher orders do not show that ardour to the cause which animates the people, but that they are borne along by an enthusiasm which they dare not resist.' There was also a lack of central authority and direction which was the result of the removal of the Royal family and Court. The various provincial Juntas were jealous of each other's powers, and had no administrative experience to help them.

As was sometimes his way, Collingwood wrote as fully to his sister about Spanish affairs as to anyone official.

Of nobility and the higher classes [he told her][3] perhaps a majority of them were either attached to the French, or doubted the ability of the country, exhausted of every necessity for war. The priests are the only people who have much influence with the people: they direct them and they are capable of it. When there appears any languor or desire to hold back from the enemy, the people, instigated by the priests, raise their voice and they must proceed.

One of the most urgent requests from Cadiz was for gunpowder. This was supplied by the ships, with spectacular results. Newnham Collingwood described it thus:[4]

[1] H., Letter 161.　　[2] N.C., 373.　　[3] H., Letter 160.　　[4] N.C., 375n.

The gunpowder which was first furnished by the English fleet was immediately fired away by the Spaniards in honour of a saint whose festival they were then celebrating; and when they requested a further supply, Lord Collingwood informed them that he could spare no more, unless they would promise to reserve it for sinners, and not for saints.

There were at this time very frequent rumours of defeats sustained by the French, in all parts of Spain; and for one of these imaginary successes the town of Cadiz was illuminated. 'I always thought that this victory,' said Lord Collingwood, on observing their preparations, 'was a doubtful and dark affair; but I see now that they are going to throw some light on it.'

The effect produced by remarks of this kind, in which he frequently indulged, was greatly increased to those who heard them by the grave humour with which he uttered them.

Having made certain that there could be no further danger from the French ships remaining at Cadiz, which surrendered to the Spaniards, the work begun at Trafalgar at last seemed complete, and Collingwood sorely needed rest. He made his first formal application to go home:

. . . lest I should fail at an important moment [he wrote to his sister on 26 August].[1] I have wrote to the Admiralty to request their Lordships will allow me to come to England and recover my shaken body, which I think you will be glad to hear. If I can but have one little finishing touch at the Frenchmen before I come it will be a glorious termination. The Spaniards are going on well, but have a great deal to do, more than people are aware of. They are a bold people, but all the avenues to their country are open, and what is the greatest evil, they have no government; the Juntas are none for the country, and can only be considered as a mere expedient to prevent anarchy.

The answer to Collingwood's application to return to England was not long in coming. 'There is only one of my propositions which is not approved,' he told his sister at the end of October,[2] 'and that gives me a good deal of uneasiness. Perhaps it is not

---

[1] H., Letter 162.   [2] H., Letter 165.

yet quite settled—that is, my request to come home. I have heard the Ministers totally disapprove of this, particularly Mr Canning, and Lord Mulgrave plainly writes to me that in the present state of affairs there is a difficulty in finding a proper person to succeed me . . . In short, it appears to me that I shall not get to England yet.'

The Government were indeed alarmed at the thought of the admiral coming home, and for all the expected reasons. 'It is a justice which I owe to you and to the Country,' wrote the First Lord, 'to tell you candidly, that I know not how I should be able to supply all that would be lost to the service of the Country, and to the general interests of Europe, by your absence from the Mediterranean.'[1]

There was yet another reason for apprehension, never known to Collingwood or indeed to anyone outside a limited circle. This was disclosed many years later, by Admiral Sir Thomas Byam Martin, who not only knew Collingwood well, and was indeed one of the last to speak to him before his final departure from England, but who had access to good information.

The Duke of Clarence [so he reported], was very anxious to serve as Commander-in-Chief, Mediterranean, when Lord Collingwood's health was so broken down as to compel him to ask relief from so anxious and arduous a charge. The Duke then pressed the point with such earnest importunity that the Minister and the First Lord of the Admiralty were put to their shifts to know how to ward off an application from a Royal personage whose rank of flag gave him as it were a professional claim.

The total unfitness of the Duke for a command of any importance was of itself a decided objection, but to place him in a position where delicate points of diplomacy frequently occurred, would have been embarrassing to the Government and hazardous to the public interest in the highest degree. It was therefore determined that Lord Mulgrave, the First Lord, should write to Lord Collingwood and state that the public interest rendered it of the highest importance that a person of his experience and distinguished services should continue for some time longer to conduct the

---

[1] N.C., 449.

duties he had hitherto managed with so much skill and benefit
to his country.

Old Cuddy, as we always called Lord Collingwood, who
had worked all his life with greater diligence for professional
applause than any other man, was tickled with the compliment, and this, acting on his devotion to the Service, procured
his assent when it was obvious to all around him that his
broken health rendered him quite unfit to retain so great a
command. He replied that if the good of the Service required
that he should remain, he was content to wait and die at his
post, for he felt his days were numbered, and this proved too
true . . .[1]

Lord Mulgrave at one stage went so far as to suggest that
if, from reasons of health, Collingwood could no longer exercise
command at sea, he might consider doing so from Plymouth,[2]
and he added later that if he stayed at his post, the Admiralty
would do their best to send him out such officers as he wished.[3]
These were extraordinary concessions and so thoroughly convinced the admiral that he was needed that, after leaving Cadiz,
he once again took up the watch on Toulon, the most arduous
service he could have chosen. This decision was the more remarkable in that he could now, had he so chosen, have established himself in a headquarters ashore, either at Gibraltar,
Malta, Palermo, Syracuse, or even possibly Minorca. There
were indeed, reasons against so doing, though not insuperable
ones. Gibraltar was overcrowded, and included a garrison as
well as a Governor with whom Collingwood might not always
have seen eye to eye. At Malta, there was Collingwood's old
friend from boyhood days, Alexander Ball, perfectly capable
of seconding any recommendations from sea, and, moreover,
rather far away; Syracuse would also have been somewhat
distant for the admiral's preoccupations; Palermo had the disadvantage of being the seat of the Sicilian Court, while the
state of Minorca was not, as yet, fully enough settled for an
official residence to be used by the highest authority of an ally.
Collingwood was indeed an unyielding man, so far as his personal standards were concerned, and although the thought

[1] *Letters and Papers of Sir Thomas Byam Martin:* ed. Admiral Sir R. V.
Hamilton (1901), iii. 304–5.
[2] N.C., 455–6.   [3] N.C.. 478.

occurred to many that he was being unnecessarily severe in the tasks he set himself and the conveniences he so rigorously eschewed, he did nothing, not even the smallest action, without due consideration, and he was nearly always right. Mulgrave went further: he told Collingwood that '*in no instance*' had the admiral failed 'to adopt the most judicious and the best-concerted measures'.[1]

In Spain and Portugal it was at last the turn of the soldiers. In August 1808, the future Duke of Wellington beat the French at Vimiero, but because he was then a comparatively junior officer, he had to acquiesce in a convention made at Cintra by two seniors which allowed the enemy to leave the country on terms which caused an uproar when they were known in England. Later in the year came Sir John Moore's advance to Salamanca, which was later followed by his retreat to Corunna and his death in the hour of a defensive victory. The war in Iberia would sway to and fro, the British armies always sustained by the Navy. Collingwood's immediate task was to see that the French at Toulon, their ships of the line seldom less than fifteen in reasonable readiness to sail, with building and repair always in progress, did not interfere either in the Mediterranean or the Atlantic. Collingwood had had bitter experience of one failure in interception: he would never risk another.

One modification he did allow himself. Owing to the dreadful gales of the previous winter, he decided to station his heavier ships off Catalonia.

> The experience of last year [he wrote to the Secretary of the Admiralty[2] in September], and the gale which we have already had, convinces me of the impracticality of keeping a station here [i.e. immediately off Toulon] during the winter and that the attempt must disable the squadron. I, therefore, propose next month to make the coast of Catalonia between Cape St. Sebastian and Barcelona (a part of the coast less subject to those storms) the Rendezvous of the Fleet, keeping two frigates to watch the enemy in the port of Toulon. The object which they appear to have now is the supply of Barcelona and their army in Spain, which I hope will be effectually prevented by keeping the station I propose.

[1] H., Letter 167: Collingwood's italics, in writing to his sister.
[2] Col., Letter Book xii, f. 41.

Yet even the new dispositions did not save the ships. After the weather of autumn and early winter, Collingwood wrote to his sister, on 17 December:[1]

My fleet has suffered so much from the constant storms we have endured, my cares are increased. This ship particularly is almost to pieces although she has not a speck of rotten timber in her. The new whimsies and absurd inventions of those who, having little science, would be thought to have it because they have an office from which science should proceed, have introduced many odd schemes in the construction of ships. And as the *Ocean* was intended to be perfection, unhappily they were all applied to her, and the consequence is that in a severe storm we had lately . . . she had like to have gone to pieces, while the old ships which escaped the philosophic plans were little injured.

Collingwood wrote to the Admiralty on the subject of 'improvements' generally, and saw no reason to modify what he had written to the Navy Office when he first joined his flagship.

This is an exceedingly fine ship [was his verdict], sails very well, stands well under her canvas and has no violent motions, yet her sides work already as much as an older ship, which undoubtedly is the effect of her topsides not falling sufficiently, and all the fastenings being ever upon the strain, and while the upright ships are for ever wanting to be caulked, those of the old construction keep constantly at sea with little defect until they rot.

Supporting this view, Collingwood wrote a letter to Captain Charles Mansfield, early in the following year, which indicated how seriously he regarded the deterioration in shipbuilding and reconstruction. Mansfield had commanded the *Minotaur* at Trafalgar, and was then at home.

If they will persist in building these wall-sided ships [said Collingwood], no power of art can keep them together. A feeble attempt is made towards it by cutting off their poops —what I consider is a step in the declension, for every officer knows the great advantage which results from so commanding a situation as the poop.

[1] H., Letter 167 and note: 259.

Would that they go back to the construction of *Venerables*, *Caledonias*, *Terribles*, and we should have ships that could carry their poops through a [hurricane]. I hope you have preserved your poop but if you had docked at Plymouth I doubt your being able to do . . .

Serres the Painter is doing pictures of the Battle [Trafalgar]: if you go to London I hope you will talk to him on the subject. Every ship in that action had a poop, though some have since been reduced. If he draws pictures of ships without poops he may keep them for I should not like to have one in my house.[1]

The weather, and the sorry condition of his own three-decker, had at least one good effect: it forced Collingwood to put in at Malta, where the dockyard had the *Ocean* 'new bolted with iron'.[2] It was there that he learnt of the last dignity which the Admiralty were ever able to confer on him, which was the occasion of a very gracious letter from the First Lord:[3]

That excellent man and highly distinguished officer Lord Gardner was lost to his family, his friends (among whom I was proud to be classed), and to his Country, last Saturday, at Bath [wrote Mulgrave on 3 January 1809]. Your Lordship's eminent services and high professional character pointed you out as a worthy successor to the dignified distinction of Major-General of Marines, and I have great satisfaction in acquainting you that I have received His Majesty's commands to notify to you, that His Majesty has been graciously pleased to appoint your Lordship to be Major-General of Marines, *vice* Admiral Lord Gardner, deceased.

It was entirely characteristic of Collingwood, that in writing to his sister, as he invariably did when any item of purely Service information was at hand which he thought would gratify her, he pointed out that although he was highly pleased at this mark of favour, yet when and if he retired from active service, the sinecure office would be set against his half pay![4]

[1] Letter, hitherto unpublished, in the collection of Sir Edward Collingwood. John Thomas Serres (1759–1825) was marine-painter to George III.
[2] H., Letter 170.
[3] N.C., 478.
[4] H., Letter 172: 'It is respectable to be so distinguished, but . . . I am jealous of their supposing such an excitement necessary to retain me.'

II

Collingwood found Malta flourishing, under the rule of Sir Alexander Ball, who was idolized by the people. The unchallenged supremacy of the Royal Navy in the Mediterranean had caused trade to flow largely through Valetta, and Collingwood described the result in a letter to his sister, dated 12 February from sea, soon after his visit had ended:[1]

> Malta is one of the gayest places in the world: the merchants having now the entire trade of the Mediterranean are become very rich and are dashing away in a great style. Nothing but feasts and festivities, which interfered a little with the young men's attention to their ships. I had little to do with it, for my mind is too much occupied to think of pleasures.

Collingwood amplified this description in what he wrote to Blackett a few days later:[2]

> Malta is the most gossiping, gormandising place I ever heard of. The merchants there, who two years since were very little men, from the extension of their trade, the exclusion of all other nations from participating in it, and the ample protection given to their speculations, are become suddenly exceedingly rich. I have heard that some of them have made a hundred thousand pounds, and several from ten to fifteen thousand a year. The ladies, who have so lately emerged from the humblest duties of domestic industry, now vie with each other in all the shining finery of tassel and tinsel, and pass their nights in routs and revels. I saw just enough of it to know that it would not do for me. Neither my health nor my occupations were suited to it, and I declined all invitations.

At least one further visit ashore had by now become almost inevitable. Sooner or later, Collingwood would have to pay his respects to the Court at Palermo, a prospect which caused him no pleasure. And for all their expressed eagerness to make his acquaintance, there can have been as little attraction to Ferdinand

---

[1] H., Letter 171.   [2] N.C., 495.

and his Queen in the thought of entertaining a powerful, but distant, disillusioned and formidable friend, yet one to whom (whatever the French might tell them) they owed the security of their island, and their current position as crowned heads. Intrigue was so much the breath of life at Palermo that the Queen had earlier dispatched a member of her family, Prince Leopold, together with the exiled Duke of Orleans, to fish in the troubled waters of Spain. Unfortunately, the royal personages could not proceed ashore without leave of Collingwood, who although he received the Duke with becoming civility[1] sent the pair and their party back to Sicily, having made it crystal clear that their presence was politically unwelcome. The Bourbon view was that anyone so adamant must be treated with the utmost circumspection; at the same time, it was essential that Collingwood's visit should pass off well, and so it did.

The first of two long descriptions was given by the admiral to his sister, on 19 February:[2]

I had appointed the General Sr Jno Stuart to meet me at Palermo, when I had much important matter to discuss with him, and I took the opportunity to pay my respects to the King and Queen. I arrived on Tuesday before Ash Wednesday, when by way of closing the jollities of the carnival the Queen gave a ball to the nobility. I rec'd an invitation the moment we anchored. We went and were most graciously received. The King is a good humoured man, free and affable in his manners, and had he not unhappily been born to be a king would have been a respectable country gentleman. Matters of state weary him, and I understand he does not attend much to them. His country amusements of hunting and shooting occupy him. On the other hand, the Queen is a great politician and is continually engaged in intrigues for the recovery of their lost [kingdom] of Naples, and I am told she maintains that tenet, that the end sanctifies the means, whatever they may be.

At her Ball she was civil to me. I supped at her table, and

---

[1] Collingwood had been reading much French, as he told his daughter Sarah in August 1808 (N.C., 428), and it is possible he conversed well enough in the language to dispense with an interpreter. French would have been one of the languages of the Sicilian court.

[2] H., Letter 171.

sat next to her. Yet through the affability she affected, I thought I could perceive the effect of the impression that I had been a bar to her son Leopold's succeeding in his mission into Spain. The thing was absurd and I only told them they had undertaken what was not practicable.

Today I have dined with the King at his country house, about four miles from the town, the prettiest thing you can conceive, built and furnished in the Chinese style. The rooms are small, but furnished and fitted up in a style so elegant, that they look like places to be admired rather than to be inhabited. He has a large farm and extensive plantations, which he has made where before was only barren rocks. It is a pity that a worthy man, so capable of being happy in his own way, should have his lot cast so distant from it.

In a letter to his wife, dated 25 February, Collingwood added some further touches:[1] Repeating that the King was intended for a country squire, Collingwood said:

. . . blundering Chance has cast his lot awry. The Queen would appear to be penetrating into the soul and mind of every body that comes near her. She would be thought a deep politician; yet all her schemes miscarry. She broods over what is impracticable with her little means, and frets herself continually that others are not as dim-sighted as herself. Her lot also has been cast awry, or, in the distribution of stations for this world, so loose a morality and such depravity of manners would never have been found perched upon a throne, from whence should issue the bright example of all that is good and great.

Returning to the King, a character with whom he found at least something in common, Collingwood continued:

We dined with him on Sunday at his country-house, and he carried us all over it. It is the prettiest thing that can be; the rooms not larger than ours at Morpeth, and the house not much bigger. We went over his grounds; and His Majesty seemed particularly desirous that I should see all his improvements, when I told him I was a great planter myself.

[1] N.C., 499.

I have also seen a great deal of the Princesses and Duchesses of Sicily; and all I shall say of them at present is, that the more I see of them, the more I bless my stars that I was born in England, and have got a darling wife who is not a Princess. They were very polite and attentive to me. I believe the Queen was relieved when I took leave of her. They had been told of the opposition which I gave to their son going to Spain . . . I do not know what possessed them on my arrival, but the consternation seemed to be general; and Sir John Stuart having come there to meet me, made an appearance of business of consequence.

There was a great alarm and suspicion that we were come to insist on all the French leaving the island; and as most of her favourites are of that nation, I do not wonder at the concern that was very visible. They never desire, I am sure, to see my face again.

Summing up the visit, as late as the end of May, to Admiral Purvis, Collingwood said:[1] 'God protect them: I wish you had seen that court. I consider it as a sort of curiosity, and how such a one can exist in civilised Europe is a matter of great astonishment.'

Collingwood had not had much satisfaction from his talks with General Stuart, who in fact never again reached such heights as he had done galloping around the victorious field of Maida, where his soldiers were winning all the glory, and he doing little of the thinking. The admiral had wanted him to ear-mark some of his army for service in Spain, but Stuart would have none of it, and it was with considerable difficulty, though with ultimate success, that Collingwood later persuaded him that something useful might be done in the Ionian Islands, and at very small expense of numbers. In due time, that was to be one of the year's successes, entirely resultant from naval initiative.

In April, Collingwood moved to a new flagship, the *Ville de Paris*. He wrote to his wife from off Minorca:[2]

---

[1] H., Letter 177.

[2] N.C., 511–12: The *Ville de Paris* (named after de Grasse's flagship captured by Rodney in 1782 and wrecked the same year) had been built in 1795, the first British built ship to be rated as a 110-gun ship. She actually carried 120 guns, including cannonades.

. . . a continuation of bad weather has brought the *Ocean* back almost to the state in which she was before her repair. I got near this island for shelter, and the *Ville de Paris* came to me. My habitation is soon changed. I have been in this ship four or five days, and like her very much; but all ships that sail well and are strong are alike to me; I see little of them, seldom moving from my desk. The Admiralty have been exceedingly kind and attentive to me; they have sent me the best ship in the Navy, and have reinforced my squadron; but what I most want is a new pair of legs and a new pair of eyes. My eyes are very feeble; my legs and feet swell so much every day, that it is pretty clear they will not last long. I am only afraid my Fleet, too, will drop off suddenly, for we have many here who are much worn.

What Collingwood said was all too true, and Thornbrough, on whom he greatly relied, was, he thought, still worse. 'I think we are both of us too long from England,' he told Purvis.[1]

Tough as I am [Collingwood told Sarah a few weeks later], I cannot last much longer.[2] I have seen all the ships and men out two or three times. Bounce and I seem to be the only personages who stand our ground. Many about me are yielding to the fatigue and confinement of a life which is certainly not natural to man.

Alas! even Bounce succumbed within two months of when these words were written. On 13 August Collingwood wrote to his sister from 'off Toulon':[3]

You will be sorry to hear my poor dog Bounce is dead. I am afraid he fell overboard in the night. He is a great loss to me. I have few comforts, but he was one, for he loved me. Everybody sorrows for him. He was wiser than [many] who hold their heads higher, and was grateful [to those] who were kind to him.

Bounce was old and worn; perhaps he had had as much as he could stand: if so, the Gulf of Lions, with the *Ville de Paris* on watch, was a notable point of departure.

[1] H., Letter 179.   [2] N.C., 529.   [3] H., Letter 184.

III

Misfortunes seldom come singly, and, having lost his pet, Collingwood also began to be seriously worried, for the first time in his life, about his home affairs. Chirton, under Sarah, seemed to be swallowing money and, what was equally bad, Blackett, who in earlier years had been such a comfort in looking after the Morpeth family, began to get into difficulties financially, and actually tried to make over to his son-in-law his share in a 'fire office'[1] in consideration of pledging the admiral's credit for an obligation he had incurred for some £2,200. Blackett was by this time an old man, and perhaps losing grip, but he chose the wrong man to upset, for Collingwood not only bitterly resented his attempted interference in his finances, but recalled that it was Blackett who had given Sarah such extravagant tastes as she seemed to be developing, without having endowed her with a head for business.

Collingwood made known his feelings in letters to his sister, and to some degree to Mrs. Stead, who, though she was not altogether free from troubles herself, since her husband was 'gay and expensive',[2] was, so Collingwood always found, an admirable confidante. In the first letter broaching the subject, written in March 1809, Collingwood felt so depressed that he told Mary:[3]

A year ashore would make me young again. I hardly wish it. I have been long enough in the world to be sick of it. The only pleasure I have enjoyed in it has been the pursuit of my duty, and the greatest satisfaction I have is that all allow I have done it faithfully, honourably, and honestly, so that my life has been quite long enough for my character, too long for my comfort . . .

I have determined to sell my house etc. at Morpeth immediately . . . You may suppose my affairs are in a very unsettled state. In short, I know nothing of them . . . I have wrote to my wife to say I entirely disapprove of my being engaged in any body's business but my own, that it is my

[1] H., Letter 172.   [2] H., Letter 194.   [3] H., Letter 172.

duty to take care of my daughters, and they shall not be disappointed.

On 22 July he wrote further to Mary:[1]

> I am sorry for the derangement, for I call it derangement where there is no order, of my house. It is what gives me great pain. I have endeavoured to restrain it. My wife would gladly confine herself to what I prescribe, but the gaiety, the vanity, and the love of feeding of her father, there is no bounds to. It has been the habit of his life, and the means, I am afraid, has never been of much consideration . . .
>
> I have been exceedingly plain with Mr. B. on the liberties taken with my fortune, and told him that if he wished his daughter to have elegancies beyond my convenience he should have provided her with a fortune.

In October Collingwood added, to the same correspondent:[2]

> I have never heard from Mr B. since I wrote him a sharp letter on the subject, and whenever he does write I dare say his hand will shake. I have written to Newton[3] to go to the Fire Office and if the share is not sold (which Mr B. told my wife was to fetch £2500 any day) to inform the gentlemen that my name has been added to their society without my authority and desire that it may be immediately erased, for that I am not, nor ever was, of the company. It is an undertaking for speculators and adventurers who have nothing to lose. I would rather lose the money than not show my resentment . . .

Newnham Collingwood naturally made no reference to this sad side of the admiral's private affairs, and the 'sharp' letter to Blackett is not preserved: moreover, Collingwood had the generosity to say that he did not really blame Blackett much, and he resumed his ordinary correspondence, in a very short time, as if harmony was unbroken.

On the larger scene, Britain had an ally in Austria, as from April 1809, and, moreover, Collingwood thought he saw signs of yet another Russian re-orientation. This indeed came about,

---

[1] H., Letter 182.   [2] H., Letter 189.
[3] Collingwood's agent in certain Newcastle matters.

though not for some time. Russian inclinations were another matter. They had some ships at Trieste, but so complete was Collingwood's control of the Adriatic that he was able to tell Lord Mulgrave:[1]

> If the Russian ships sail ... I do not think they can escape from our squadron; but unless that nation takes a part against Austria, the ships will probably remain where they are. The officers profess to be averse to any co-operation with the French. The Russian Commodore told the Governor of Trieste, that while he received orders from Paris, he did not think his ships sea-worthy; but were they to come from Russia, and direct him to join the English, he would be ready the next day.

Collingwood's proposals about sending a force to the Ionian Islands was first put forward in a letter to General Stuart written from off Toulon on 15 July:[2]

> I would propose ... there should be despatched 1000 men to Cephalonia and Zante, which are said to be ripe for insurrection. From the information which I have, the Islanders are all averse to the French, and would heartily join in expelling them. In forming an administration for their government afterwards, there would possibly be more difficulty; but an officer of temper and judgment would have great influence in deciding them. Such a measure would exceedingly distract the French in their operations, and probably open the way to the reduction of Corfu. Many and great advantages would result from the liberation of those islands, and from attaching them to us, and to us alone.

Writing the same day to Rear-Admiral Martin, who was in direct touch with Stuart, he asked him to consult the general *privately*[3] 'for if it were known at Messina it will pass to Calabria, and a resistance be prepared in the islands, which will defeat the undertaking.' All went well, though there was a sticky start. Stuart, so Collingwood told his sister[4] lost much time, but during the early autumn Zante, Cephalonia, Ithaca, and Cerigo were taken, 'restoring the Septinsular Republic,' as

[1] N.C., 527.   [2] N.C., 536.   [3] N.C., 540.   [4] H., Letter 191.

Collingwood joyfully reported. 'The people are delighted at
their emancipation and it is to be tried whether they can
maintain their independence with such protection as we can
give them. I am very anxious on this subject, because having
undertaken this without instructions from England and wholly
on my own responsibility, I am yet to learn how it is approved.'
It was indeed approved, and led to the liberation, later, of
Corfu, as Collingwood hoped it would. It was a venture well
within the resources of the army and the Fleet, sensible, un-
costly in life or treasure, and it made a pendant to news of the
last success which Collingwood was ever able to achieve at
sea. This he described in a letter to his wife written on 30
October:[1]

> You will have great pleasure in hearing of my success, and
> particularly of its having been effected without a hair of any
> body's head being hurt, and almost without a shot being
> fired. I told the Admiralty what my plan was in September,
> and it has succeeded to a marvel.
>
> I knew, from the intelligence which I had received, that
> the French were impatient to supply Barcelona with pro-
> visions, and that while I was off Toulon, they would not
> attempt it until the squadron was blown off; and, in that
> case, I should not be able to prevent them.
>
> After one of those strong gales I retired to Minorca, sent
> several of my ships into the harbour, where they remained
> just long enough to seem settled, and for the intelligence to
> go to Toulon that we were there, when I called them out and
> proceeded to Cape Sebastian, to which place the frigates,
> stationed at Toulon, were to bring me intelligence.
>
> On Sunday night, the 22nd, one of them came with the
> signal that the enemy was approaching. Every soul was in
> raptures; I expected their whole fleet, and that we should
> have had a dashing business.
>
> The next morning between eight and nine o'clock, they
> came in sight; but they were few, one Rear-Admiral, with
> three sail of the line, two frigates, some other armed things,
> and a convoy of about twenty vessels.
>
> As soon as they discovered us, they made off. Night came

[1] N.C., 551–3.

on, and I thought we had lost them; but as the fleet separated in different parties, by good luck Admiral Martin's division fell in with them, near their own shore, in the Gulf of Lyons, where he chased them on shore on the 25th; and on the 26th, the French Admiral set fire to his own ship, the *Robuste* of 80 guns, and the *Lion* of 74. The *Borée* of 74 guns, and one of the frigates, run on shore at Cette. It blew almost a gale of wind, and our own ships were in a very dangerous situation.

The first day of the chase, the *Pomona* burnt five vessels of the convoy, and one has since been taken; the rest are in a port near to which I have sent a good squadron to endeavour to destroy them or bring them off; and if they are to be come at, I know that it will be done.

Two days later, from 'off Rosas Bay,' Collingwood wrote the last of many purely naval letters to his sister, giving her a special version of the news for the house at Newcastle. After repeating much of what he had said to Sarah, he added:[1]

Last night a squadron was sent in, to bring them out or destroy them [the French in Rosas Bay] and this morning, a little after four, I saw the flames rising. At half past five a ship blew up which I suppose is a transport laden with powder, for I know there was one. One of the frigates has got into Marseilles and that, I believe to be the only vessel that has escaped of the whole convoy. They (the *Robuste, Borée* and *Lion*) were all new, the two first had never been at sea except in the spring for five days when they carried a convoy to Barcelona and then had a very narrow escape. I now see our squadron coming out of Rosas Bay with four or five of the enemy's vessels with them, so that they are not all burnt.[2]

'I saw the flames rising . . .' wrote the old warrior, this time from the actual scene of action. Mary did well to cherish her letter, for it was a last gleam. Collingwood had very few months to live, and no more excitement would come his way.

[1] H., Letter 191.

[2] The final reckoning was two (not three) ships of the line and thirteen transports destroyed; four transports taken.

IV

During the autumn there was an extension of the flag-list, the object of which was to introduce some new blood into the lower part of it. Promotion did not extend upwards to the senior Vice-Admirals, and Collingwood was convinced that it was because George III had heard about the business of the 'fire office', though this was in fact improbable. At the end of the year he wrote to his sister from Minorca:[1]

> God help me! I hear nothing of being relieved but, at Malta, they say, the King has expressed his desire that I may not be recalled. His Majesty knows every thing about every body and I dare say having read the advertisement in the Newcastle paper (for he reads all provincial papers) is unwilling that an insurance broker should sit in his house of peers.
> There is the cause of my illness and broken spirit . . . and now my character is established as a mercantile jobber, without my even knowing about it. Every body expresses surprise that the promotion did not give a flag at the main top.[2] I am not surprised at all, but am ashamed to tell them why. The King jealous of the dignity of his flag cannot be very anxious to have it an insurance beacon.

Collingwood was wrong in his diagnosis of the situation, and the King would certainly not have extended his reading as far as the admiral supposed: yet it was sad that he never reached the rank of full admiral, and the chance had now gone for ever.

Collingwood was at Port Mahon, and mortally stricken. His doctor realized it. 'I have been very ill ever since I came here,' he told his sister,[3] and the physician has much difficulty in determining on the nature of my complaint, which is in my stomach, and they say entirely the consequence of the sedentary life I must have. I have lost digestion and have a constant pain, and my spirits are so bad, and so low, that I am become indifferent to every thing.' The diagnosis was 'a contraction of the

---

[1] H., Letter 197.
[2] Collingwood would have flown a full admiral's flag there.
[3] H., Letter 197.

pylorus'.[1] If, as is very possible, he had cancer of the stomach, his way of life had actually not much to do with his condition.

He was still capable of pleasing letters, and in his less melancholy moments he saw his affairs in a truer perspective than he had sometimes done in writing to his sister. For instance, in his final letter to Blackett there was no indication of any bitterness between them. As it was the last of any note to his family which has survived, it merits quotation in full, so far as it is given by Newnham Collingwood.[2]

Ville de Paris, Minorca, Jan. 1, 1810

Thus the years roll on; and as the season comes round, I congratulate you, at the same time, on entering a new year of the world and of your life, which, I hope, you will enjoy in health, and pass in happiness and comfort.

I have been in port longer than I ever was since leaving England, and have saved my ships very much from a great deal of extreme bad weather. This I have been enabled to do by having luckily reduced the enemy's fleet, as you will have heard, in October, and given them a check which will make them very cautious. I am not without hope that they will make another attempt to victual Barcelona, which is straitened for provisions, and that we have another meeting with them. It would have been a happy day if they had all come last time. I expected them, and was well prepared for them.

In Sicily they are delighted; for as they are always in danger, whatever reduces the enemy's force diminishes their fears. I have a very handsome letter from the Prime Minister, who writes, in the King's name, to congratulate me. The Court there is very gay at present, the Duke of Orleans being lately married to the Princess Amelia, who appeared to me to be a mild and pleasing woman. The old Duchess, who is a delightful old woman, seems to have forgotten her misfortunes, and they have been great—and is very happy in the choice which her son has made of a wife.

I have been very unwell lately. The physician tells me that it is the effect of constant confinement, which is not very comfortable, as there is little chance of its being otherwise.

---

[1] N.C., 570.   [2] N.C., 557-8.

Old age and infirmities are coming on very fast, and I am weak, and tottering on my legs.

I had a great loss in the death of Sir Alexander Ball. He was an able and industrious man; and I fear Malta will never be so well governed again. We were Midshipmen together, and have always been on terms of the greatest friendship. The islands which we took will very much add to the commerce of Malta. That business was done particularly neatly. In a letter from a French Governor at Cerigo, he informs his Chief, that some Albanians, about 600, had come to that island, and that he was determined to get clear of them by some means. In the next letter he tells him that he found himself under the necessity of poisoning the waters, by which many died, and the rest, alarmed, went away—a deed worthy of the Devil.

Collingwood sent a letter of resignation to Lord Mulgrave on 22 February, and then only when it was apparent, even to himself, that he was no longer capable of managing his command.

It has given me much concern [he wrote][1] that I have been under the necessity of writing to the Secretary of the Admiralty, stating the ill condition of my health, and requesting their Lordships' permission to return to England; and this, I can assure your Lordship, I have not done until I am past service, being at present totally incapable of applying to the duties of my office. My complaint is of a nature to which I apprehend it is difficult to apply a remedy, for I have hitherto received no benefit from medical advice. Since November it has been daily increasing, so that I am now almost past walking across my cabin; and as it is attributed to my long service in a ship, I have little hope of amendment until I can land.

Three days later, he went ashore for the last time, accompanied by Captain Benjamin Hallowell, an old and trusted friend, who left his ship to attend the Commander-in-Chief. Collingwood had been recommended to try the effects of gentle exercise on horse-back, but it was by then too late. He had

[1] N.C., 560.

become incapable of bearing the slightest fatigue, and on 25 February he surrendered his charge to Admirals Martin and Sir Samuel Hood, the latter an officer for whom he had specially asked.[1] On 3 March he tried to sail.

The two following days [wrote Newnham Collingwood],[2] were spent in unsuccessful attempts to warp the *Ville de Paris* out of Port Mahon; but on the 6th the wind came round to the westward, and at sunset the ship succeeded in clearing the harbour, and made sail for England.

When Lord Collingwood was informed that he was at sea again, he rallied for a time his exhausted strength, and said to those around him, 'Then I may yet live to meet the French once more.' On the morning of the 7th there was a considerable swell, and his friend Captain Thomas, on entering his cabin, observed, that he feared the motion of the vessel disturbed him. 'No, Thomas,' he replied, 'I am now in a state in which nothing in this world can disturb me more. I am dying; and I am sure it must be consolatory to you, and all who love me, to see how comfortably I am coming to my end.'

He told one of his attendants that he had endeavoured to review, as far as possible, all the actions of his past life, and that he had the happiness to say that nothing gave him a moment's uneasiness. He spoke at times of his absent family, and of the doubtful contest in which he was about to leave his Country involved, but ever with calmness and perfect resignation to the will of God; and in this blessed state of mind, after taking an affectionate farewell of his attendants, he expired without a struggle at six o'clock in the evening of that day . . .

In his account of Collingwood's last moments, Mr. Macanst, surgeon of the *Ville de Paris*, stated:[3]

Those who were about his Lordship's person, and who witnessed the composure and resignation with which he met his fate, will long remember the scene with wonder and admiration. In no part of his Lordship's brilliant life did his

---

[1] Col. 13b. 0311.   [2] N.C., 568-9.
[3] N.C., 569-70: in his Obituary (*N. Chron.* xxiii. 350) it is stated that Collingwood died at 8 o'clock on 7 March.

character appear with greater lustre than when he was approaching his end. It was dignified in the extreme. If it be on the bed of sickness and at the approach of death—when ambition, the love of glory, and the interests of the world are over—that the true character is to be discovered, surely never did any man's appear to greater advantage than did that of my Lord Collingwood.

For my own part, I did not believe it possible that any one, on such an occasion, could have behaved so nobly. Cruelly harassed by a most afflicting disease, obtaining no relief from the means employed, and perceiving his death to be inevitable, he suffered no sigh of regret to escape, no murmuring at his past life, no apprehension of the future. He met death as became him, with a composure and fortitude which have seldom been equalled, and never surpassed.

The man of discipline had become the martyr to duty.

12 *Characteristics and Achievement*

If Collingwood had chosen his family's motto, it could scarcely have been more appropriate—*ferar unus et idem*: 'always one and the same', the traditional amplification being 'diligent in small or great matters'.[1] He exemplified it in precept and practice; in precept, as when he wrote to his daughter Sarah, 'never do anything with indifference,'[2] in practice in his notable care for detail and his exceptional breadth of view.

Collingwood's attention to detail was remarked throughout his career, and sometimes it showed itself in curious ways. A typical instance from his later days, when he had more responsibility than almost anyone else in his profession, may serve to demonstrate it. On 20 August 1807, when he was in the *Ocean* off the Dardanelles, wrestling with the intricate affairs of Turkey, he wrote in his Journal:[3] '. . . directed the Purser to exchange the Hides of the slaughtered Bullocks with the native Greeks for Sheep, for each of which he got three sheep, which were distributed in the Fleet for the sick men.' These few words illustrate four distinct traits: an almost absurd care for the particular; the habit of doing everything himself; his pleasure in following everything up; and his consideration for his men.

Two successive letters to Rear-Admiral Purvis, written in November and December 1809, afford other striking examples, in this case when Collingwood was very near collapse. In the first of them[4] he was suggesting action to be taken in case guns

---

[1] Horace, *Epist*. Lib. II. Ep. 2, line 200:
      . . . ego utrum
    Nave ferar magna an parva, ferar unus et idem.
[2] N.C., 493.   [3] Add. MSS. 14280.   [4] H., Letter 195.

on the Spanish coast became in danger of falling into the wrong hands:

> I recommend [he wrote], that you secretly and privately in your own ship prepare spikes for the guns on the north side of the bay, and carcases for burning whatever cannot come away; in knocking the trunions off guns the gun should be rolled upon a chock on which it will balance, if it lies solid on the ground, the trunions are not to be knocked off.

The next instance shows that his judgement of personnel descended far down the ranks. 'The boatswain of the *Tuscan*,' he told Purvis, 'is said to be a good man but wants nerves to bear a brig.'[1] This indicated that Collingwood had heard, and understood, that while the petty officer in question would be satisfactory in a big ship, he had not the initiative necessary for the very different type of service demanded in a smaller, swifter vessel. When his numerous observations on his 'younkers' are recalled, it is clear that, however busy and remote he may have appeared to be, Collingwood missed nothing in his observation of people, to the very end of his life. He was a rare judge of character, never better shown than in the way that he addressed his extraordinarily ramified correspondence to fit the recipient.

If George III was one of his warmer admirers in this respect, so were His Majesty's chief ministers. About one particular public letter, Collingwood wrote to his sister:[2] 'I have been told by a gentleman from England that Mr. Canning said, "If Mr Pitt had lived to read the letter I wrote to the Capitan Pasha (when I took the Turkish business out of the hands of the Ambass'r) he never would have lost sight of the person who wrote it." ' The letter in question, as printed by Newnham Collingwood,[3] reads as follows:

TO THE MOST ILLUSTRIOUS ALI, CAPITAN PACHA

Most Illustrious Pacha,

It is now a month since I arrived in these seas with a squadron of His Britannic Majesty's ships. Your Excellency knows that it is the duty of British fleets to present themselves to the enemies of their Country; but I had entertained the hope that God would have inspired the Sultan of the

---

[1] H., Letter 196.   [2] H., Letter 167.   [3] N.C., 306–7.

Turks with the same holy desire which has ever animated the breast of my King, that peace may be established among all nations; and that in the Turkish fleet I should have found not enemies, but that friendship renewed, which has most unhappily been suspended for a time by the convulsions which have shaken the Governments of Europe.

His Majesty, with this impression of friendship for the Sublime Porte, had sent his Embassador to propose a renewal of that harmony and friendly intercourse that he wished to maintain with a nation, whose interests and preservation from the intrigues of ambition have ever been a subject of his solicitude, and which a few years since called forth the exercise of his arms. The Sublime Porte, professing a desire that this friendship which we offer should be established, have not yet proceeded one step towards it; and this irresolution calls on me, most illustrious Pacha, to propose to the Sublime Porte the following questions, which, as the Turkish Ministers are already fully informed on the subject, I expect that they will reply to promptly, and with that ingenuousness and truth with which they are proposed.

Will the Sublime Porte accept the friendship offered by England, with a renewal of all the relations of peace and amity, the particular terms of which may be settled by the Plenipotentiaries?

Or do they reject the proposal, and, influenced by malign councils, determine on a state of war?

If the Sublime Porte accepts the proposal to establish friendship, in what place shall His Majesty's Embassador meet the Plenipotentiary whom the Sultan may appoint to conclude the treaty which is necessary to declare the renewal of former engagements, and seal the bond of friendship between our nations?

I have said before, most illustrious Pacha, that the subject is not new to the Ministers of the Porte. They have already, doubtless, determined in their minds the conduct to be pursued; and I expect in their reply that ingenuousness and truth with which God inspires the hearts of honest men, and that they give it immediately. If, in a short period, I have not an answer, I shall conclude that they intend to take such a part, or are under such influence, as they cannot without regret reveal. I cannot omit this opportunity of assuring your Excellency of my high respect for your person, that I am, most illustrious Pacha, your most humble servant, and that I desire to be your friend.

This letter referred to the events of 1808, when Britain was making such strenuous efforts to retain Turkish friendship, on account of which Collingwood had himself gone to Imbros. 'The measure was bold,' he commented to his sister,[1] 'but it seems it was approved. He [the 'Embassador'] was tenacious of diplomatic forms. I overthrew them to maintain the country's honour and determined in a day what he would have prosed over for a year.' Although Collingwood's success with the Turks was in fact inconsiderable, one effect of this particular letter was notable in the extreme. He had an acknowledgement almost by return.

On 'diplomatics' in general Collingwood could be as scathing as St. Vincent and Nelson had been in their days in charge of the Mediterranean Fleet. On 25 April he wrote to his sister:[2]

No creature can have an idea of the torment I have with all sorts of people, not so much with the fleet, for really the captains of the ships seem to me to be the only sensible people in the King's service. I am sure they are the most zealous and disinterested, but your diplomatics. God keep me from the diplomatics! I have no idea of any thing more frivolous, more perplexing, than a young Minister, what they call a sucking ambassador. They imagine that the fate of Europe depends on them—and bless them, poor dears, if they would be moderate in the exercise of their talents, Europe would perhaps be the better for it.

Mr. Adair [Ambassador at Vienna] is not one of those young men, but he dearly loves a little hostile intrigue. In my mind there cannot be a greater error than to introduce chicane and deceptions into politics. I am persuaded from what I have seen that honesty is the best policy, and yet the great art of diplomacy is, that nothing they do should be understood, always to have an object that is not [to] be discovered by the person with whom they treat.

Consuls were not much better. 'It is very extraordinary,'

[1] H., Letter 167.   [2] H., Letter 175.

wrote Collingwood to Sir Alexander Ball,[1] 'that consuls, peaceful ministers, sent abroad to promote friendship and maintain harmony amongst nations, never think they have done half their business until they can stir up a little mischief.'

Never did Collingwood lose sight of the purpose of war, which was honourable peace. 'War is not a subject to be considered with levity,' he wrote in July 1808, 'it is not a subject in which the personal resentment of an individual should be allowed to have any weight—and the person who makes an honourable peace for his Country is more its friend than he who adds to its splendour by many victories in a cause which was not of strict necessity.'[2]

Strangely enough, Collingwood's own skill as negotiator as well as fleet commander was paralleled in his own day by Sir James Saumarez, who from 1808, for some five years, with his flag in the *Victory*, was as much an arbiter in the Baltic as Collingwood in the Mediterranean. Saumarez had as many interests to cherish and knots to unravel. Both men were as redoubtable in battle as at the desk, but Saumarez was younger, and he spared himself in ways which Collingwood's temperament seemed to forbid, so that he survived into old age.

Of generals, as opposed to the private soldier, Collingwood thought little. His early experience at Bunker Hill had given him no inclination to think highly of military capacity when applied to that 'option of difficulties' which Wolfe once described as the essence of war. His one close army friend, Sir Hew Dalrymple, however charming a man, was scarcely a Wellington. Sir John Stuart he found, as did all that general's subordinates, a far from easy colleague; brave enough, but not remarkable for intelligence or insight.

Writing once to Mrs. Stead about a mutual acquaintance, a certain General Clavering about whose career history is mercifully silent, Collingwood remarked: 'What a delightful head that man must have for the front rank of an army! It needs no helmet. They [the enemy] might hack their swords to saws— without harm to it.'[3]

[1] N.C., 340.   [2] N.C., 403.   [3] H., Letter 176.

II

Collingwood held strong views on the vital importance of family life and unity, the basis of his own happiness. Fate so willed it that, through the death in reduced circumstances of his father, the comfort of his mother and sisters should fall upon him and his brothers, of whom only John lived into and beyond middle life. Collingwood's attention to his sisters was unceasing, as was his care for their maintenance in every comfort he could afford. Though they never married, they were sociable ladies, and Collingwood could always rely on a shrewd view about those in Northumberland on whom he sought their advice. They were also assiduous in sending him potential officers, with very mixed results.

In his ships, while Collingwood applied the principle of sub-ordination strictly, and was all too inclined to do much that might safely have been left to others—'I have ever acted on the principal of never employing others in what I could do myself,' he told Mrs. Stead[1]—yet the sense of family was very marked. When he became a Commander-in-Chief, although he lived in strict isolation so far as official business was concerned, he entertained whenever possible, and his small staff, flag-captain, doctor, secretary, were rightly described as 'my family'. They were truly attached. The bond certainly extended to Smith, who proved so much more satisfactory than Ireland as a personal attendant, and who became as valued a part of his master's life as had 'old Scott', the Morpeth gardener of whom he thought so much. 'I hope Smith will stay with me when I go on shore,' Collingwood wrote to his wife in 1808,[2] 'for he is quiet and well educated, and suits me very well. I have not had occasion to find fault with him these four years; indeed never.'

The bringing up of the young was always a grave care, and Collingwood's remarks on some of the aspirants to the quarter-deck (his 'monkey things' as he once called them) were remark-able for shrewdness. Writing to his sister from off Toulon in October 1808 he remarked:[3] 'I have no time to look after boys and they soon grow to weeds, if not taken care of.' Yet almost

[1] H., Letter 190.   [2] N.C., 450.   [3] H., Letter 165.

in the same breath he continued: 'Stanhope breakfasts with me every day and is a signal midshipman. Currell is so heavy that I do not know what he is. His mother had better have made something else of him for he will never be a seaman. He never opens his mouth and does nothing—stupid . . . Stanhope has sense and can take care of himself.' A few months later Collingwood amplified his verdict. Of Stanhope he said:[1] he is 'a fine boy, good dispositioned, and good sense, but it is astonishing how little educated. He will be a useful officer, a good one, but never a great one.' As for Currell: 'I can do nothing with Currell; he had better come home; he is very *odd*.'[2] Pursuing the matter still further, he remarked to Mrs. Stead:[3] '. . . he [Currell] has something very odd in his manner, or rather, no manner at all, but saunters a melancholic for a week altogether, unnoticing and unnoticed, except when I give him a little rally to make his blood circulate, and this I do, not in the expectation that it will make him better in his profession, but merely for his health's sake. It is a pity she [his mother] had not put him apprentice to Jno Wilson, the apothecary; he might have gone on very wisely. His gravity would have established his reputation as a learned doctor, and if he did poison an old woman now and then, better do that than drown a ship's company at a dash by running on the rocks.'

'You may have heard,' Collingwood said in the same letter, 'that I am reckoned rather queer in the promotion of young men. I advance a great many who have not a friend to speak for them, while those I most respect in the world sometimes plead in vain. Those who are diligent and promise to be useful officers never miscarry.' 'My business,' he explained to his sister, 'is to look for officers capable of doing the duty of the Service. When I find them, and find them gentlemen, I do not care who they belong to.'[4]

Even Mrs. Moutray, one of Collingwood's oldest and most knowledgeable friends, so far as the Navy was concerned, became inured to shock with regard to her favourites. Writing to her early in 1801 from the *Barfleur*, Collingwood said of a young man for whom she had solicited his interest:

I will tell you my opinion. He is as well-bred, gentlemanly

---

[1] H., Letter 175.   [2] H., Letter 172.   [3] H., Letter 174.   [4] H., Letter 175.

a young man as can be, and I dare say an excellent fox hunter, for he seems skilful in horses, dogs, foxes and such animals. But unluckily . . . these are branches of knowledge not very useful at sea, we do not profit by them off Ushant. For the rest he has no great taste or application, but on your account I will show him all the favour I properly can.[1]

Collingwood's wife, and his father-in-law, were not always more fortunate in their recommendations than his sisters or Mrs. Stead. He told his wife that a certain lady had written:

. . . that her son's want of spirits is owing to the loss of his time when he was in England, which is a subject that need give her no concern, for if he takes no more pains in his profession than he has done, he will not be qualified for a lieutenant in sixteen years, and I should be very sorry to put the safety of a ship and the lives of the men into such hands. He is of no more use here as an officer than Bounce is, and not near so entertaining. She writes as if she expected that he is to be a lieutenant as soon as he has served six years; but that is a mistaken fancy; and the loss of his time is while he is at sea not while he is on shore. He is living on the navy, and not serving it.

In the same letter, Collingwood remarked of another young man, that he was applying to go home. 'If he goes he may stay,' was the unsparing verdict, 'for I have no notion of people making the Service a mere convenience for themselves, as if it were a public establishment for loungers.'[2]

A year later Collingwood told Blackett:[3] 'I was surprised to see Mr —— come out again. They think, when they have served six years at sea, they should be made Lieutenants, and never deem it necessary to qualify themselves. He is a good, quiet young man, and walks about, doing no harm; but he has no activity in him. Such people become rather pensioners upon the Navy, than officers in it.'

In one important respect Collingwood's views modified with time. He came to believe that he could make something of the Irish, if caught young enough.

Lord Collingwood [wrote his son-in-law],[4] had ever been

---

[1] N.C. (Additional letter; 1837 edition.)
[2] N.C., 417.   [3] N.C., 497.   [4] N.C., 535.

adverse to impressment, and early after the mutiny at the Nore had been studious to discover some means of avoiding the too frequent recurrence to that system. He had found that Irish boys, from twelve to sixteen years of age, when mingled with the English sailors, acquired rapidly the order, activity, and seaman-like spirit of their comrades; and that, in the climate of the Mediterranean they often, in less than two years, became excellent topmen; while adults, who had been little habituated to the sea, but torn by impressment from other occupations, were generally ineffective and discontented. He accordingly proposed to the Admiralty to raise yearly five thousand Irish boys, and to send a large proportion of them to his command, where he would have them taught and prepared in ships of the line, before they were sent into smaller vessels. By these means, and by the extension throughout the Navy of that humane and temperate discipline for which he was ever distinguished . . . he was convinced that a large and effective force might be maintained . . .

As for the men in general, Newnham Collingwood noted:[1]

. . . in the latter years of his life he had carried his system of arrangement and care to such a degree of perfection, that perhaps no society in the world, of equal extent, was so healthy as the crew of his flag-ship. She had usually 800 men; was, on one occasion, more than one year and a half without going into port, and during the whole of that time never had more than six, and generally only four on the sick-list. This result was occasioned by his attention to dryness, (for he rarely permitted washing between decks,) to the frequent ventilation of the hammocks and clothes on the booms, to the creating of as much circulation of air below as possible, to the diet and amusement of the men; but above all, by the contented spirits of the sailors, who loved their commander as their protector and friend, well assured that at his hands they would ever receive justice and kindness, and that of their comforts he was more jealous than of his own.[2]

[1] N.C., 357.

[2] The punishment records of Collingwood's Mediterranean flagships make a striking contrast with those of the *Victory*, in the same area, during the Nelson-Hardy regime, when the cat-o'-nine-tails was in all too frequent use.

Collingwood's later Journals certainly bear this testimony
out, and the health record of his ships was indeed remarkable;
the regular issue of lemon juice (not, as sometimes believed,
lime juice) having at last put a term to scurvy in the British
fleets. How little the cause of this disease was still known, even
among people of Collingwood's experience and advantages, is
illustrated by a postscript in a letter addressed to Sir Alexander
Ball on 27 August 1808:[1] 'if the *Standard* has any Egypt water
on board, she must start it, as there is a suspicion that it may
be the cause of the scurvy, which her men are afflicted with.'

It is noteworthy that when he became a landowner, as he did
after inheriting Chirton, Collingwood was as considerate to his
tenants as to his sailors. 'One thing . . . interests me,' he wrote
to Blackett:[2] 'that no person should be removed from a house
or farm, unless his conduct has made him very obnoxious. It is
the interest of an old tenant to give a fair rent; and when he
does, it is shameful to have him subjected to a higher bidder.
I have lived long enough without wealth to be very indifferent
about it; and I hope I may always be comfortable without putting others to difficulty.'

III

Collingwood paid such attention to the education of his beloved
children that he sometimes overdid it. If he had returned home
in 1810, when the girls were almost launched into Society, the
suspicion is allowable that Sarah and Mary Patience would
have found it hard to live up to all their father's precepts.
Moreover in one matter, that of the search after knowledge, he
did not allow for difference of character and outlook in those
less remarkable than himself. His idea of never wasting time,
of inquiry into the roots of everything, of fostering a sense of
wonder about the universe in all its aspects has been the secret
of many a well-filled life: but there are signs in Collingwood's
later letters, particularly in those to Mrs. Stead and his sister,
that his wife and children, with prosperity and expansion before
them, and without his own firm and guiding presence, were
not going in the direction he wished. For instance, when old
Mr. Henry Blackett, the Rector of Bolden, died, Collingwood

---

[1] Add. MSS. 14287, f. 7.   [2] N.C., 496.

wrote to his sister:[1] 'I thought it very unkind in Mr H. Blackett
not leaving my children something, but perhaps he thought,
what I by experience know, for every thousand pound he left
them, two would have been spent on the credit of it.'

These were hard words, written in September 1809 and therefore towards the end of his life, but they were not singular.
The truth was that no governess, or maiden aunt, or indulgent
father-in-law, or even Mrs. Stead, could make up what he himself would have supplied to his own household. It was part of
the price that was paid for the admiral's devotion to the service of his country, and when he said, as he did more than
once,[2] that he no longer wished to go home, it arose from a
sense of disappointment for which, if anyone was to blame, it
was himself.

Collingwood's letters to his children make a series from which
Victorian moralists loved to quote. This was one of the reasons
for the continuing popularity of his son-in-law's Memoir. The
first important missive was addressed jointly to Sarah and
Mary Patience from sea on 26 December 1807, when the girls
were fifteen and fourteen respectively.

It is exactly at your age that much pains should be taken
[wrote their father],[3] for whatever knowledge you acquire
now will last you all your lives. The impression which is
made on young minds is so strong that it never wears out;
whereas, every body knows how difficult it is to make an
old snuff-taking lady comprehend anything beyond Pam or
Spadille.[4] Such persons hang very heavy on society; but you,
my darlings, I hope, will qualify yourselves to adorn it, to
be respected for your good sense, and admired for your gentle
manners.

Remember that gentle manners are the first grace which
a lady can possess. Whether she differ in her opinion from
others, or be of the same sentiment, her expressions should
be equally mild. A positive contradiction is vulgar and ill-
bred; but I shall never suspect you of being uncivil to any
person . . . Should I return to England and find you less

---

[1] H., Letter 186.   [2] H., Letters 184, 186.   [3] N.C., 327–8.
[4] Pam is the knave of clubs in the game of loo; spadille is the ace of spades
in the games of ombre and quadrille.

amiable than my mind pictures you, or that I have reason to expect, my heart would sink with sorrow.

Your application must be to useful knowledge. Sarah, I hope, applies to geometry, and Mary makes good progress in arithmetic. Independently of their use in every situation in life, they are sciences so curious in their nature, and so many things that cannot be comprehended without them are made easy, that were it only to gratify a curiosity which all women have, and to be let into secrets that cannot be learned without that knowledge, it would be a sufficient inducement to acquire them. Then do, my sweet girls, study to be wise . . .

On 23 July 1808, from off Cadiz, advice continued:[1]

My dearest Sarah and Mary [Collingwood wrote], it gave me great pleasure to find, from your letters, that you were well, and I hope, making good use of your time. It is at this period of your lives that you must lay the foundation of all knowledge, and of those manners and modes of thinking that distinguish gentlewomen from the Miss Nothings. A good woman has great and important duties to do in the world, and will always be in danger of doing them ill and without credit to herself, unless she has acquired knowledge. I have only to recommend to you not to pass too much of your time in trifling pursuits, or in reading books merely of amusement, which afford you no information, nor any thing that you can reflect upon afterwards, and feel that you have acquired what you did not know before.

Never do any thing that can denote an angry mind; for although every body is born with a certain degree of passion, and from untoward circumstances will sometimes feel its operation, and be what they call 'out of Humour,' yet a sensible man or woman will not allow it to be discovered. Check and restrain it; never make any determination until you find it has entirely subsided; and always avoid saying any thing that you may afterwards wish unsaid. I hope, Sarah, you continue to read geography. Whenever there are particular events happening, examine the map and see where they took place. At Saragossa, in Arragon, the Spanish army was composed mostly of the peasants of the country, and

[1] N.C., 404-5.

the priests (who take a great interest in this war), were officers. The Bishop headed the army, and with his sword in one hand and a cross in the other, fought very bravely, until he was shot in the arm . . .

What was perhaps the fullest expression of Collingwood's wishes for his girls was sent to Sarah from the *Ocean* when the ship was at Malta on 5 February 1809. He had more than his usual snatched opportunities for writing, and although he was seldom tedious in his admonitions, for once he allowed himself to descend into some detail.[1]

The greatest pleasure I have amidst my toils and troubles [he wrote], is in the expectation which I entertain of finding you improved in knowledge, and that the understanding which it has pleased God to give you both has been cultivated with care and assiduity.

Your future happiness and respectability in the world depend on the diligence with which you apply to the attainment of knowledge at this period of your life, and I hope that no negligence of your own will be a bar to your progress.

When I write to you, my beloved child, so much interested am I that you should be amiable, and worthy of the friendship and esteem of good and wise people, that I cannot forbear to second and enforce the instruction which you receive, by admonition of my own, pointing out to you the great advantages that will result from a temperate conduct and sweetness of manner to all people, on all occasions.

It does not follow that you are to coincide and agree in opinion with every ill-judging person; but after shewing them your reason for dissenting from their opinion, your argument and opposition to it should not be tinctured by any thing offensive.

Never forget for one moment that you are gentlewomen; and all your words and all your actions should mark you gentle. I never knew your mother—your dear, your good mother—say a harsh or a hasty thing to any person in my life. Endeavour to imitate her. I am quick and hasty in my temper; my sensibility is touched sometimes with a trifle, and my expression of it sudden as gunpowder: but, my

[1] N.C., 492–4.

darling, it is a misfortune, which, not having been sufficiently restrained in my youth, has caused me much pain. It has, indeed, given me more trouble to subdue this natural impetuosity, than any thing I ever undertook.

I believe that you are both mild; but if ever you feel in your little breasts that you inherit a particle of your father's infirmity, restrain it, and quit the subject that has caused it, until your serenity is recovered.

So much for mind and manners; next for accomplishments. No sportsman ever hits a partridge without aiming at it; and skill is acquired by repeated attempts. It is the same thing in every art: unless you aim at perfection, you will never attain it; but frequent attempts will make it easy. Never, therefore, do anything with indifference. Whether it be to mend a rent in your garment, or finish the most delicate piece of art, endeavour to do it as perfectly as it is possible.

When you write a letter, give it your greatest care, that it may be as perfect in all its parts as you can make it. Let the subject be sense, expressed in the most plain, intelligible, and elegant manner that you are capable of. If in a familiar epistle you should be playful and jocular, guard carefully that your wit be not sharp, so as to give pain to any person; and before you write a sentence, examine it, even the words of which it is composed, that there be nothing vulgar or inelegant in them.

Remember, my dear, that your letter is the picture of your brains; and those whose brains are a compound of folly, nonsense and impertinence, are to blame to exhibit them to the contempt of the world, or the pity of their friends. To write a letter with negligence, without proper stops, with crooked lines and great flourishing dashes, is inelegant: it argues either great ignorance of what is proper, or great indifference towards the person to whom it is addressed, and is consequently disrespectful. It makes no amends to add an apology, for having scrawled a sheet of paper; of bad pens, for you should mend them; or want of time, for nothing is more important to you, or to which your time can more properly be devoted.[1]

[1] 'It is folly to say that any man, let his business be what it may, has not time to write.' Nelson to Collingwood, 18 August 1796. (Col. 15.)

I think I can know the character of a lady pretty nearly by her hand-writing. The dashers are all impudent, however they may conceal it from themselves or others; and the scribblers flatter themselves with the vain hope, that, as their letter cannot be read, it may be mistaken for sense. I am very anxious to come to England; for I have lately been unwell. The greatest happiness which I expect is to find that my dear girls have been assiduous in their learning.

May God Almighty bless you, my beloved little Sarah and sweet Mary too.

There was one further considerable letter on the same lines, written in April 1809 from near Majorca. In this, Collingwood summed up what he thought to be the essence of all he had expressed before.[1] Education, so it seemed to him, could be divided into three distinct parts: 'the first part is the cultivation of the mind . . . a knowledge of right and wrong . . . a habit of doing acts of virtue and honour.' The second is 'to acquire a competent knowledge how to manage your affairs, whatever they may happen to be; to know how to direct the economy of your house; and to keep exact accounts of every thing that concerns you.' The third is: 'how to practise those manners and that address which will recommend you to the respect of strangers. Boldness and forwardness are exceedingly disgusting, and such people are generally more disliked the more they are known; but, at the same time, shyness and bashfulness, and the shrinking from conversation with those with whom you ought to associate, are repulsive and unbecoming.'

If Collingwood had an ideal for girls, based in large part on the character of his wife, he knew a great deal about boys from having been their mentor for most of his professional life. Writing in October 1809 to Mrs. Hall, daughter of his old captain, Braithwaite, who had a flourishing family of three, he said:[2]

The temper and disposition of most people are formed before they are seven years old; and the common cause of bad ones is the too great indulgence and mistaken fondness which the affection of a parent finds it difficult to veil, though the happiness of the child depends upon it.

[1] N.C., 513–14.   [2] N.C., 548–9.

Your measures must be systematic: whenever they do wrong, never omit to reprove them firmly, but with gentleness. Always speak to them in a style and language rather superior to their years. Proper words are as easily learned as improper ones. And when they do well, when they deserve commendation, bestow it lavishly. Let the feelings of your heart flow from your eyes and tongue; and they will never forget the effect which their good behaviour has upon their mother, and this at an earlier time of life than is generally thought.

This letter, the original of which survives,[1] provides an instance of Newnham Collingwood's excisions on the grounds of 'taste', for the admiral continued: 'I consider young children, before they have any reasoning faculty, to possess an instinct that is very little inferior to a young dog—and you know how soon a puppy is taught good behaviour by proper treatment.' He added later, thinking of his Sarah's long grass widowhood: 'Don't you think Lady Collingwood is well prepared for her widowhood: she will make an admirable widow. I suppose she must go through all the ceremony just as if she had a husband all this time.'

War had shown Collingwood that women could be as brutally exposed to the hazards of the time as men. Writing to Mrs. Stead in October 1809 he gave her (in one of his expansive postscripts),[2] an idea of the siege of Gerona, not far from the Costa Brava, off which some of his ships were then stationed.

The garrison behave with the greatest valour. The town is a ruin; the walls all thrown down in many places, yet they repulse the enemy. The women are dressed in the habits of men, are armed with muskets and behave with the greatest gallantry. The soul of a woman is the excellence of creation, but how they would spoil it by foolish fashion, affecting a timidity which they do not feel. I wish my girls were taught their exercise and to be good shots. I think it will be useful to them before long. I am sure Sarah would be a sharp shooter, a credit to any Light Corps.

[1] Col. 15.   [2] H., Letter 190.

IV

As regards the second part of his scheme for education, the management of personal affairs, Collingwood set a fine example. He husbanded what belonged to him in shrewd fashion, and he was equally well known for his economy in naval stores and equipment. A story circulated of how, in the heat of action, he once ordered Clavell to save a badly torn sail, helping him to place it in safety. Some nineteen years after his death, a writer, George Pryce, contributed a note to a popular educational journal which has the ring of truth.[1]

> One of the most striking features of this distinguished British Admiral [wrote Pryce], was his strict economy in every thing relative to the public service. The sails of his own ship were literally worn to rags before he suffered them to be condemned. He kept a close watch over his fleet in this respect, and was highly displeased whenever he observed any expense incurred where there was not a strict necessity. A vessel in his fleet having displayed new sails, he ordered the old ones to be brought to him for inspection; and finding them in far better condition than his own, he commanded the fore-sail to be hoisted in place of the tattered one that was in use. His Lordship then invited the captain of the gay vessel to dinner, and carelessly asked him what he thought of his fore-sail: 'In fair condition, my Lord,' was the unwary answer. 'If it be good enough for an admiral's ship, I think it might have served a captain's,' said Collingwood.
>
> On another occasion, in the midst of an action, seeing that one of the masts was shivered, he ordered out the boat, and being asked for what purpose, 'To take that spar into the store-ship,' was the reply. By this unrelaxing spirit of economy, he saved thousands to the revenue.

Economy, as well as his firm belief that his own capacity was equal to any situation he was likely to encounter, made him so ardent a champion of the principle of 'do it yourself'. It was not pride, he once said, and he attempted to explain

---

[1] *The Youth's Instructor and Guardian*, Vol. xiii, No. 145, Jan. 1829.

what he felt in a letter of 18 April 1809 to Mrs. Stead:[1]

> While I can serve to the satisfaction of my King, and benefit of the country, I feel the reward in my act, and look no further for it. But my fear, my only fear is, that my strength of body, impaired by length of days and weight of years, should unfit me for the arduous duties I have to fulfil.
>
> Fourteen or sixteen hours of every day I am employed. I have about eighty ships of war under my orders, and the direction of naval affairs from Constantinople to Cadiz, with an active and powerful enemy, always threatening, and though he seldom moves, keeps us constantly on the alert.
>
> I leave nothing undone that I can devise for the public good. Where I fail it will be my misfortune, not my neglect. Where there is fault it will be all my own. In the plan, I involve no one, for I never ask for council, and this I do from principle, not pride. But I look for success, and I know I shall glad your heart when the world allows I deserve it.

As for his personal fortune, although Collingwood never considered himself outstandingly lucky in the matter of prize, and his letters were filled with complaints on the subject, he had in fact very little to worry about. He left a sum of £163,743 exclusive of his interest in Chirton and Hethpool,[2] and although this was not one of the greater naval fortunes of its time, it was a very handsome one by any standards. He left £40,000 to each of his two daughters, every penny of which he had earned for himself.

V

If Collingwood stressed, in writing to his daughter, that his temper was explosive, yet over the years he brought self-discipline to an enviable pitch. Close observers were astonished that, in the tension of battle, the admiral's voice and manner were precisely as usual. This was the result, not of phlegm but of deliberate control, for by temperament he was fretful. In February 1808, in the course of a letter to Admiral Purvis,

---

[1] H., Letter 174.   [2] Hughes, p. 306n.

otherwise almost entirely about matters of business, Colling-wood confessed:[1] 'the constant anxiety of my mind, and per-petual study to do the best I can for the publick service, keeps me on a constant stretch: men with nerves like cables, that can never be made to vibrate are certainly happier, but they are more like sticks and not to be envied.'

Collingwood was described as follows in his obituary:[2]

His lordship was of middle stature, but extremely thin, and temperate in his general habits; ate always with an appetite, drank moderately after dinner, but never indulged afterwards in spirits or in wine; while his personal attention to the lowest guest at his table was always universally ob-served. It was his general rule in tempestuous weather, and upon any hostile emergency that occurred, to sleep upon his sofa in a flannel gown, taking off only his epauletted coat. The writer . . . has seen him upon deck without his hat, and his grey hair floating to the wind, whilst torrents of rain poured down through the shrouds, and his eye, like an eagle's, on the watch. Personal exposure, colds, rheumatisms, ague, all nothing seemed to him when duty called.

Writing to his wife from off Cadiz in July 1808 about the evidently startling effect of his portrait on those at home whom he had not seen for so long, he said:[3]

I am sorry to find my picture was not an agreeable sur-prise: I did not say any thing to you about it, because I would always guard you as much as I could against disap-pointment; but you see, with all my care, I sometime fail. The painter was reckoned the most eminent in Sicily; but you expected to find me a smooth-skinned, clear-complexioned gentleman, such as I was when I left home, dressed in the newest taste, and like the fine people who live gay lives ashore.

Alas! it is far otherwise with me. The painter was thought to have flattered me much: that lump under my chin was but the loose skin, from which the flesh has shrunk away;

---

[1] H., Letter 148.   [2] N. Chron. xxiii. 351.
[3] N.C., 415–16. The painting referred to was completed at Syracuse on 18 December 1807 and signed Guiseppe Polite Sorcevani.

the redness of my face was not, I assure you, the effect of wine, but of burning suns and boisterous winds; and my eyes, which were once dark and bright, are now faded and dim.

The painter represented me as I am; not as I once was. It is time and toil that have worked the change, and not his want of skill. That the countenance is stern, will not be wondered at, when it is considered how many sad and anxious hours and how many heartaches I have. I shall be very glad when the war is over.

Sarah's own appearance, about this time, was referred to in a letter to Mrs. Stead sent a few months later:[1] 'Sarah tells me she has become moderately fat, a good round, portly gentlewoman, but seems to intimate some doubt of her having arrived at that perfection to which Mrs Ingham has attained. I was glad to hear it, because it looks as if she was happy, her heart at ease, no corroding cares wasting her midnight hours, but her natural suavity of disposition gently gliding her through life.'

George Pryce, in the *Youth's Instructor*,[2] bore out the testimony of others, in describing Collingwood's salient characteristics.

Though his attention was . . . alive to every minutia, he gave his orders in the heat of an engagement as calmly as on an ordinary occasion. To his men he was always attentive and kind; but strict with the officers, particularly with young nobility. He could not bear to see promotion, unless arising from merit, and used to say: 'I like a man to get in at the port-hole, not at the cabin window.' He was perfectly plain in his dress, and retained the old fashion. A small cocked hat; a square cut blue coat, with tarnished epaulettes; blue waistcoat and small clothes; with boots, guiltless of blacking, but occasionally greased, formed his costume on state occasions. In his diet he was strictly temperate, and even abstemious. So long as his health permitted, he constantly regulated the motions of his own vessel: leaving his officers scarcely any duties to perform.

As a pendant to this delineation, it is to be noted that Collingwood was as alive to aristocratic merit as to any other. Captain

[1] H., Letter 168.　　[2] Vol. xiii, No. 145.

Waldegrave, son of his friend Lord Radstock, got the praise he deserved, and so did others of high birth, if their talents and zeal were exceptional.

One characteristic of Collingwood's was often remarked. He was a great reader, but he detested cards. Once he let himself go on the subject to Mrs. Stead:[1]

> ... cards [he wrote], which I do so truly abominate, that I hope my children will never use them but to wind their threads upon. There is no excuse for them but by acknowledging a vacuity of mind, fit only to entertain trifles, or an avidity for money, that would take from their neighbours what they have not got perhaps by honest industry.
>
> I have known this passion for cards so corrupt the mind that it was unfit for anything else . . . and so increase as to induce people to invent a game at which they could play by themselves when a partner could not be found. Would you not be amused to peep through a hole and see a person playing for hours a serious game at cards, and even at last to engage so much in it as to feel a real interest in such nonsense? How much better was he employed who amused himself by picking the grey hairs out of his asse's tail. To immerse my poor girls in such a society, the thought gives me a chill even in the heat of summer.

In general, Collingwood's obituarist is not to be doubted when he wrote, of other characteristics:

> His lordship's judgement was sound and firm, his mind acute and penetrating, his wit so very lively, it led him constantly to pun; and though general punsters must be frequently insipid, he seldom failed to produce the playful equivoque he wished.
>
> To his religious duties he constantly attended; his religion, like himself, was without terror, pure without fanaticism, and gentle without levity. The Latin he learned at school he had never forgotten, and though he knew but sufficient French to maintain a general correspondence on the coast,

---

[1] H., Letter 178: though judging by a reference in A. M. W. Stirling's *The Letter-bag of Lady Elizabeth Spencer-Stanhope* he had not, in younger days, been averse to a game of whist.

and could scarcely manage Spanish at all, he was notwithstanding a good scholar, but a scholar of the old school.

He was always perfectly dignified in his deportment, without that execrable pride which we so often see assumed as a cloak to conceal a want of worth. A rich vein of native worth within him, its assumption was unnecessary.

There is a surface brightness about the style of these observations which might argue polite platitudes, but in the main they are true. The writer could have added that Collingwood was a convinced believer in the hand of Providence guiding his country's endeavours in times of crisis. Like so many great captains, he believed God was on his side, and as his most constant enemies were the French, who in the early days of their Revolution officially eschewed religion, he had more grounds for this ingenuous faith than some of those who have held it.

Shortly after Trafalgar, Mrs. Moutray sent Collingwood the text of a sermon she had heard, the occasion and substance of which are now forgotten. In the course of his address the preacher referred in warm terms to the General Order to the Fleet in which the admiral had issued immediately following the battle.

Who would have thought [replied Collingwood],[1] that my orders for the conduct of a fleet should ever have been preached from a pulpit. It seems so odd a thing. God knows it never struck me that there was anything particular in them. The expressions were merely those that flowed naturally from a heart full of thankfulness to God for the happy issue of a great contest; for under all our circumstances it was impossible for any one to consider them, and not to feel a consciousness of Divine aid.

The language of the sermon is fine, the doctrine of it highly instructive. It teaches us where we may safely rest our hope of a happy issue to our endeavours, but not to sit with arms across crying: 'God help us!' He has given us certain powers, and it is in the exercise of them, to the best of our understanding, that we may reasonably hope for help.

[1] N.C. (Additional letter, 1837 edition.)

Collingwood wrote an instructive passage in a letter sent on 18 April 1809 to Mrs. Stead:[1]

To tell you the truth, my dear sister, I have lived long enough in the world to know that there is no sense in lamenting the death of people; indeed, to consider it not as a subject of lamentation. I do not know of any thing the mind can dwell upon with more pleasure than the idea of dying comfortably. I think it has got all its horror in weak minds, by the same sort of operation that the soul shrinks at the story of a ghost. In infancy we get the impression that death is horrible, but I believe if the same pains were taken to combine the ideas of death and delight, we should wait as impatiently for it as they do for a Guild ball, or a Lord Mayor's feast, or any other of those great events which make people perfectly happy.

Shortly before Collingwood died, he thought the general prospect for Europe dismal. A few weeks after he had written to her about death, he confessed to Mrs. Stead:[2]

When I look abroad, the prospect is bad: when I look to home, it is worse. And unless mankind can be made honest, and to act from public spirit, uncontaminated by their individual interest, and reconcile themselves to justice though to their own disadvantage, the longer we live, the the worse we shall see it.

I am thankful my head is grey. The people in England know nothing of war but the taxes, and when they read in a newspaper of the destruction of twenty-eight or thirty thousand men, the impression is slightly felt at Charing Cross. But were we to witness the inhabitants flying from their town in flames, and before they gain the next discover it in the same state, women and children running from death and when they come to the Po or the Pavia find the bridges broken down, it was scenes like these, to which human creatures are now daily exposed, that made me so desirous my girls should learn to swim, then they might set such chance and circumstance at defiance, and a river or two would have been no bar to their safety.

[1] H., Letter 174.   [2] H., Letter 176.

Dark as the times were, yet in due course the clouds did disperse, though not in Collingwood's own life-time, or for some years afterwards. In future decades, the country he loved was once again to know prosperity and greatness, and he had helped to re-create it. In a notable summary of what he had achieved in his final years (the ones which mattered most), Mr. Piers Mackesy wrote:[1]

He was the only man in the Mediterranean, sailor, soldier or diplomat, who could survey the whole theatre and see its unity. From Finisterre to the Dardanelles, his cruisers' ceaseless activity brought him information of the enemy's forces and agents, of events going forward in Egypt and Morocco, in Trieste and Tunis, in Albania and Corsica. His diplomatic correspondence covered the theatre: the Sultans of Barbary, the Pachas of Albania and Egypt, the Kings and Ministers of Sicily and Sardinia, the British representatives in Palermo, Vienna and Constantinople, all looked to him as the fountain of British power and policy on the southern edge of Europe...

Napoleon blamed much of his defeat on what he called the 'Spanish ulcer'. Collingwood had been responsible for ensuring that, from the very first moment she attempted to throw off the yoke which France had placed upon her, Spain was supported, and the activities of the French fleet nullified in every sphere where it could aspire to operate with effect. He was one of the supreme examples of the selfless leader, utterly single minded in his pursuit of victory, entirely understanding of the relentless, all-demanding nature of total war. He could have learnt nothing even from his most professional and accomplished enemies, while few of them could have matched that amazing tenacity which led Collingwood to write to Lord Northesk, exactly a year before he died:[2]

My dear Lord, I shall never come home; and the only fear I have is, that my diminished strength cannot maintain the war as the circumstances of it require. Had I strength, such as Lord St. Vincent had, I should never think of England, but how I could serve her.

---

[1] *The War in the Mediterranean: 1803–1810*, Piers Mackesy (1957), p. 395.
[2] N.C. (Additional letter; 1837 edition.)

18

Collingwood's great work had been achieved far from home and those he loved, and the final paragraph of his letter to the *Naval Chronicle*, composed in 1806, in which he attempted the only summing up of his own career, remained true to the end.[1]

In this sketch of my life you may perceive, Sir, how great a part of it has been spent at sea; since the year 1793, I have only been one year at home; to my own children I am scarce known; yet while I have health and strength to serve my country, I consider *that* health and strength due to it; and if I serve it successfully, as I have ever done faithfully, my children will not want friends.

'Fame's trumpet makes a great noise,' Collingwood once wrote to Mrs. Moutray, 'but the notes do not dwell long on the ear.'[2] Collingwood did not care greatly for fame, and nothing at all for popularity. To him, reputation, personal and professional honour, were all in all. His honour was unblemished; his reputation is unassailable; and there are those who find in his personality a number of lovable qualities which have not always distinguished the greater commanders.

Leadership in part derives from example, and Collingwood gave it, but his gifts did not include the magic which Nelson possessed, and which Collingwood so much admired, the inspiring force which causes other men to rise above themselves. If, as on one occasion seemed likely, Collingwood had held chief command in a fleet action, victory would have been achieved, but it would have been won through strict control, not through that wider freedom which Nelson allowed his captains.

'I often wish I was peaceably settled in heaven,' wrote Collingwood to Purvis six months before the end. 'I am sure I may say "few and evil have been the days of my pilgrimage."'[3] This was a sad retrospection, wrung from a failing man who had always found it hard to share his burdens. In this respect, his deep reserve carried its own penalties.

Collingwood's wisdom and courage were apparent in his

---

[1] *N. Chron.* xxiii. 382.
[2] N.C. (Additional letter; 1837 edition.)
[3] H., Letter 185.

actions, and the essential nobility of his mind is recorded in what he wrote, in public and private correspondence alike. Even in his age of great sea officers, he stands out as one who served his country with high distinction.

Epilogue

Lord Collingwood's body was taken to England, as Nelson's had been some four years earlier, and it was landed at Greenwich, where it lay in state from 26 April to 11 May 1810. Then a flag from the *Ville de Paris* was draped over the coffin, and eight officers carried their burden to the funeral car, the procession to St. Paul's being by land, not by river. Lord Hood, Lieutenant Governor of Greenwich Hospital, paid his last respects as the carriages moved off.

Among the mourners was Collingwood's old school-fellow, Lord Eldon, who had risen to become Lord Chancellor, his presence a touching courtesy, since he had scarcely met the admiral since youth. Lord St. Vincent, still with years of life before him, Sir Peter Parker, early patron and life-long friend, Lord Cochrane, one of the most brilliant of Collingwood's frigate captains, and two First Lords of the Admiralty whom Collingwood had served well, Lord Mulgrave and Thomas Grenville, were also present. Some thirty admirals and captains from the Fleet were in the procession, as was Collingwood's signal lieutenant, George Brown, who had been in the *Victory* at Trafalgar. Mr. Brown was one of the three officers for whom Collingwood had requested promotion in his last official letter on the subject. He was made a commander, as were the others.

Collingwood's devoted servant Smith, later to become a schoolmaster, was allowed to perform the final rite by placing the coronet on the coffin. Only the barest legend was chiselled on the tomb: 'Cuthbert Lord Collingwood, Died 7 March 1810: Aged 61.' The economy of words would have appealed to the admiral; less so, perhaps, the melancholy monument by Westmacott which stands in the body of the cathedral.

Sarah Collingwood survived her husband by nine years, and

became known to the forlorn Lady Nelson. Her elder daughter married G. L. Newnham, later Newnham Collingwood, in 1816, and lived to be sixty. She was of help to her husband in compiling the Memoir which kept Collingwood's achievements before posterity, but in her widowhood she became increasingly eccentric, particularly in the dispersal of her inheritance. Mary Patience was at one time betrothed to W. R. Cosway, her father's secretary. The engagement was broken off, largely at the instigation of her uncle, John Collingwood, who considered that a baker's son was no fit match for a peer's daughter. Mary was married in 1817 to Anthony Denny, and although she herself died young, her family continues the admiral's line of descent.

APPENDIX

The Trafalgar Dispatch

Collingwood's Trafalgar dispatch took the form of two letters to William Marsden, Secretary of the Admiralty, which were printed in the *London Gazette*, on 6 November 1805.

> To William Marsden, Esq, Admiralty.
> *Euryalus*, off Cape Trafalgar,
> October 22nd, 1805

Sir,

The ever to be lamented death of Vice-Admiral Lord Viscount Nelson, who, in the late conflict with the Enemy, fell in the hour of victory, leaves to me the duty of informing my Lords Commissioners of the Admiralty, that on the 19th instant it was communicated to the Commander in Chief from the Ships watching the motions of the Enemy in Cadiz, that the Combined Fleet had put to sea. As they sailed with light winds westerly, his Lordship concluded their destination was the Mediterranean, and immediately made all sail for the Streights' entrance with the British squadron, consisting of twenty-seven Ships, three of them sixty-fours, where his Lordship was informed by Capt. Blackwood, (whose vigilance in watching, and giving notice of the enemy's movements, has been highly meretorious,) that they had not yet passed the Streights.

On Monday the 21st instant, at daylight, when Cape Trafalgar bore E. by S. about seven leagues, the Enemy was discovered six or seven miles to the eastward, the wind about west, and very light; the Commander in Chief immediately made the signal for the fleet to bear up in two columns, as they are formed in order of sailing; a mode of attack his Lordship had previously directed, to avoid the inconvenience and delay in forming a line of battle in the usual manner. The Enemy's line consisted of thirty-three Ships (of which eighteen were French and fifteen Spanish), commanded in chief by Admiral Ville-neuve; the Spaniards, under the direction of Gravina, wore, with their heads to the northward, and formed their line of battle with great closeness and correctness; but as the mode of attack was unusual, so the structure of their line was new;—it formed a crescent convexing to leeward—so that, in leading down to their centre, I had both their van and rear abaft the beam. Before the fire opened, every alternate Ship was about a cable's length to windward of her second a-head and a-stern, forming a kind of double line, and appeared, when on their beam, to leave a very little interval between them; and this without crowding their Ships. Admiral Villeneuve was in the *Bucentaure* in the centre, and the *Prince of Asturias* bore Gravina's flag in the rear; but the French and Spanish Ships were mixed without any apparent regard to order of National squadron.

As the mode of our attack had been previously determined on, and communicated to the Flag-officers and Captains, few signals were necessary, and none were made except to direct close order as the lines bore down.

The Commander in Chief in the *Victory* led the weather column; and the *Royal Sovereign*, which bore my flag, the lee.

The Action began at twelve o'clock, by the leading Ships of the columns breaking through the Enemy's line, the Com-mander in Chief about the tenth Ship from the van, the Second in Command about the twelfth from the rear, leaving the van of the Enemy unoccupied; the succeeding Ships breaking through in all parts, a-stern of their leaders, and engaging the Enemy at the muzzles of their guns, the conflict was severe. The Enemy's Ships were fought with a gallantry highly honour-able to their Officers, but the attack on them was irresistible; and it pleased the Almighty Disposer of all events to grant His Majesty's arms a complete and glorious victory. About three P.M. many of the Enemy's Ships having struck their colours, their line gave way; Admiral Gravina, with ten Ships, joining their Frigates to leeward, stood towards Cadiz. The five head-most Ships in their van tacked, and standing to the southward to windward of the British line, were engaged, and the sternmost of them taken; the others went off, leaving to His Majesty's squadron nineteen Ships of the line, (of which two are first-rates, the *Santissima Trinidada* and the *Santa Anna*,) with three Flag Officers; viz. Admiral Villeneuve, the Commander in Chief; Don Ignatio Maria d'Alava, Vice-Admiral; and the Spanish Rear-Admiral, Don Baltazar Hidalgo Cisneros.

After such a victory it may appear unnecessary to enter into encomiums on the particular parts taken by the several Commanders; the conclusion says more on the subject than I have language to express; the spirit which animated all was the same; when all exert themselves zealously in their country's service, all deserve that their high merits should stand recorded; and never was high merit more conspicuous than in the battle I have described.

The *Achille* (a French 74), after having surrendered, by some mismanagement of the Frenchmen took fire, and blew up; two hundred of her men were saved by the Tenders.

A circumstance occurred during the Action, which so strongly marks the invincible spirit of British seamen, when engaging the enemies of their country, that I cannot resist the pleasure I have in making it known to their Lordships. The *Téméraire* was boarded by accident, or design, by a French ship on one side, and a Spaniard on the other: the contest was vigorous; but in the end the Combined ensigns were torn from the poop, and the British hoisted in their places.[1]

Such a battle could not be fought without sustaining a great loss of men. I have not only to lament, in common with the British Navy and the British Nation, in the fall of the Commander-in-Chief, the loss of a hero whose name will be immortal, and his memory ever dear to his Country; but my heart is rent with the most poignant grief for the death of a friend, to whom, by many years' intimacy, and a perfect knowledge of the virtues of his mind, which inspired ideas superior to the common race of men, I was bound by the strongest ties of affection;—a grief to which even the glorious occasion in which he fell, does not bring the consolation which perhaps it ought: his Lordship received a musket ball in his left breast about the middle of the Action, and sent an Officer to me immediately with his last farewell, and soon after expired.

[1] On further investigation, this incident proved to have been imaginary.

I have also to lament the loss of those excellent Officers, Captains Duff of the *Mars* and Cooke of the *Bellerophon*: I have yet heard of none others.

I fear the numbers that have fallen will be found very great when the returns come to me; but it having blown a gale of wind ever since the Action, I have not yet had it in my power to collect any reports from the Ships.

The *Royal Sovereign* having lost her masts, except the tottering foremast, I called the *Euryalus* to me, while the Action continued, which Ship lying within hail, made my signals, a service Captain Blackwood performed with great attention. After the action I shifted my flag to her, that I might more easily communicate my orders to, and collect the Ships, and towed the *Royal Sovereign* out to seaward. The whole fleet were now in a very perilous situation; many dismasted; all shattered; in thirteen fathoms water, off the shoals of Trafalgar; and when I made the signal to prepare to anchor, few of the Ships had an anchor to let go, their cables being shot; but the same good Providence which aided us through such a day preserved us in the night, by the wind shifting a few points, and drifting the Ships off the land, except four of the captured dismasted Ships, which are now at anchor off Trafalgar, and I hope will ride safe until those gales are over.

Having thus detailed the proceedings of the fleet on this occasion, I beg to congratulate their Lordships on a victory which, I hope, will add a ray to the glory of His Majesty's crown, and be attended with public benefit to our country.

I am, &c,

C. COLLINGWOOD.

THE ORDER IN WHICH THE SHIPS OF THE BRITISH SQUADRON ATTACKED THE COMBINED FLEETS ON THE 21ST OF OCTOBER 1805

Van	Rear
Victory	*Royal Sovereign*
Témeraire	*Mars*
Neptune	*Belleisle*
Conqueror	*Tonnant*

Leviathan		Bellerophon
Ajax		Colossus
Orion		Achille
Agamemnon		Polyphemus
Minotaur		Revenge
Spartiate		Swiftsure
Britannia		Defence
Africa		Thunderer
Frigates: Euryalus	Naiad	Defiance
Sirius	Pickle Schooner	Prince
Phoebe	Entreprenante Cutter	Dreadnought

C. COLLINGWOOD.

Euryalus, October 24th, 1805

Sir,

In my letter of the 22nd, I detailed to you, for the information of my Lords Commissioners of the Admiralty, the proceedings of His Majesty's Squadron on the day of the Action, and that preceding it, since which I have had a continued series of misfortunes, but they are of a kind that human prudence could not possibly provide against, or my skill prevent.

On the 22nd, in the morning, a strong Southerly wind blew, with squally weather, which however did not prevent the activity of the Officers and Seamen of such Ships as were manageable from getting hold of many of the Prizes (thirteen or fourteen), and towing them off to the Westward, where I ordered them to rendezvous round the *Royal Sovereign*, in tow by the *Neptune*; but on the 23rd the gale increased, and the sea ran so high, that many of them broke the tow rope, and drifted far to leeward before they were got hold of again; and some of them, taking advantage of the dark and boisterous night, got before the wind, and have perhaps drifted upon the shore and sunk. On the afternoon of that day the remnant of the Combined Fleet, ten sail of Ships, who had not been much engaged, stood up to leeward of my shattered and straggled charge, as if meaning to attack them, which obliged me to collect a force out of the least injured Ships, and form to leeward for their defence. All this retarded the progress of the Hulks, and the bad weather continuing, determined me to destroy all the leewardmost that could be cleared of the men, considering that keeping possession of the Ships was a matter of little consequence compared with the chance of their falling again into the hands of the Enemy: but even this was an arduous task in the high sea which was running. I hope, however, it has been accomplished to a considerable extent. I entrusted it to skilful Officers, who would spare no pains to execute what was possible. The Captains of the *Prince* and *Neptune* cleared the *Trinidad* and sunk her. Captains Hope, Bayntun, and Malcolm, who joined the Fleet this moment from Gibraltar, had the charge of destroying four others. The *Redoubtable* sunk astern of the *Swiftsure* while in tow. The *Santa Anna*, I have no doubt, is sunk, as her side was almost entirely beat in; and such is the shattered condition of the whole of them, that unless the weather moderates, I doubt whether I shall be able to carry a Ship of them into Port. I hope their Lordships will approve of what I (having only in consideration the destruction of the Enemy's Fleet) have thought a measure of absolute necessity.[1]

I have taken Admiral Villeneuve into this Ship; Vice-Admiral Don Alava is dead.[2] Whenever the temper of the weather will permit, and I can spare a Frigate (for there were only four in the action with the Fleet, *Euryalus*, *Sirius*, *Phoebe* and *Naiad*; the *Melpomene* joined the 22nd, and the *Eurydice* and *Scout* the 23rd), I shall collect the other Flag Officers, and send them to England with their Flags, (if they do not all go to the bottom), to be laid at His Majesty's feet.

There were four thousand Troops embarked, under the command of General Contamin, who was taken with Admiral Villeneuve in the *Bucentaure*.

I am, Sir, &c

C. COLLINGWOOD.

[1] The *Santa Anna* was retaken by the enemy in their sortie.
[2] Admiral Alava in fact survived.

SOURCES

Manuscript:

There are scattered manuscript items in various public collections, *e.g.* the National Library of Scotland, but the bulk of material relating to Lord Collingwood is in the Public Record Office, London, the National Maritime Museum, Greenwich, the British Museum, and in the collection of Sir Edward Collingwood.

(1) The Public Record Office contains the logs of a series of ships which Collingwood commanded, the earlier ones in his own hand, others in those of clerks who, working under his eye, wrote with uniform legibility without losing individuality. Adm. 50/41, 45, 46, 49, 53, 74 comprise Journals of Admirals Collingwood and Duckworth. C.O. 152/64 comprises correspondence relating to illicit trading by American merchants with the Leeward Islands. C.O. 173/2 comprises Collingwood's correspondence relating to Spanish affairs, 1808. F.O. 70/21–27, 29, 30, 32, 33, 36 and 39 relate to Naples and Sicily, F.O. 42/5, 7, 8–12 relate to affairs of the Ionian Islands, F.O. 78/51, 52, 55, 60, 62–5 relate to Turkey.

(2) An extensive series at Greenwich, Col. 1–15, includes letters to Consuls and general Correspondence, Collingwood's Journal, 1801–1810, and the series of letters to Dr. Carlyle and Mrs. Stead included by Professor Hughes in his edition of the admiral's private correspondence.

(3) In the British Museum, Add. MSS. 14273–80 comprise Collingwood's Letter books, copies of orders and a Journal, 1807–8, not in his own hand. Add. MSS. 40096–8 comprise letters and reports received 1805–9. Add. MSS. 37425 includes signed orders and autograph letters. Add. MSS. 52780

comprises the important short series addressed to Edward Collingwood of Chirton. There are various letters to and from Collingwood in the great collection of Nelson Papers, Add. MSS. 34902–92.

(4) Sir Edward Collingwood's collection comprises the originals of the long series of letters to the Misses Collingwood, letters to Rear-Admiral Purvis, logs of the *Liverpool* and *Portland* and extensive material relating to Lord Collingwood, Commander Wilfred Collingwood, and other members of the family.

Printed Books containing original material:

Memoirs of the Professional Life of the Rt. Hon. Cuthbert Lord Collingwood (?1806)
> Published at Gateshead soon after Trafalgar, this pamphlet, which is full of invention and misinformation, is of interest as being the first attempted biography of any description.

The Naval Chronicle: Vol. 15 (1806) and 23 (1810)
> Vol. 15 contains a fulsome biographical article which Collingwood disliked, and with reason. Vol. 23 contains the original version of the sketch of his life which Collingwood supplied to the publisher in 1806, an obituary, and a brief account of his state funeral.

A Selection from the Public and Private Correspondence of Vice-Admiral Lord Collingwood interspersed with Memoirs of his life, by G. L. Newnham Collingwood (1828)
> The fifth edition, published in two volumes in 1837, includes valuable additional letters which are indicated in the list of Contents by an asterisk.

The Dispatches and Letters of Vice Admiral Lord Viscount Nelson, edited by Sir Harris Nicolas (7 vols.: 1844–6)

A Fine Old English Gentleman Exemplified in the Life and Character of Lord Collingwood: a biographical study, by William Davies (1875)

Collingwood, by W. Clark Russell (1891)

The Letter-bag of Lady Elizabeth Spencer-Stanhope, by A. M. W. Stirling (formerly Pickering) (2 vols.: 1913)

The Life of a Sea Officer, by Jeffrey Baron de Raigersfeld, edited by L. G. Carr Laughton (1929)

The Life of Admiral Collingwood, by Geoffrey Murray (1936)

Admiral Collingwood and the Problems of the Naval Blockade after Trafalgar, by D. F. Stephenson (1948)

Nelson's Letters from the Leeward Islands and other Original Documents, edited by Geoffrey Rawson (1953)

Landsman Hay: the Memoirs of Robert Hay 1789–1847, edited by M. D. Hay (1953)

Archaeologia Aeliana, or Miscellaneous Tracts Relating to Antiquity: published by the Society of Antiquaries of Newcastle-upon-Tyne. Fourth Series: Vol. xxxii (1954)
    This volume includes 'The Letters of Lady Collingwood and others to Miss Mary Woodman' (of Morpeth) by M. Hope Dodds and A. Howard Hall, a pedigree of the Collingwood family, and reproductions of portraits.

The War in the Mediterranean 1803–1810, by Piers Mackesy (1957)

The Private Correspondence of Admiral Lord Collingwood, by Edward Hughes (1957)
    This volume belongs to the series published by the Navy Records Society, in which there is liberal though scattered documentation concerning Lord Collingwood. The most important individual volumes are xviii (*Logs of the Great Sea Fights:* Vol. ii) which includes Collingwood's Trafalgar Journal; xxiv (*Journals and Letters of Sir T. Byam Martin:* Vol. i), and xxviii (*The Correspondence of Admiral John Markham*, 1801–7)

Note: *The Mariner's Mirror*, the Journal of the Society for Nautical Research, indexes a number of items relating to Collingwood, including, in Vol. xxiv (p. 237) one on the admiral's important annotations made in his copy of William Beatty's *Authentic Narrative of the Death of Lord Nelson* (1807) now in the library of the National Maritime Museum.

Index